1/25/17

# Metamedia

American Book Fictions and
Literary Print Culture after Digitization

**Alexander Starre**

University of Iowa Press ¶ Iowa City

University of Iowa Press, Iowa City 52242
Copyright © 2015 by the University of Iowa Press
www.uiowapress.org
Printed in the United States of America
Design by Sara T. Sauers

The University of Iowa Press is a member of Green Press
Initiative and is committed to preserving natural resources.
Printed on acid-free paper

Library of Congress Cataloging-in-Publication Data
Starre, Alexander.
Metamedia : American book fictions and literary print culture
after digitization / Alexander Starre.
pages    cm. — (Impressions: Studies in the art, culture, and
future of books)
Includes bibliographical references and index.
ISBN 978-1-60938-359-6 (pbk),
ISBN 978-1-60938-360-2 (ebk)
1. American literature—21st century—History and
criticism. 2. Books and reading—United States.
3. Digital media—United States. 4. Literature and society—
United States—History—21st century. I. Title.
PS231.B66S73   2015
810.9'357—dc23   2015005560

I have no more made my book than my book has made me.
—Michel de Montaigne, *Essais*

# Contents

## Acknowledgments

"LIFE PASSES INTO PAGES if it passes into anything," novelist James Salter writes in his memoir *Burning the Days*. I came across this line during the final stages of revising my manuscript and found that it perfectly captures the moment when one lets go of a work long in the making. This book has been a part of my life for a number of years, so its opening lines are the proper place to express my gratitude toward those wonderful people whose support has not just passed into these pages, but who helped to initiate, shape, and complete the entire project.

*Metamedia* began as a doctoral dissertation at the University of Göttingen, where I had the great fortune to find Frank Kelleter as my advisor and mentor. From the moment I presented him the first scattershot ideas for this project, he provided essential input, critical perspective, and encouragement. Frank's vast knowledge of American literary and cultural history and his admirable talent for teaching others have left a permanent imprint on this book and on my thinking in general. Philipp Schweighauser was an excellent coadvisor throughout. Despite moving from Göttingen to a new position at the University of Basel in the early stages of my research, he was always on call when I needed someone to discuss the finer points of systems theory or the aesthetic dimensions of contemporary literature. I also wish to thank Claudia Stockinger for joining my doctoral committee. The English Department at Göttingen proved to be the perfect environment for my first few years in academia. Barbara Buchenau and Harald Kittel were generous sources of motivation and professional advice. Andreas Jahn-Sudmann philosophized with me about what media were, are, and should be. In the final stages of my work, Babette Tischleder provided further feedback on materiality in literary studies. I am indebted in various ways to many other former Göttingen colleagues, among them Claudia Georgi, Ralf Haekel, Klaus Herrgen, Christy Hosefelder, Andreas Lemke, Katharina Nambula, Johannes Schlegel, MaryAnn Snyder-Körber, Peer Trilcke, and Nicole Waller. I am especially thankful to everyone in the tightly knit group of doctoral students and junior faculty in American Studies: Susanne Hamscha, Kathleen Loock, Birte Otten, Emily Petermann, Frederike Rathing, Diana Rosenhagen, Bettina Soller, Stephanie Sommerfeld, and Maria Sulimma. Finally, I have to single out Daniel Stein not only for reading large parts of the manuscript, but also for being such an inspiring presence throughout my work. It was Daniel who encouraged me to trim and revise a sprawling dissertation manuscript and submit it to an American publisher.

In 2013, I joined the faculty of the John F. Kennedy Institute for North American Studies at the Freie Universität Berlin. The new position brought with it a welcome influx of intellectual support and I wish to thank my colleagues with specific mention to Laura Bieger, James Dorson, Winfried Fluck, Ulla Haselstein, Martin Lüthe, Simon Schleusener, Florian Sedlmeier, Ahu Tanrisever, and Sarah Wasserman. Regina Wenzel went out of her way to make my transition to Berlin a smooth one. Throughout, I have benefited immensely from the input of the students in several classes I taught both in Göttingen and in Berlin.

Many other individuals and institutions from Germany and abroad helped along the way. Bill Bell invited me to present my work at the Edinburgh Book History Seminar, generously shared his expertise in the field, and assisted with the book proposal. For stimulating conversations and helpful advice, I wish to furthermore thank Shane Denson,

Kathleen Fitzpatrick, Florian Groß, Ruth Mayer, Christina Meyer, Jason Mittell, and Fabian Stroth. Fred Schmalz, who has a way with words, meticulously edited the manuscript and gave guidance in my revisions.

None of the following chapters have been published before, but I have based some of my arguments on two previously published essays: "'Little Heavy Papery Beautiful Things': McSweeney's, Metamediality, and the Rejuvenation of the Book in the USA." *Writing Technologies* 3 (2010): 25–41; "The Materiality of Books and TV: *House of Leaves* and *The Sopranos* in a World of Formless Content and Media Competition." *The Metareferential Turn in Contemporary Arts and Media: Forms, Functions, and Attempts at Explanation*. Ed. Werner Wolf. Amsterdam: Rodopi, 2011. 195–215. I am grateful to the colleagues who invited me to contribute to conferences, symposia, and publications, and shared their feedback with me, among them Astrid Bracke, Lan Dong, Doris Lechner, Stefanie Lethbridge, Karla Nielsen, Corinna Norrick-Rühl, Marc Priewe, Christian Quendler, Tatiani Rapatzikou, Arthur Redding, and Werner Wolf. The Göttingen Graduate School of Humanities (GSGG) supported my work with several travel stipends, as did the German Academic Exchange Service (DAAD).

Matthew Brown took an interest in my work when we first met at SHARP 2013 in Philadelphia and has since been a frequent and supportive correspondent. I am very glad that this book now appears in his new Impressions series. Catherine Cocks at the University of Iowa Press was the most helpful editor one could wish for. She advised me during the tough process of editing and shortening the manuscript and provided expert advice on illustrations and permissions. Thanks are also due to Jim McCoy for his commitment and support. The two anonymous readers commissioned by the press supplied lucid and deeply thought-out reports that guided me to the finish line. Further thanks go to Laura Howard at McSweeney's for providing permission to reproduce material from several publications, as well as to Chip Kidd and Jon Gray for letting me include selections from their artwork. Harald Wenzel added some flair by shooting two gorgeous photographs of books.

This work would not have been possible without the support of my parents Ulrike and Christian. They nourished my fascination with American culture from early on and have come to share it. Even though I cannot fully express my gratitude here, I am sure that the book itself represents it better than words can. I also thank Grete Starre for assisting me throughout my education. The company of my "other" family Beate, Bernd, and Moritz Rose made the years of writing much richer.

About a year before the text went to press, I became a parent myself. I am eagerly anticipating the day when our daughter, Klara, will first be able to read her own name printed here. Finally, with love and respect, I wish to thank my wife, Nina-Marie, for being at my side and keeping me afloat throughout everything. She endured countless hours of conversation about my topic and still had the energy to read drafts and give suggestions, sustaining me with food, coffee, and rounds of Carcassonne. This is because of her; this is for her.

# Metamedia

## Introduction: From Text to Book

CAN COMPUTERS READ, UNDERSTAND, and critically analyze literature? The brilliant neuroscientist Philip Lentz thinks they can. His research associate, prolific but heartbroken novelist Richard "Rick" Powers, disagrees. To distract himself from a recent breakup, Rick is spending an extended period of writer's block at the computer science research center of a midwestern university in the mid-1990s. Throughout Richard Powers's novel *Galatea 2.2* (1995), we follow the uneasy relationship between the author's pseudo-autobiographical persona, Rick, and the obsessive scientist, Lentz, who lures the novelist into a wager regarding the likelihood of creating artificial intelligence. Using state-of-the-art supercomputers, they start training a program named Helen in the special skills needed to successfully pass a master's examination in English literature. In their feverish but often entertaining

1

debates over knowledge and academic practices, Lentz and Rick act as representatives for the two cultures of the sciences and the humanities. During one of the training sessions, Lentz teasingly asks: "What do the literary theorists say about reading books these days?" (91). Rick, who holds a graduate degree in English literature, cannot help but ironically castigate the profession:

"First off, they're not books anymore."

"Texts," Lentz corrected himself. "Excuse me." As always, he knew more than he let on.

"Well, let's see. The sign is public property, the signifier is in small-claims court, and the signification is a total land grab. Meaning doesn't circulate. Nobody's going to jailbreak the prison house of language." (91)

Both seem to agree that the abstract detachment of literary studies from the object of the book has taken on excessive proportions, as visible in the discursive expansion of the concept "text." However, Lentz believes that the academic jargon of high theory bodes well for their adaptation of the famous Turing Test. To win the bet, he would need the computer program to produce analytic prose indistinguishable from the writing of a human. He boasts, "We can get our supernet to sound exactly like a fashionable twenty-two-year-old North American whiz kid imitating a French theorist in translation by, say, this time next month" (91). Without mentioning specific names, Powers here ridicules the American reception of post-structuralism, as embodied in the works of Roland Barthes and Jacques Derrida.

A few years earlier, the book historian G. Thomas Tanselle had mounted similar criticism against major post-structuralist scholars. His essay "Textual Criticism and Deconstruction" (1990) parses the usage of the word "text" in *Deconstruction and Criticism*, the programmatic publication of the "Yale School" of critics. Tanselle takes Harold Bloom, Paul de Man, and Jacques Derrida to task for blurring the distinction between the intangible idea of a "work" and the tangible form of physical documents, such as books. To accuse Derrida of neglecting the physical text, however, means to disregard important parts of his work. His late writings show that French theory has engaged with the complexities of book culture in a more nuanced way than the fictional Richard Powers and Tanselle could anticipate. In 1997, Derrida mused about his academic legacy in an interview with *Les Cahiers de Médiologie*: "Seeing all these questions emerging on paper, I have the impression (the *impression!*—what a word already) that I have never had any other subject: basically, paper, paper, paper" ("Paper" 41).[1] Derrida's retrospective glance at his philosophical interests does not seem to align with his oft-cited pronouncement "*There is nothing outside of the text*," (*Grammatology* 158). It appears that a fundamental shift has taken place between these two moments of his career.

With *Of Grammatology* (1967/1976), Derrida undertook a reevaluation of writing that decentered and exploded the notion of "text" while pronouncing the death of the book. The main deconstructive idea of *différance* reoriented the scholarly focus away from concrete textual instances to the endless deferral of meaning inherent in every textual artifact. Merely counting the occurrences of the term "book" in *Of Grammatology*, one may expect this seminal text to devote significant space to bibliographical concerns. But Derrida never really claims to be writing about the book as a material object. To the contrary, what interests him is the *metaphor* of the book in Western intellectual history; for Derrida, the metaphorical book is intricately bound up with the practice of writing (*écriture*), which he also ponders as a trope. To be sure, Derrida's work itself still included lucid commentary on the history and transformation of book culture. Yet the reception of his and other post-structuralist writings largely discarded the material underpinnings of texts in favor of discourse, *différance*, and deconstruction.[2]

As we can see in another interview from 1996, Derrida's reassessments of book culture spring from the evolution of his own writing practices. In an anecdotal aside, he mentions that he can hardly imagine anymore how he composed longer texts without his "little Mac" ("Word" 20). The progression of Derrida's writing tools—from pen to electric typewriter to computer—mirrors that of many professional writers, literary or otherwise, during the past decades. Digitization

3

has been encroaching on literary communication ever since visual user interfaces began to represent electronic texts in sufficiently convenient ways on personal computer screens in the 1980s. Yet, as I will explain below, the technological ensemble of carrier media for digital texts passed a crucial threshold in the late 1990s, prompting an ever-growing number of American writers and readers to acknowledge the changing media environment and respond to it.

When Derrida relates how he saw "questions emerging on paper," he is consciously observing his own reading experience. As if by epiphany, he recognizes that his own writings are more than mere texts; he now perceives them as durable marks on a specific inscription surface. With this experience, Derrida turns into a prototypical reader at the turn of the millennium. A few years after Derrida gave this interview, scores of American readers may have found themselves similarly transformed. For the sake of argument, let us briefly imagine a fictive American reader in the year 2000. This reader has bought the novel *House of Leaves* (2000) by Mark Z. Danielewski because many of her college friends already own it. Besides, reviews in the press celebrate the work and the Internet is full of fan chatter. Our reader descends the novel's layered architecture into a mysterious house somewhere in Virginia, where the protagonist, photojournalist Will Navidson, records his daily life on film. As it turns out, the gothic house contains a hidden labyrinth, stretching into infinity behind an inconspicuous door in the living room. Navidson's video recordings will later be edited into a documentary feature film, *The Navidson Record*. Here, Danielewski's twofold editorial fiction sets in: an old man with the telling name Zampanò becomes obsessed with this film and chronicles its genesis and its reception in an extended scholarly essay. After Zampanò's death, manic-depressive drug addict Johnny Truant discovers the essay, along with the notes and typescripts of the deceased. Johnny sets out to prepare the disordered textual archive for publication.

Our fictive reader enjoys the reading experience, mostly since *House of Leaves* unfolds like an intricate puzzle. She expects that all its pieces will eventually fit together and reward her for the strenuous hours spent with the nonlinear and multilayered text. In the last third of the book, she witnesses Will Navidson losing his way in the labyrinthine hallways inside his own home. Our reader progresses through chapter XX, which stretches across sixty-eight pages, but disperses its text on the pages in short passages so that she turns the pages in quick succession. Finally, as Navidson faces his own death in the darkness, she reads the following: "Taking a tiny sip of water and burying himself deeper in his sleeping bag, he turns his attention to the last possible activity, the only book in his possession: *House of Leaves*" (Danielewski, *House* 465). Narratologists have labeled this embedded mirroring of a text within a text "mise en abyme." Yet, this surprising appearance of a copy of *House of Leaves* in the protagonist's hands functions in a peculiar way, as Navidson lights several matches to read the pages in the dark:

> With only 24 matches plus the matchbook cover . . . Navidson had a total of five minutes and forty-four seconds of light. The book, however, is 736 pages long. Even if Navidson can average a page a minute, he will still come up 704 pages short (he had already read 26 pages). To overcome this obstacle, he tears out the first page, which of course consists of two pages of text, and rolls it into a tight stick, thus creating a torch, which . . . will burn for about two minutes and provide him with just enough time to read the next two pages. (465–67)

What does our reader do now? Granted, we can never know exactly what an individual reader felt and did more than a decade ago. Still, it appears reasonable to expect that this meticulous narrative description of the artifact would give her pause.

As the immersive suspense of Navidson's solitary fight against death fades, our reader wonders: do the page numbers in the passage correspond to those in the actual book? At first glance, they do not. She flips back to the last page in her book, but it carries the number 709. Navidson's book seems to be a different version of *House of Leaves*. Then again, her book has a fictional preface by Johnny Truant, which is paginated with Roman numerals. Adding the pages for this preface and all other printed matter—title page, copyright page, endorsements—the reader finally arrives at the 736 pages indicated in the quote. At the most submerged level of its narrative, Danielewski's novel thus contains an exact replica of itself—a self-description destined to confound the reader. If the fictional world accounts for the entire stack of pages that forms her book, does this mean that everything about her copy is supposed to be part of the literary work? Reenacting Derrida's epiphany, the anonymous reader has just seen *House of Leaves* reemerge on the paper of the physical book published by Pantheon. This novel is not just a book *of* fiction; it is a minutely calculated "book fiction" that interweaves text, design, and paper into an embodied work of art. Digital production tools combined with today's print technologies have enabled Danielewski and many other writers to produce such book fictions, thus enhancing text-based narrative with an added layer of metatextual meaning. In recent American book fictions, as I show in the following chapters, literary works attempt to push their reality effect outward into the readers' hands. More than just the container of a story, the physical codex here comes to function as a narrative device in and of itself.

For now, this representative reading scenario generates a number of questions and observations, which will be taken up in Chapter 3. These issues also delineate the central concerns of *Metamedia*: Which tools and institutional contexts allowed the author to inhabit the material book of *House of Leaves* so completely? How can we account for the book's intricate design, extravagant typography, and its physical reading experience, which feels simultaneously disordered and carefully orchestrated? Why does an expert user of computer technology like Mark Z. Danielewski publish his experimental debut novel as a printed book when it seems so appropriate for digital hypertext environments? Other questions transcend this specific context and touch upon tenets of aesthetics and literary studies: How does the idea of a literary work change when we think of it not as a text, but as an embodied artifact? Can hermeneutics and close reading explicate the narrative elements and the formal structures of such a book fiction? What difference does the carrier medium of a literary work make? Is literature a medium, or does it have a medium? Finally, then, we may ask: Is *House of Leaves* merely a unique product of one authorial genius or does it relate to the larger evolution of American literature at the beginning of the twenty-first century? As the title of this book indicates, I support the latter idea.

Beyond *House of Leaves*, a number of contemporary literary works react to the challenges of digitization in creative and often unlikely ways. *Metamedia* explores the history of recent American literature along several lines of inquiry, which one may group under three headings: authors, forms, and objects. For one, this book presents an account of individual authors and their contributions to millennial American literature. The texts covered here are some of the most prominent examples of literary metamediality to come out of the U.S. in the past decade. In the collocation of these works, we can perceive the tremendous functional scope of metamedial devices, transcending the limits of particular styles and genres. Best-selling novelists such as Mark Z. Danielewski and Jonathan Safran Foer figure strongly in this argument, but so do less prominent authors like Salvador Plascencia or Reif Larsen. This generation of authors is the first to have come of age in a time of omnipresent screen media and casual computation. Debuting in the early twenty-first century, these writers did not have to adapt to digital composition tools—they had them at their disposal all along. As many of their works show, young American novelists use computers with unprecedented ease and proficiency. In their social circles, flickering displays and shiny gadgets hardly raise an eyebrow. Conversely, they approach the mass-produced commodity of the printed book with a sense of wonder. In and through their texts, American literature has begun to confront the unlikely amalgam of fixity, permanence, and aesthetic flexibility embodied in its traditional papery container. We might think of this as the literary dialectic of digitization, threatening to supersede printed artifacts while simultaneously enabling them to appear as artistic media. Beyond individual authors, however, the field of actors discussed here extends to graphic designers, editors, and publishers. The recent evolution of American literature rests not only on authorship, but also on such aspects as Dave Eggers's literary patronage and Chip Kidd's typography and visual design.

Alongside these personal histories, this book also follows formal and thematic strands. Specifically, it traces a particular literary phenomenon that lends the title to this text: metamediality. Broadly speaking, a literary work becomes a metamedium once it uses specific devices to reflexively engage with the specific material medium to which it is affixed or in which it is displayed. The main concern of this book is to examine the specific forms and effects of metamediality in relation to the respective texts, their material embedding, and their function in the larger media ecology.[3] During a recent interview, Mexican American author Salvador Plascencia explained his discontent with the standard book format: "Somehow this led me to Lawrence [sic] Sterne, to early books, and to the realization that the way we understand the book is only a domesticated version of the wild, feral, origins of the book. We have housecats, when we once had sabertooths" (M. Baker). To become such a Sternean "sabertooth," Plascencia's debut novel The People of Paper (2005) employs unconventional book design, typography, and page layout, as detailed in Chapter 4. Laurence Sterne's The Life and Opinions of Tristram Shandy, Gentleman (1759–67) is indeed the locus classicus of literary metamediality. In one scene, Tristram Shandy for example enlists the help of the reader to draw an image of the beautiful widow Wadman. He suggests that the reader "call for pen and ink" and adds, "here's paper ready to your hand" (482). Throughout its publication history, the book has included a blank page intended for the reader's drawing right next to these directions. To playful effect, Sterne hereby turned Tristram Shandy into a metamedium. The text of his book appears to know about its immediate material context—the physical book—and freely communicates this knowledge. Like a faint echo through the centuries, Sterne's ur-text inspired The People of Paper, whose author dislikes the industry standard of a modern book. Yet, as suggestive as the link to Sterne's early modern anticipation of postmodern aesthetics appears to be, it provides little insight as to the cultural work bibliographic metamedia are currently performing in American literature.

Within and beyond the story of individual actors and textual devices, all chapters investigate a number of material objects. Building on impulses from the fields of book history and media theory, my aim is to read literary texts not as abstract renderings of a narrating voice, but as concrete, tangible artifacts. The signifying potential of any text owes some debt, however small, to its bibliographic form. In novels that use metamedial forms of representation, this share may grow to such an extent that the individual copy of the book itself becomes an embodied fiction. The physical book thus enters the liminal space that separates the empirical world from the fictional diegesis. As the subject matter of literary scholarship, the material book is at once more challenging and more accessible than mere text. It is more challenging because hermeneutic methods like close reading do not apply easily to nonlinguistic phenomena like paper size or typefaces. Still, I wish to show that the material copy of a book provides insights into the approximate aesthetic experience of large audiences who have read the text in the form of a specific edition. The qualities of place-bound design and tangibility endow the book with a robust frame whose function as a creative catalyst has received comparatively little attention in literary studies. This is what makes the book so accessible to scholars, as opposed to authors, writing tools, and the anonymous mass of readers. Unlike these complex domains of research, the book itself is present within close reach for every reader—including every academic reader.

Taken together, these three lines of inquiry converge in the idea of literature as a form of social communication. As an expansive system of communication, American literature continually evolves in and through individual works. This system extends across a wide network of elements loosely ordered by a common language, a geographical location, and a set of intertextual relationships. In adopting this systemic perspective, my aim is not to assess the validity of the wide-ranging theoretical work of Niklas Luhmann and other scholars in this field. Still, I do believe that systems theory holds immense functional value both for literary studies and for book history, as it provides sufficiently complex terminological tools to elucidate the communicative processes of modern societies. My argument uses systems theory to explain contemporary literature—not vice versa.

Within this theoretical framework, instances in which literature communicates about itself are of prime interest. Such reflexive moments make visible the self-reproductive evolution—the "autopoiesis," in Luhmann's terms—of a specific form of art.[4] American literature has arrived at a point where it cannot help but reflect on its relationship to the book. Since every unpublished text now faces both screen and printed page as potential distribution media, authors as well as readers need to distinguish whether the material medium belongs to the inside or the outside of a literary work. In the modernist avant-garde, the prominent art critic Clement Greenberg argues in his influential essay "Towards a Newer Laocoon" (1940), visual artists began to confront the material substrate of painting. In modernist aesthetics, Greenberg conjectured, the "purely plastic or abstract qualities of the work of art are the only ones that count" (34). A similar preoccupation with medial purity pervades the literature of the time, with Ezra Pound as one of the most outspoken advocates. The modernist battles over literary and poetic form, however, were waged on the immaterial plane of language and style.

Greenberg's fascination with the constraints of individual media soon chafed against expansive postmodern self-descriptions of art. Within the literary system, electronic writing tools arrived on the scene at a time when borders between high and low, or visual and verbal, were deconstructed with much rhetorical panache. Accordingly, hypertext theoreticians singled out the limitations of printed media as their prime target. Derrida's metaphorical assertions concerning "the end of the book" (*Grammatology* 6–26) as well as his experiments with print led hypertext critic George P. Landow to read him as an early advocate of digital networks and e-texts. Landow argues, "Among major critics and critical theorists, Derrida stands out as the one who most realizes the importance of free-form information technology based upon digital, rather than analogue, systems" (67). In an ironic twist, though, Derrida would later explain that *Of Grammatology* was merely meant to describe the end of the "onto-encyclopedic or neo-Hegelian model of the great total book, the book of absolute knowledge linking its own infinite dispersion to itself, in a circle" ("Book" 15). Writing in 2001, he claims that the digital technologies celebrated by Landow have not brought about the end of this model. Instead, they have transposed the idea of the total book into the digital realm, where the Internet now emerges as "the ubiquitous Book finally reconstituted, the book of God, the great book of Nature, or the World Book" (15). Derrida perceptively anticipated the rhetoric of digital visionaries such as Kevin Kelly who now predict the coming of a vast, singular electronic book that digitally swallows up all existing texts.

Notably, Landow misreads Derrida's experimental book *Glas* as an expression of the wish "to escape the confinements of print" (66). Derrida explicitly counters this viewpoint: "[T]he typographic experiments . . . particularly the ones in *Glas*, wouldn't have been interesting to me any more; on a computer, and without those constraints of paper—its hardness, its limits, its resistance—I wouldn't have *desired* them" ("Paper" 47). Derrida himself is nevertheless partly responsible for Landow's assumptions, as his rhetoric celebrates notions of expansion and deferral, which have become central characteristics of vast, hyperlinked digital environments. Yet, in line with Greenberg's aesthetics of medial limitations, Derrida insists on the interrelation of constraints and innovation. In their aesthetic visions, Greenberg and Derrida thus share the preoccupation of contemporary systems theory with limitations, distinctions, and boundaries.[5] From the perspective of second-order cybernetics, there is indeed a direct correlation between (systemic) closure and (communicative) openness, as Chapter 1 shows.

Greenberg's "New Laocoon" also prefigures the systems-theoretical insistence on the historicity of (artistic) communication. The renegotiation of mediality within abstract art, Greenberg holds, does not spell out a timeless aesthetic truth. Instead, the avant-garde's self-reflexive use of paint, brush, and canvas only emerges "in conjunction with a particular moment reached in a particular tradition of art" (Greenberg 37). The same holds for authors such as Mark Z. Danielewski, whose commitment to typography and book design emerges out of concrete developments in the cultural and technological environment of American literature. I will therefore not attempt to build a normative case for the aesthetic superiority of either print or electronic literature. The literary system itself provides ample space for debates on whether the screen or the book is a "better" medium for literary texts.

While it is a common rhetorical reflex in the humanities to expand definitions that are deemed "too narrow" or "too limiting," the word field "medium/medial/mediality" will occur throughout this book in a relatively restricted manner pertaining largely to the material dimensions of individual medial constellations. This is not to suggest a regressive perspective that would oppose evolving fields like intermedia studies or transmedial narratology, which emphasize the interconnectedness and the multipolarity of media. Rather, this materialist framework is used as a heuristic tool. The extensive entry in the *Oxford English Dictionary* bears witness to the ambiguities inherent in the word "medium." One of its subsections defines medium as "physical material (as tape, disk, paper, etc.) used for recording or reproducing data, images, or sound" ("Medium" def. 11.4.e). I favor this definition with its focus on the physicality of paper, since I am interested in the book mostly as a material carrier medium. By positing the "recording and reproducing" of data as the prime function of a physical carrier medium, the definition accounts for both the encoding operations on the sender's side and the (potential) decoding on the receiver's side. I therefore understand the printed and bound book as a carrier or storage medium that allows inscription on and reception from its material surface.

Media scholars rarely employ such a narrow definition. For Lisa Gitelman, to cite just one example, media are "socially realized structures of communication, where structures include both technological forms and their associated protocols, and where communication is a cultural practice, a ritualized collocation of different people on the same mental map, sharing or engaged with popular ontologies of representation" (7). This definition has its merits insofar as it widens the field of media history to include aspects of cultural history. But Gitelman's media concept introduces ambiguity and contingency at the level of terminology, and she freely acknowledges that it "keeps things muddy" (7). While I agree that critical engagement with media needs to account for the complex cultural frameworks and influences they are enmeshed in, I have reservations as to the value of Gitelman's decision to lump together materialities, technologies, and social practices. If the field itself is full of cultural and historical complexity, it appears far from effective to opt for a "muddy" perspective that augments the opacity of the phenomena in question.

Adding "associated protocols" to the term "media" introduces a pluralistic component that prevents a clear understanding of an individual medium, such as a specific book at a specific point in time. There is of course little fault to find with the conviction that the larger field of media studies should confront the cultural contexts that surround media like the phonograph record or the DVD. But if protocols are "supporting" and "associated" (Gitelman 7), we may as well perceive them as necessary additions, not as genuine components of a medium. Strategic concerns also motivate such spacious conceptualizations of "media," since they can be used to expand the boundaries of one's own discipline. The result is different when scholars approach books neither as communication channels nor as parts of sociocultural macro-formations, but as material objects of analysis. In the burgeoning field of book history, a narrower media concept is the norm, as David Finkelstein and Alistair McCleery show in their *Introduction to Book History*: "Medium, as used here, is a generic term for the material form of a text" (3).

While *Metamedia* focuses exclusively on American literature and its relationship to one medium—the printed book—in the early years of the twenty-first century, my argument about medial self-reference in these writings takes on its full significance when sketched out against the background of a different medium. This other medium has many names: It manifests itself in concrete technologies such as "computer," "laptop," or most recently "tablet." It also includes more fundamental mechanisms such as "networks" or "the Internet." Finally, it is contained in new processes such as "digitization" or "computation." To order this vast field, we may ask whether the "digital revolution" has introduced a specific new carrier medium that can be equated with the book. A provisional answer should take into account the functional and material divide between carrier media on the one hand and recording and reproduction technologies on the other.

As early as 1972, the journalist and communication scholar Harry Pross distinguished between various media according to their respective dependence on technologies. In his tripartite typology, voice, gestures, and facial expressions are "primary media" that originate in the body of the sender and can be directly decoded by the sensorium of the receiver (Pross 128–49). "Secondary media" introduce technology, i.e. external apparatuses, at the level of production (145–224). The sender of a particular message needs some type of tool or machine capable of producing externalized artifacts, such as scrolls, printed books, newspapers, magazines, flyers and other printed ephemera. Literate readers, however, can consume the printed product without additional mechanical or electronic aids. "Tertiary media" add another layer of technology (224–262). This class of more recent media consists of communication and reproduction technologies like the telegraph, the telephone, radio, and TV, as well as new encoded storage or recording media such as phonographic records, audio cassettes, VHS tapes, CDs and DVDs. For each of these storage media, both the sender and the receiver need apparatuses to encode and decode the content.

Recent studies that contrast books and electronic media have implicitly taken up Pross's arrangement. The French media philosopher Bernard Stiegler distinguishes the "literal synthesis" of writing and print from analog and digital recording: "The literal reader is herself an apparatus, 'equipped' and independently able to access the content of a literal recording . . . With analog and digital technologies, however, the functions of coding and decoding are delegated to machines" (81). The embodied reader surrenders her independence vis-à-vis the medial object to various automated mechanisms performed by machines. N. Katherine Hayles arrives at the same conclusion with regard to e-texts, which is "that with electronic texts there is a conceptual distinction—and often an actualized one—between storage and delivery vehicles, whereas with print the storage and delivery vehicles are one and the same" (My Mother 101).

In a comparative approach to literary texts in book form and their new-media counterparts, the work of Pross, Stiegler, and Hayles helps to stress the techno-phenomenological difference between these media: A Penguin Classics edition of *Moby-Dick* is an artifact that can be read and understood directly by humans via their senses, provided they are literate and proficient in the English language. However, if the full text of Herman Melville's novel is digitized and stored in any of the available tertiary media—a CD-ROM, a USB flash drive, a laptop's hard drive, a webserver on a university campus, etc.—its letters and sentences are transcoded into a different "language," unintelligible (and invisible) to humans. While all these electronic incorporations fall under my material definition of a medium, none of them is a secondary medium like the book. As tertiary media, they need decrypting technology to transfer the e-text of *Moby-Dick* into an intelligible form; they also need visualization tools to display the text in a concrete form so that a given person can read the novel.

Large portions of the contemporary discourse on the book in the digital age fall into the trap of confusing secondary and tertiary media. Various vehicles such as "hypertext," "digital text," "the Internet," or "the e-book" may act as alternative dissemination channels for literature. Still, with Pross, Stiegler, and Hayles, we have to doubt the viability of pairing any of them with the traditional book. Electric, electronic, and digital technologies have not introduced a new *secondary* medium in which to disseminate texts. Even though book production has undergone massive changes in the wake of technological advances, the "medium" or "medial object" of the printed book as it is sold in bookstores or shelved in university libraries is essentially the same as it has been since Gutenberg invented movable type printing. The bound codex has been around even longer, its earliest forms having evolved in the second century A.D. Digital technologies have instead created new *tertiary* media for storage and display, as well as new technologies for transmitting binary codes over great distances instantaneously.

Often overlooked in the commotion surrounding the Internet is the new physical medium that provides a viable alternative to printed texts:

the screen. The electronic screen distills digitally encoded text into a quasi-finite form, which is intelligible to readers through its emulation of the printed book's conventions of line orientation, typography, and page layout. The screen may imitate book visuality. It may even include three-dimensional visual effects like page-turning animations. Still, the individual picture displayed on the screen can never transcend the medial framework of the screen. Screen readers do not turn pages; they swipe their fingers across glass. Referencing the screen as a malleable interface, Roger Chartier points out: "In the digital world, all texts, whatever their genre, are produced or received through the same medium and in very similar forms, usually decided on by the reader him- or herself. Thus a textual continuity is created that no longer differentiates discourses on the basis of their materiality" ("Languages" 142). TVs based on the cathode-ray tube (CRT) already offered the viewer several tools—brightness, hue, contrast—to customize the visual image to their liking. Today's prevalent screen technology, the liquid crystal display (LCD), further extends the viewer's options. Even more, screens built with this display technology drastically augment the spectrum of possible screen sizes and shapes, inhabiting tiny contraptions like smartphones or iPods as well as enormous wall-mounted television screens that allow panoramic views in the private home. In a general sense, then, text displayed on a screen is never an artifact.[6] Instead, we may call it a performance—a performance, that is, by a programmed machine working in conjunction with a display technology and possibly initiated by human input. One would expect new media scholars to devote extended attention to the screen as the carrier medium of almost everything that is understood as "new media." But this is decidedly not the case.[7]

In a way, this media-theoretical trend has its precursor in the fixation on Gutenberg's print shop. The technology of printing arrives as the key revolution of Western society both in McLuhan's work, and in many of his descendants'. Yet, as Lothar Müller suggests, Gutenberg's invention merely forms a milestone in a more extended era of paper (122–23). Perhaps, the history of media technologies appears so fascinating because it is so ripe with revolutions and upheavals. Measured against this, the history of display and carrier media proceeds at a crawl. If we perceive the screen as a display medium, we can see how its adjacent technologies replace each other in quick succession—broadcasting airwaves, cable lines, satellite dishes, fiberglass networks, personal computers, smartphones, and so on. Beyond this ever-changing infrastructure, the concept of the electric screen has progressed gradually. It has already passed its first centenary. Measured against the recording medium of paper, however, that is still a very limited timeframe. The concept of paper originated with the papyrus roll sometime around 2000 B.C. (Kilgour 29). Since then, the media history of paper has been one of slow evolution, mostly without decisive revolutions or upheavals. Paper was ready at hand when Gutenberg invented movable type printing; it was still there when Ira W. Rubel invented offset printing in 1903 (136). The history of technology is fast. Media history is slow.

In addition to a media history, the following chapters also contain an American history. But why limit the scope of the book, one might ask, to a specific nation? After all, many industrialized and developing nations have to face the effects of digitization, albeit in different degrees of magnitude. Especially from a systems-theoretical angle, the frame of observation could be much larger, as the recent past has seen the rise of global networks of data traffic, commodity exchange, and personal mobility. Beyond the pragmatic decision to select a focused field of study, I nevertheless refrain from a transnational focus as it would override the self-descriptions occurring within the communication system in question. In contrast to fields such as economy or science, the domain of literature still largely orders itself along national lines. Transnational approaches have considerably enriched the disciplinary perspectives of literary studies; yet, as an observational stance, transnationalism works best when it supplements, rather than replaces, smaller-scale analysis. It is not per se a more advanced, more valid, or more appropriate approach, although it underscores the preferred self-description of American Studies at the present time.

Mark McGurl has recently addressed the value of nation-based scholarship after the transnational turn. Anticipating criticism of his own national and regional focus, he proposes complementing extensive frames of observation with a turn "inward to the regions and localities, not to mention the institutions, that are equally corrective to the thoughtless assumptions of disciplinary nationalism" (401). I wish to adopt this sensible framework in my readings of literary texts as locally produced and locally consumed material artifacts. Not even in the hyperconnective present do literary texts easily transgress national borders. First of all, the vast majority of the international readership encounters texts in translated form. In addition to this linguistic shift, however, physical books differ in their outward form as they are reprinted in various countries of the world. Copyright law and local distribution chains diversify even the otherwise formidable integration of the U.S. and British literary marketplaces. In several important respects, my analyses would read differently were they based on British editions of the same literary texts. Through metamedial aesthetics, the technological advances of digitization enable a renewed interest in locality, embodied interaction, and the flipside of informational mobility.

Regarding the technological and cultural trajectory of digitization, American developments and contributions cannot merely be conflated with those of the rest of the world. A large share of the inventions that shape today's digital media ecology either originated in the U.S. or first gained widespread acceptance there. Thus, this nation was one of the first that had to cope with the impact of "new" media in the late twentieth century. As has been the case with the development and proliferation of television equipment, the United States had a head start on other nations in the realm of digitization. The giants of the trade—Apple, AT&T, Google, Microsoft, etc.—all firmly reside in the U.S., thus sharing a primary attachment to American communication regulations, Internet standards, and engineering norms. Since a great share of technological innovation in the digital realm occurs on the North American continent, American society has to react to advances in hard- and software relatively early. This allows cultural discourses to form around the new technologies that take longer to develop elsewhere. Even if we were to choose a transnational perspective on contemporary communication networks, it would still have to be, in many ways, a transnationally American one.

One burst of discursive activity occurred when e-book readers became available in the United States in 1998 with the widely publicized introduction of the first portable e-book reader, the Rocket eBook. I take this event as pivotal for the medial context of American literature, which is why the timeframe under consideration here begins with the year 1998. Coincidentally, this was also the year Larry Page and Sergey Brin founded Google. The first generation of e-reading devices included all-but-forgotten brands such as the Millennium Reader, the SoftBook, and the EveryBook. These ancestors of the iPad and the Kindle offered the screen as an alternative display medium for the content of books and they also made it possible to think of books themselves as digital content.[8] The advent of these devices did not initiate mass consumption of e-books at the time, yet it forms a crucial threshold in the development of digital textuality. Many commentators offered a teleological vision of future books, in which one technology would supersede the other. In late 1999, the *New York Times* published a report by Dinitia Smith on the evolving e-book technology. Her article is remarkable in two ways: first, it clearly distinguishes the concepts of the e-book and hypertext; second, it shows how the appearance of an alternative medium for long-form texts leads to reevaluations concerning the printed book. Referencing several software and hardware projects at Microsoft and other companies, Smith points out that developers of e-books share a common goal, which is to "recreate the experience of reading a printed book." This ambition of American e-book entrepreneurs breaks with the program of radical innovation pronounced by advocates of hypertext.

Even though the buzz surrounding hypertext in the 1980s and 90s seemed to upset the literary system, readers and critics could still make sense of hyperlinked forms of writing via recourse to genre. Hypertext fiction assimilated well into transmedial classifications of textual forms, as in Espen J. Aarseth's influential concept of "ergodic literature," which denotes nonlinear, fragmented narratives that active readers assemble into a customized whole (1–5). Aarseth traces the openness and dynamism of hypertext back to experimental novels by writers like Marc Saporta and B.S. Johnson, thereby supplanting medial differences with formal ones. The introduction of e-book readers, conversely, affected the entire literary system precisely because it seemed so far from revolutionary: e-books merely imitate the printed page on their screens. At base, this is a much more radical shift since it promises to offer a portable, easy-to-use medial alternative for *every* book. Hypertext mostly affected the genre of ergodic literature. The Rocket eBook and its progenies, however, offer an informational infrastructure that can potentially channel all literary communication.

As to Smith's second noteworthy point: almost half her article is not about the new e-books at all, but about the traditional print book. Drawing on interviews with the historians Robert Darnton and Anthony Grafton, Smith relates a miniature history of the book, stretching back to the invention of the bound codex. She maps out the specificities of the physical book that distinguish it from the screen, noting the differences in the use of serif type, letter kerning, and ligatures. Smith's article exhibits a nascent cultural semantics of medial difference that counteracts the imitative visual design of e-books. This semantics is fueled by the realization that emerging technologies might restructure the entire economic and logistical infrastructure for printed texts. The Rocket eBook completed a digital communications circuit that went full circle from the author's computer, through fiber optic cables or wireless Web services, to the customer's portable reading device. From this point on, the printed communications circuit—well theorized in book historical scholarship—lost its monopoly on the transmission of authoritative texts.

The search company Google became the harbinger for the e-book's return to the center of attention after an extended lull in the wake of the dot-com crash. Following the precedent of early e-book designers, the aim of the Google Books project started in 2004 was not formal innovation. Rather, this venture concentrated on replicating physical books as accurately as possible to make them available for screen reading.

Google's e-books do not contain intricate hypertext; rather they want to provide an image faithful to the original book on the digital screen. On top of this, however, Google sends all images through Optical Character Recognition (OCR) software to render their text machine-readable. While retaining bibliographic visuality and thereby leaving many associated usage protocols in place, scanned e-books make full use of the strength of computation in networking and indexing data.

In 2006, Kevin Kelly—senior consultant to *Wired* magazine—published an op-ed piece in the *New York Times Magazine* in which he mused about these developments. "Scan This Book!" mounts a utopian wake-up call to the print community reminiscent of McLuhan's anti-Gutenberg prose. For Kelly, digitizing books means overcoming the physicality of the codex toward a blissful, dematerialized hyperspace. Printed and bound, the book languishes on the shelf. As a digital file, the book not only encourages active readership, it becomes active by itself: "The static world of book knowledge is about to be transformed by the same elevation of relationships, as each page in a book discovers other pages and other books. Once text is digital, books seep out of their bindings and weave themselves together." Kelly's rhetoric contains two underlying assumptions. First, his argument correlates computational activity with human activity and favors a state of relatively high activity over a supposedly inactive, "static" state. Second, as he sees editing and linking as inherently intelligent processes, he perceives virtualized convergence processes as superior to finite artifacts. As an overarching trope for the basic features of digital books, Kelly employs the metaphor of water. The liquid essence of e-books freely flows and seeps through digital networks, unimpeded by the borders of the bound codex. The essay thus weaves a liberalist strain into its key assumptions, presenting the online world as the technological fulfillment of the idealized free flow of communication that ought to form the backbone of modern nation states.

In a wider framework, "Scan This" conveys an underlying ideology of expansion. This model disapproves of borders and localized phenomena while valuing complexity and perpetual movement. In Kelly's vision of the universal library, size matters. His rhetoric reveals an astonishing fascination with large numbers; one of the most frequently used words in the essay is "millions." For him, an ultra-complex agglomeration of networked texts—the Internet—provides the ultimate playing field of an ever-expanding digital culture. The act of reading itself, however, recedes to the sidelines once networking activities become the primary goal of cultural interaction. Readers of e-books, Kelly holds, have obligations far transcending the consumption of texts. Hopping through the virtual library, traveling between links, swapping digital bookshelves, manipulating individual passages, and compiling snippets are the principal pursuits of Kelly's digital culture. As all of these activities are executed through computer code, Kelly must employ these concepts as metaphors. Highlighting a text in a computer program basically entails adding textual code to the source file. The visual effect, then, is a performance of the computing machine and the monitor used to render the code into an intelligible display. Kelly accepts the surface functions of current software interfaces as equal to the original body- and materiality-bound interactions with secondary storage media. Inevitably, his essay follows a discursive notion that does not grant bodily existence to software. In Kelly's digital culture, copies of books exist in an imagined space that is free of bodily constraints. "Digital bits" figure as "intangible assets" that multiply ad infinitum (Kelly). The physicality and the economic relevance of the technological infrastructure do not enter the equation.

"Scan this!" drew a fierce rejoinder from novelist John Updike, published in the *New York Times* about a month later in 2006. In his personal essay, Updike recalls his reading life in college. Central to his anecdotes are the local bookstores around the Harvard campus in Cambridge, Massachusetts, such as The Grolier and Mandrake, where young Updike scrounged "books with purely typographic jackets and cloth-covered boards warping from the damp of their trans-Atlantic passage." Reading here figures as a multisensory experience, in which the external form of the book merges with the poems or prose contained within it. Even deficiencies such as the damaged covers of imported books become memorable as they serve to locate the books in time and space. Updike then counters Kelly with a concise media theory of the book: "Books traditionally have edges: some are rough-cut, some are smooth-cut, and a few, at least at my extravagant publishing house, are even top-stained. In the electronic anthill, where are the edges?" His central metaphor of the "edge" entails a reconsideration of the specific medial properties of books vis-à-vis screen display technologies. Set squarely against the "open" paradigm in literary theory, which privileges multiplicity, open-endedness, and author-reader negotiations, his Greenbergian media concept emphasizes the borders of the material text as a defining feature.[9] Updike apparently believes that it is exactly the closure achieved by this medial container that allows for successful communication to evolve.

The Kelly–Updike debate presents two extreme positions in the discourse on future forms of the book.[10] The historian Anthony Grafton suggests a compromise in his New Yorker piece "Future Reading" (2007), arguing that the Internet and the codex book will have to arrange themselves through "a long series of new information ecologies." Grafton refutes Kelly's piece as utopian and instead presents the book and the Internet as components of "the long saga of our drive to accumulate, store, and retrieve information efficiently." His synthesis comes through a methodological decision: the differentiation between search and storage. In terms of search, Grafton argues, Internet technologies trump any previously existing system of categorization and retrieval. However, as far as storage is concerned they will merely complement localized, fully materialized secondary media. As long as there are places where "knowledge is embodied" (Grafton) in a form other than hard drives, Kelly's vision of the disembodied total book will remain incomplete.[11] These essays, along with countless other opinion pieces and reports on the effects of digitization, pose a challenging question to literary authors: Does your art need a specific medium?

Works such as House of Leaves, The People of Paper, and Tree of Codes directly respond to this query. They enter the debate on the future of the book as active social agents that perform cultural work not merely as discursive, but also as material interventions. My readings make no overarching claim for newness and formal innovation with regard to the novels, short stories, and other types of literary communication under consideration here. Historical precursors are in fact many and varied— from Samuel Richardson to Laurence Sterne, from William Morris to William Addison Dwiggins, from Octave Uzanne to Marc Saporta. While all these names will reappear, the following historical account concentrates on the aesthetics and the cultural work of one specific mode of artistic communication within American culture from 1998 to the present. Throughout, I develop three closely related arguments concerning metamedial phenomena in recent American literature: First, American literary texts increasingly merge the medial properties of the printed book with their discursive content, a phenomenon that fosters the aesthetic experience of metamediality. Second, this metamedial form of expression is neither fully determined by the production technology and the medial object, nor by the encoding and decoding strategies of author and reader. Rather, metamediality emerges as a communicative phenomenon at the intersection of all these spheres. Third, the bond between literature and the book medium may historically seem strong, but it is not a natural given. In the face of digitization, literary texts can no longer take a specific medium for granted. The advent of the e-book has generated complexities and irritations that the literary system has to address in order to uphold and foster its autopoiesis.

Instead of addressing these three central arguments individually, the individual readings oscillate among them. Chapter 1 stakes out a heuristic framework for dealing with the mediality of literature. It first provides a macro-frame for my argument via Niklas Luhmann's systems-theoretical outlook on the social significance of self-reference and media evolution. The core part of Chapter 1 then deals with the emerging field of "textual materialism," with a critical focus on seminal works by Marshall McLuhan and N. Katherine Hayles. In various forms, these scholars promulgate a technology-centered philosophy that fails to account for the agency of secondary media. As I show, the bibliographic features of works by McLuhan and Hayles in themselves illustrate the aesthetic primacy of the material text over its production technologies. The work of Bruno Latour usefully points beyond the opposition between technological and social determinism. In its final section, Chapter 1 shows how a materialist hermeneutics built upon the work of book historians such as Jerome McGann and Johanna Drucker can introduce the material substance of print culture into literary readings. Based on McGann's and Drucker's accounts of avant-garde writers and artists, the chapter also shows that central aspects of digital print culture such as typographic experimentation and little magazines manifest the enduring relevance of literary modernism.

Chapter 2 chronicles and analyzes the evolution and the aesthetics of the literary journal *Timothy McSweeney's Quarterly Concern* from its inception in 1998 to about 2010. The journal forms both a symptomatic reaction to and a seminal influence on the coevolution of literature and media in American print culture after digitization. During its first decade, the McSweeney's venture evolved into an extensive publishing universe, owing much to the entrepreneurship of its founder Dave Eggers.[12] My account of the literary magazine also comments on Eggers's autobiographical debut and on his first novel, *You Shall Know Our Velocity* (2002), both of which renegotiate the mediality of prose writing. Overall, the chapter approaches American literature by decentering the traditional preoccupation of literary studies with the novel. Instead of ordering the field into individual authors and their long-form products, my argument focuses on serial production, cultural networks, and creative coteries, as well as on paratextual experimentation and the publisher's house style.

Building on this, chapters 3, 4 and 5 trace the impact of metamediality in the dominant literary art form of the novel. In several obvious intersections with the McSweeney's phenomenon, however, this part of the book emphasizes the notions of connectivity and mutual interrelation that fuel the autopoiesis of American literature. Here, the increasingly canonized novels by Mark Z. Danielewski (Chapter 3) and Jonathan Safran Foer (Chapter 5) bracket the work of writers who have received little scholarly attention so far. As outlined in Chapter 4, Chip Kidd, Salvador Plascencia, and Reif Larsen represent the convergence of writing, design, and bookmaking—a convergence that affects American literature more profoundly than the technological convergence that scholars such as Henry Jenkins have observed in contemporary screen media. In the work of these writers, the full potential of metamedial narration is on display, spanning across a wide range of narrative functions and effects. In general, metamedial writing extends the self-description of the literary work in a way that encompasses the full bibliographic artifact. Beyond this overarching function, however, each novel employs metamedial devices differently, leading to multiple forms of engagement with the materiality of the book that pertain to diverse themes, such as cultural memory, identity, or romantic love. The roughly chronological progression of these chapters also stresses the evolution of metamedial writing into an increasingly self-aware and accessible form. Where *House of Leaves* is a searching meditation on and experimental reconfiguration of the book form, later works by Larsen and Foer possess a much more assertive ideology of bibliographic realism.

American literature will not be able to recede behind the digital chasm that divides the new millennium from the old. Richard Powers could not yet anticipate the escalating dynamics of computation in *Galatea 2.2*. His vision of information overload simply projected the status quo into the future. Having been fed scores of canonized texts, the artificial intelligence Helen at one point asks her tutor Rick, "How many books are there?" The novelist patiently explains the swelling print market: "I told her that the number of new books published increased each year, and would soon reach a million, worldwide. That a person, through industry, leisure, and longevity, might manage to read, in one life, half as many books as are published in a day" (Powers 290). From this scenario, Helen deducts that the world "will fill with unread print" unless print itself dies (291). Rick, conversely, imagines how society might bury itself in a mountain of books: "History would collapse under its own accumulation. Scope would widen until words refused to stray from the ephemeral present" (291). Powers simply extrapolates predigital print culture into the future. The actual evolution of communication media quickly diverged from the path suggested in Rick's vision, promising obsolescence not in heaps of paper but in clouds of data. Yet below this spectacular scenario, recent media evolution also projects the antithesis: the literary dialectic of digitization may stimulate a resurgence of the book. In this resurgence, however, the book may no longer figure as transparent carrier of information, but as an aesthetic agent within material networks of communication.

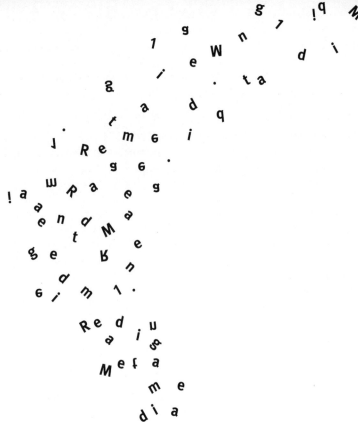

## 1. Reading Metamedia

AROUND THE TURN OF THE MILLENNIUM, American literature could well have ignored the new e-book devices that promised to conveniently store and display any text. However, a significant number of influential works registered these reorientations in literary communication as a paper-based system came to be complemented by a screen-based one. Such medial reflexivity is not an inevitable effect of media change, except of course if one has a determinist perspective on the power of media and technologies within human communication. With recourse to the theory of social systems by Niklas Luhmann, I instead wish to frame media change as a process that does not penetrate the core of social communication but occurs within its environment. Luhmann argues that the appearance of new media technologies does not directly affect the ways in which individuals communicate. Instead, system-internal irritations reconstruct certain external developments, while other factors are ignored (Theory 66–67). Luhmann uses this concept of "irritation" to account for this relationship, highlighting that spheres like politics, economics, or law tend to react to certain changes in their environment while ignoring others. In a way, a communication system has to choose to be irritated.

The emerging infrastructure for screen reading opened up a discursive frame for American literature, allowing for inquiries that could not well be formulated during the monopoly of the physical book. In the introduction to her study Beauty and the Book from 2000, the print specialist Megan L. Benton directly referenced the early e-book devices SoftBook and Rocket eBook and wondered:

> Does the form of a book matter? Is the text all that counts? Is the book merely a package, or is it a cultural creation in its own right, with layers of meaning and value independent from, though intermingled with, those of its text? Questions that might have seemed idle musings a century ago now lurk with growing immediacy as fundamental notions of "the book" are no longer so familiar and ubiquitous as to be culturally invisible. (vii)

Benton's remarks exemplify the sense of irritation that follows when innovations call into question seemingly natural conventions. In this manner, changing environmental conditions tend to give rise to new semantics that adapt social discourse to the status quo.[1] The complex phenomenon of metamediality exhibits the irritations that media change initiated in recent American literature. Much as a perceived epistemological crisis fostered postmodernist metafictions, a swelling sentiment of medial crisis now informs narrative metamedia.[2] Beyond the confines of primary texts, however, literary communication extends to the actors and institutions in the fields of criticism and academia. The ongoing debate about the future of the book in the American public sphere as discussed in the Introduction is thus recursively entwined with the signification processes of individual literary artifacts. In addition to this, literary scholars actively construct their object of study, especially because the contested concept of "the literary" is subject to constant renegotiation.

For as long as the physical book was a redundant, neutral component literature, critics tended to regard it as a negligible impediment to be overcome through one's imagination during the reading process. One of the most pointed versions of this argument is Georges Poulet's "Phenomenology of Reading," published in the inaugural issue of *New Literary History* (1969). Associated with the influential Geneva School, Poulet championed the *nouvelle critique* that used intrinsic methods of literary analysis. In his romantic and anthropocentric conception of literature, the book figures as a portal to transcendence. Recounting the reading experience in the first-person voice, Poulet claims that the reception of literature occurs on the immaterial level of the mind:

> Where is the book I held in my hands? It is still there, and at the same time it is there no longer, it is nowhere. That object wholly object, that thing made of paper, as there are things made of metal or porcelaine, that object is no more, or at least it is as if it no longer existed, as long as I read the book. For the book is no longer a material reality. It has become a series of words, of images, of ideas which in their turn begin to exist. And where is this new existence? Surely not in the paper object. Nor surely, in external space. There is only one place left for this new existence: my innermost self. (54)

The Belgian scholar predicates his reception theory on this immersive understanding of reading. For Poulet, literary communication is the direct meeting of two minds—that of the reader and that of the author. Later in the essay, he claims that the author kidnaps the readers to such a degree that they eventually lose their self-reliant subject status: "This I who thinks in me when I read a book, is the I of the one who writes the book" (58). Where subjectivities are supposed to communicate directly, intervening media and technologies are indeed a nuisance.

In a recent iteration of Poulet's immersive aesthetics, Elaine Scarry compares reading to dreaming. As readers decode the author's printed "instructions" (Scarry 6), they envision the true work of art in their minds so that the dream becomes the essence of literature. Narrative, she holds, "is almost bereft of any sensual content" (5). Its few stimuli are black inscriptions for the readers' eyes and pages to hold in their hands. "More important," Scarry continues, "these attributes are utterly irrelevant, sometimes even antagonistic, to the mental images that a poem or novel seeks to produce (steam rising across a windowpane, the sound of a stone dropped in a pool, the feel of dry August grass underfoot), the ones whose vivacity is under investigation here" (5). For large areas of literature, Scarry's description may prove to be adequate. Yet, there is a range of "mental images" for which these sensual attributes of the book turn out to be not only relevant, but essential. The metamedial effect which recursively intertwines language and book, diegesis and medium, relies on the "meager" attributes Scarry dismisses.[3]

Such metaphysical framings of poetic expression have not remained unchallenged. In the late 1980s, a group of loosely associated academics surrounding the critic Hans Ulrich Gumbrecht became vexed by the interrelation between meaning and substance. At a number of conferences, specialists from across the humanities and social sciences formulated a post-hermeneutic, in some ways even anti-hermeneutic critical program that would transcend classical literary scholarship and encounter head-on the "materialities of communication." Using this phrase as title, Gumbrecht and his colleague Karl Ludwig Pfeiffer published a collection of essays with Stanford University Press in 1994, which established "materialities of communication" as a tagline in the field. In his concluding contribution to the volume Gumbrecht articulated "A Farewell to Interpretation." The main target of this essay is the "hermeneutic paradigm" that values "subjective interiority" over and above "any material surface" (397). After having dismissed hermeneutics, however, members of this nascent school "didn't quite know how to deal with this interface of meaning and materiality," as Gumbrecht later concedes (*Production* 11–12).

In *Production of Presence* (2004), Gumbrecht proposed to remedy this conceptual problem through the notion of presence. If something is present, he holds, "it can have an immediate impact on human bodies," and this impact has to be initiated or "produced" by certain interactions (xiii). In his view, aesthetic experience is characterized not simply by meaning-based interaction with representations; rather, he argues, perceptive interaction with aesthetic objects calls up an "oscillation" between what he calls "meaning effects" and "presence effects" (107). He insists that works of art enforce the possibility to experience meaning and presence simultaneously, so that neither effect will cancel out the other one. Over the course of the book, Gumbrecht probes the aesthetic experience of dance, music, painting, and sports. According to him, all of these intrinsically emphasize the presence dimension. But even in language-based formats, meaning is never the sole component, as literary texts can trigger presence effects by "bringing the presence-dimension of the typography, of the rhythm of language, and even of the smell of paper into play" (109). In rather broad strokes, Gumbrecht thus stakes out a field of inquiry that he himself does not invest much energy into—probably due to his self-imposed abstinence from hermeneutics.

In this chapter, I wish to suggest that the materialities underlying contemporary literature in no way require us to forsake hermeneutics. Making sense of the aesthetic experience of metamedial texts will instead necessitate an extension of hermeneutics to the carrier medium of the printed page. Gumbrecht's philosophy of presence locates aesthetic experience deep within the human subject and seeks to engage with it directly. Yet, to communicate about primal experiences with the physical world always entails a hermeneutic operation, transposing sensual impressions like touch, smell, or taste into linguistic expressions. As the subject of critical inquiry, the tension between presence and meaning cannot remain unresolved, for in order to talk about it, one has to wonder: what is the meaning of presence? Faced with this dilemma, the best way forward may be to give objects a more central role in textual analyses, so as to reflect their agency in communicative processes. As Bruno Latour has observed, objects tend to shrink from view all too quickly: "To be accounted for, objects have to enter into accounts. If no trace is produced, they offer no information to the observer and will have no visible effect on other agents. They remain silent and are no longer actors: they remain, literally, unaccountable" (79). The object of the book becomes visible as an actor in literary communication whenever its material presence plays a nontrivial role in its meaning.

In order to account for the agency of media, literary studies needs to do more than merely import the material book as a device or trope. With recourse to the fields of systems theory, media studies, and book history, this chapter develops a critical perspective on the role of media in literary communication. It is my overall contention that an account of print culture in the present should resemble the ideal envisioned by Latour as a "narrative or a description or a proposition where all the actors *do something* and don't just sit there" (128). In this manner, not only do media become active social agents—or "mediators," as Latour terms them—but so do theories of the media. Accordingly, there is no decisive conceptual distinction between this chapter and the ones to follow. Just as scholarship has formulated media theories, so has American literature generated ideas and ideals about its own mediality. As such, Marshall McLuhan and N. Katherine Hayles effectively merge theory and practice in their work, so that their theories of media are simultaneously bound to a medial aesthetics. Yet, in a first move that may seem counterintuitive, I wish to expel objects from the realm of the literary. "Understanding system formation via communication," Luhmann holds, "requires excluding the material embodiment of artworks from the system" (Art 79). Especially for such seemingly accessible and commonplace artifacts as books, the abstract discourse of systems provides an alienating perspective that helps to grasp mediated communication in all its strangeness.

## ¶ The American Literary System: A Macro-Perspective

Luhmann's work on social systems is more than a theory. According to Hans-Georg Moeller, it is also an affront. Luhmann, Moeller holds, heaps a fourth insult on humanity after Copernicus, Darwin, and Freud disenchanted the human role in cosmology, biology, and psychology. His sociological insult relegates the notion of the human subject to the sidelines: "Just as we cannot control the universe, our bodies, or our minds, we are also unable to shape the social world we inhabit according to our ideals, wishes, or intentions" (Moeller 28). For Luhmann, human beings are of course necessary for societies to form, but these humans do not constitute society: "The system of society consists of communications. There are no other elements, no further substance but communications. The society is not built out of human bodies and minds. It is simply a network of communication" (Luhmann, "Modes" 100). Physical groups of people form a basic prerequisite for any higher-order social structures to emerge, but in no way do they determine communicative social processes. In Luhmann's theory, this relationship is called "emergence," referring to new levels of order that have no causal relation to the physical or energetic base on which they appear to be built. In the process of emergence, humans are thus demoted from the center of communication to its periphery, where they crowd together with technologies, media, and the entire nonhuman environment.

The appeal of this program for literary studies lies in its strictly anti-deterministic stance. Contingency, improbability, and unlikeliness are key terms for systems-theoretical accounts. In his radical leap beyond the work of his early mentor Talcott Parsons, Luhmann asks us to see everyday life foremost as something very strange. For this goal, systems theory strategically defamiliarizes the familiar, as David Wellbery writes, "Given the contingency of the start-up situation (the fact that a large number of outcomes are possible), we ask, How is it that this one outcome, improbable as it is, comes about?" ("Systems" 305). At times it does seem uncanny that literary writers can turn the chaos of the world into a coherent narrative, fix it in time and space, and distribute it as a printed novel to readers via a publisher. Systems theory may momentarily redirect scholarly attention away from the textual features of a given work and toward the improbability of its very existence.[4] After all, the unintelligible complexity of the external world is the prime reason why ordering systems appear to develop in the first place. Systems theory often appears to fight fire with fire—it creates theoretical models that are intricate enough to not seem inane in the eye of this overarching complexity. Yet, the ultimate goal is of course to reduce complexity in such a form that overcomplex phenomena may be broken down into simpler, more intelligible elements.

A comprehensive sketch of Luhmann's expansive theory outlined in dozens of monographs and countless essays is hardly possible here.[5] Aside from the systems of politics, law, and economics, which traditionally figure strongly in sociology, Luhmann devoted much attention to art as a social system. Wellbery holds that, while warmly received in literature departments in Germany, systems theory has been viewed as "marginal and recondite" in American literary scholarship ("Systems" 307). Hans-Georg Moeller blames Luhmann's "extremely dry" and "unnecessarily convoluted" writing style for the obscure status of his work in the English-speaking world (10). Contrary to these assessments, several literature and media scholars such as Cary Wolfe, Bruce Clarke, and Mark B.N. Hansen promote the approach. Their work has only now been bolstered by the English translation of the two-volume *Theory of Society* (*Die Gesellschaft der Gesellschaft*), Luhmann's final book published shortly before his death in 1998, which presents an extensive synthesis of his previous work on various social domains such as law, science, and politics.

Cary Wolfe has pointed to the affinities in the premises of deconstructionist theoreticians—foremost Jacques Derrida—and Luhmannian systems theory, aiming "to nudge the reception of systems theory in a different direction by strategically bringing out some of its more 'deconstructive' (if you will) characteristics" (222). Both approaches present a post-logocentric understanding of culture in which the key operations of human societies are not inherently attached to human beings. Rather, they come about in higher-order forms such as "writing" (Derrida) or "communication" (Luhmann). As similar as this core premise appears, there is a wide gap between the respective analytical practices of Derrida and Luhmann. The starting point of contemporary systems theory, as mentioned earlier, lies in the notion that from chaotic environments something like temporally ordered communicative systems may emerge at all. Systems theorists start with chaos and inquire into the "autopoietic," that is self-creating, processes that establish islands of meaning within this vast sea of disorder.[6] The deconstructionist perspective is an "exact mirror image" as Dietrich Schwanitz points out, taking as its "main point of reference . . . the discourse of Western metaphysics, seen as the reduced order of phonetically motivated logocentrism." Proceeding from this perspective, the main question of deconstruction became: "how is the subversion of this structure made possible?" (155–56). Reversing the direction of inquiry, the deconstructionist attempts to show that within any given meaningful system, the underlying chaos is still visible and threatens to undermine the superficial stability. In the end, Derrida would hold, all closed structures necessarily self-subvert their seeming stability. His method has been very influential in fields such as gender studies and various ethnicity-related approaches, which set out to prove that even literary texts that advocate a certain ideological position contain inherent contradictions and polyvalences that overthrow their unity at the level of meaning-making.

Systems theory does not offer such an appealing tool to express social or cultural grievances, which is why it has often been charged with political conservatism. However, according to Luhmann, stabilizing and maintaining a system does not equal stifling dissent: "This theory is not concerned, like the classical theories of equilibrium, with returning to a stable state of rest after the absorption of disturbances, but with securing the constant renewal of system elements—or, more briefly, not with static but with dynamic stability" (Social 49). Cary Wolfe calls the charge of political conservatism a "category mistake," residing in the assumption that the distinctions and models created on the level of the theory are to be used as normative enforcements vis-à-vis the entities to be observed (229).[7] Accordingly, systems theory sees openness and closure not as polar opposites, but as a differential pair in constant need of balancing each other out. Luhmann aimed to overcome the debates surrounding open and closed systems within the early phase of cybernetics by refocusing on the "question of how self-referential closure can create openness" (Social 9). I concur with Clarke and Hansen, who claim that literary and cultural studies still have to grapple with the full extent of this methodological shift in second-order cybernetics: "What is needed is a generalization of the openness-from-closure principle that is capable of addressing the full complexity of contemporary systems operations and environmental couplings ("Introduction" 10–11). In its apolitical and anti-normative thrust, Hans-Georg Moeller maintains, Luhmann's grand theory actually qualifies as one of the most radical departures from modern Western philosophy (106–11).

Pioneering American scholars in the field of systems-theoretical literary studies include William R. Paulson, Tom LeClair, and Joseph Tabbi.[8] William R. Paulson's *The Noise of Culture* (1988) posits literature as the residual noise in a hyper-efficient, information-driven culture. LeClair's *In the Loop* (1987) uses the work of Don DeLillo as an exemplar of a genre he calls "the systems novel." Both Paulson and LeClair co-opt the descriptive vocabulary of systems theory as a prescriptive device within their aesthetic argument. The idea of systems in their respective arguments works mainly through analogy. Tabbi's *Cognitive Fictions* (2002) explicitly addresses literature as a communication system, specifically "a print-based system existing at the margins of the defining media of our time." This precarious existence, Tabbi argues, accords literary art a subversive function, which "might allow the artist to resist the largely communicative purposes of other media" (Tabbi xi). Where Paulson conceptualizes literature as noise, Tabbi likens it to a form of cognition. Based on the tenets of second-order cybernetics, processes of self-reference and self-observation take center-stage in Tabbi's readings of metafictional novelists such as Thomas Pynchon, Richard Powers, Paul Auster, and David Markson.

We need to nevertheless complicate Tabbi's notion of the "print-based system" of literature. The supposedly inherent linkage between literary text and printed book is much more insecure than he suggests. If we understand literature as a communicative social system, this will imply that its basic building blocks are communicative acts. From a Luhmannian perspective, it appears counterintuitive to introduce the medial components of literature at this initial point. In this model, communication is not medially predetermined. It is a system-specific and highly contingent process, which Luhmann describes as a set of three selective operations in the realms of "information," "utterance," and "understanding" (*Social* 141–43). Through this subdivision, he stresses that neither the informational content, nor the external form, nor the recipient's way of thinking wholly determine the communication's outcome. All three are interwoven so that no one element can dominate the others. Tabbi assumes that literature is based within and bound to the medium of the printed book as if by nature. Michael Wutz takes up this thread of reasoning when he juxtaposes the novel and the "postprint mediascape," as if these were non-negotiable opposites (203). This premise appears alluring in the context of the readings that I will present in the following, but it postulates natural cohesion where rifts and uncertainties dominate. The contemporary mediascape in fact teaches us that any bond between the novel and the printed book is not given, but earned.

Even though the communicative system of art consists of much more than just paintings, novels, or musical performances, the individual work of art still holds a privileged position. Semiotic multiplicity sets apart literary works from everyday speech acts, as Roman Jakobson pointed out in his well-known model of linguistic functions. While pointing outward to the world, texts are taken to become literary when they refocus attention to themselves, thus making self-reflection a foundational concern for the system of art. Literature as communication is taken to be concerned with communication to achieve the artistic effect: "[W]e claim that the work of art is produced *exclusively* for the purpose of communication and that it accomplishes this goal or fails to do so by facing the usual, perhaps even increased, risks involved in all communication. Art communicates by *using perceptions contrary to their primary purpose*" (Luhmann, Art 22). In everyday communication, the main purpose of words and sentences is usually the transmission of some informational content from sender to receiver. Textual art distinguishes itself, Luhmann holds, from such goal-oriented communication in that it enforces self-reflexive attention to its own medium, combining "elements of sound, rhythm, and meaning" (26). He uses the term "medium" to denote words as primary components of literature. Luhmann's understanding of literary art thus turns out to have a distinctive modernist bias. This bias fits well into his contention that the genre of the novel migrated from the system of mass media to the art system only when it ceased to function merely as entertainment.[9] The "sensuous perceptibility of words" only extends to the oral dimensions of prose and poetry (26). Yet, by introducing medial self-reference as a catalyst for autopoiesis, Luhmann's work proves conducive to the approach presented here.

Aside from his aerial view of art discourse, Luhmann also assessed the functional relevance of individual works. His definition of the nature of such a work—a painting, a sculpture, a novel, a poem—combines two components: "[W]e can consider the work of art, if need be, as a compact communication or as a program for innumerable communications about the work of art. Only thus does it become social reality" (Luhmann, "Work" 194). Within this short sentence, I see a basic guiding scheme for the analysis of individual works in their relationship with literature as a system. According to Luhmann, a literary text—i.e. a text that presents itself as literature *and* is processed within the literary system as such—can be said to have two functions: First, it is an instance of "compact communication," a type of crystallizing point in which information and utterance are present in a distilled form. Secondly, literature is also a "program," a set of instructions and a collection of material for encouraging "connecting communications."[10] These are communicative acts sparked by the act of reading, viewing, or otherwise experiencing the artwork and subsequently commenting on it. Reviews, critical scholarship, and newspaper coverage all fall into this category, as do contributions to online forums, instant messages on mobile phones, or Tweets. At this stage, the material medium employed for the purpose of connecting communications is insignificant. In their references to the initial work, all of these communications foster the autopoiesis of the literary system.

From this perspective, the recent advent of computers and digitization took place in the environment of the literary system—as did the invention and evolution of letterpress printing, typesetting, and bookbinding. Understood as a communicative entity in Luhmann's sense, the literary system is operationally closed to all these external factors.

Like other systems, however, it does rely on environmental influences, such as the influx of materials or energy. The interrelation between system and environment should not be understood as a simple input/ output mechanism; rather, this relationship means that change in one place will inevitably lead to change in another place (Luhmann, *Social* 177). Consequently, it is not enough to posit change in technologies and medial forms as a given and explore literary texts to identify possible effects of this development. In order to become meaningful in the social system of literature, these environmental factors need to enter its communicative processes. We can only speak of a true interrelation between literature and media when this aspect is addressed within communicative operations.

Although systems theory does not put forth a fully formulated media theory, Luhmann nevertheless undertakes a redefinition of the concept "medium." As with many other terms, he presents not an intrinsic or normative definition, but a differential and functional one. In a first step, he correlates medium with another concept—that of "form"—and holds that the theoretical value of this distinction lies in the difference, or more specifically, in the notion that this difference can be processed within various systems. While systems theory acknowledges that matter exists, it holds to the premise that materiality cannot enter a system as an a priori entity. In order for the medial properties of a given work to enter the communicative system of art, they must be operationally processed by the observing system. This happens, Luhmann holds, in the correlative differential between medium and form. Within this distinction, "medium" is understood as an ensemble of "loosely coupled elements" (*Art* 104). Forms, conversely, are "tightly coupled"; they select from the large but finite repertoire of the medium. This shift entails a move toward intelligibility and visibility as forms "are always stronger and more assertive than the medium" (105). While artistic forms—poems, statues, books—are of main interest in literary and cultural criticism, they nevertheless depend on underlying media, such as words, marble, or paper.

Luhmann's differential media concept is based on other premises than the materialist perspective developed here, but it still suggestively models the relationship between art and media:

> For its part, a medium—the material of which the artwork is crafted, the light it breaks, or the whiteness of the paper from which figures or letters emerge—can be used as form, provided that this form succeeds in fulfilling a differentiating function in the work. In contrast to natural objects, an artwork's material participates in the formal play of the work and is thereby acknowledged as form. The material is allowed to appear as material; it does not merely resist the imprint of form. Whatever serves as medium becomes form once it makes a difference, once it gains an informational value owing exclusively to the work of art. (Art 108–09)

A medium that makes a difference, to extrapolate from this, turns into a form that can be appreciated as art. During this process, communication becomes more likely as the work of art is imbued with "informational value" that may spark connecting communications. If a literary text therefore stages its aesthetic illusion not merely in the ethereal realm of language, but also on the printed page, it impels its readers toward recognizing the materiality of the book and possibly communicating this recognition to others.

It helps at this point to take a closer look at Luhmann's description of media history and the social impact of printing (Buchdruck).[11] Theory of Society features a long chapter on the evolution of dissemination media, in which the author explains the basic terminological building blocks of systems theory, such as "meaning," "complexity," and "environment." As such, the monograph that stands at the apex of his theory presents media history as its fundamental organizing principle. In general, Luhmann aligns the various evolutionary stages of communication with a tripartite historical scheme of segmentary, stratified, and functionally differentiated societies: the first goes along with language and speech, the second with writing, and the third with printing. To preempt any simplifying cause-and-effect mapping, he emphasizes that these dissemination media are just one factor within a network of other historical variables, such as impulses from the economy, law, or politics

(*Theory* 311–12). All of these aspects taken together form a repertoire of possibilities from which social systems can select; there is no inherent determining force in media technologies.[12]

With the institutionalization and the worldwide spread of the printing press, modern society achieved an unprecedented potential for functional differentiation. Yet, in tandem with this potential came a strong restriction—social systems of communication became reliant on technology so that, Luhmann holds, "any breakdown of technology (especially energy supplies) would also lead to the breakdown of our familiar society" (*Theory* 321). Once more, Luhmann stresses in this context that technologies and media do not determine the outcome of communication. To formulate their mutual dependence, he imports the concept of "structural coupling" from the work of Humberto R. Maturana and Francisco J. Varela. Structural coupling accounts for the seeming disparity between the ideas of operational closure and environmental coevolution: "It does not determine what happens in the system, but must be presupposed, because autopoiesis would otherwise come to a standstill and the system would cease to exist. To this extent, every system is adapted to its environment (or else it does not exist); but within the given scope, it has every possibility to behave aberrantly" (Luhmann, *Theory* 54–55). Modern societies use communication technology in such an essential and basal function that they cannot afford to retreat from this state of structural coupling. Still, there is no simple logic of technological cause and social effect at work in this bond.

How can Luhmann's insights be transported into literary and cultural studies? These fields have for the longest time been, as Hayles aptly describes it, "[l]ulled into somnolence by five hundred years of print" (*Writing* 29). It used to be a common, almost natural fact that texts are processed by the critic in the form of printed characters on a page. Critical schools such as the New Criticism, the New Historicism, or intertextuality studies have by and large taken for granted the concrete material existence of texts. This naturalizing tendency is the prime reason why enthusiasts of "book literature" often posit an intrinsic link between literature and the codex. However, the outlook changes if we rethink literature as a system based on contingent acts of communication. The current scenario of insecurity and reorientation, rather than the improbable phase of medial stability that preceded it, should be the historical norm. New screen media and their corresponding forms of representation (e-books, hypertext) irritate the timeworn communications circuit of literature.

No writing technology or reproduction surface can determine the outcome of autopoietic communication processes. Yet, authors and readers still have to confront the increasingly complex publication scenario in which every text faces a choice between two radically different medialities. Through metamediality, literary texts enforce and make visible the structural coupling between their communicative operations and their carrier medium. They integrate their medial basis into their utterances, potentially fostering reflection in readers and thus strengthening the reproduction of the literary system by turning external complexities into system-internal operations. In simpler terms: Literature never naturally adhered to the book. The bond between the two is not a given. If it seemed like this for a long time, it is because dissemination of literary communication was not practical through other media. To make a difference in the media ecology of the present, this bond needs to be activated through literary communication. As literary autopoiesis becomes imaginable without printed paper, the precarious structural coupling between text and page—which had been latent all along—comes to the fore.

## ¶ Textual Materialism

For the longest time, the answer to the question "what is the medium of literature?" appeared straightforward to writers. To take just one example, William H. Gass held in *Fiction and the Figures of Life* (1970): "It seems a country headed thing to say: that literature is language, that stories and the places and people in them are merely made of words" (27). Soon enough, however, the tendency to speak of writing *and* the media was complemented by a growing interest in viewing writing *as* a medium. To this point, one of the most ambitious studies concerning the mediality of representations is *Remediation* (1999) by Jay David Bolter and Richard Grusin. The two media scholars propose an expansive theory of media: "We offer this simple definition: a medium is that which remediates. It is that which appropriates the techniques, forms, and social significance of other media and attempts to rival or refashion them in the name of the real" (65). This definition underscores the teleological thrust of their argument in that it privileges newer media over older ones. As such, remediation functions best in the computer environment: "Again, we call the representation of one medium in another *remediation*, and we will argue that remediation is a defining characteristic of the new digital media" (45). Inherently, a medium that can emulate many different medial forms through visual representation takes on a heightened value because of its multipurpose operations of mimicry. If the representation of one medium in another is defined as remediation, and a medium is taken to be that which remediates, Bolter and Grusin's concept of mediality is built on a tautology. By privileging visual representation and multimodal displays, they prepare the ground for their contention that the pinnacle of remediation occurs in hypermediate virtual realities and the layered architecture of software suites. With this bias, they of course fulfill the objective formulated in the subtitle of their book: Understanding *New* Media.

The theory of remediation usefully elucidates shifting processes of communication. Fundamentally, however, it interrogates mediacy and mediation, not mediality. In recent years, scholars from several disciplinary backgrounds have begun to relocate literature as a particular staging ground of material culture. In a 2010 issue of *PMLA*, Bill Brown called this emerging field "textual materialism," which serves well as a preliminary umbrella term for studies of the "embodied text" (25). A traditional approach to a literary text, for example a novel, will largely be concerned with its linguistic features, treating language as a primary medium of literary communication. The underlying idea of the text-as-speech disregards the secondary aspects of the mediated text, i.e. the fact that it has been given the medial form of a book by a technological production process. As readers often overlook medial differences, literary scholars are inclined to do so, too. The production and reception practices of fictional texts encourage the sense that the artistic quality of literature lies less in the object than in the content. Most readers would agree that a canonized novel retains its aesthetic quality even if it is reproduced in a cheap paperback edition. In no small part, the contested relationship between literature and popular writing genres owes to their mutual origin in the same production technology.

Textual materialism asks us to step beyond the insight that a text is mediated toward an inquiry about how it confronts the recipient in its material form. Brown holds that this type of interpretive activity will need to engage in "objectification," i.e. it will need to conceptually process the material contexts which it observes. In practical terms, the study of material can only be a study of materiality effects, so as to depict objects like the book not as a priori givens, but as potential agents that may have certain effects upon the observer or reader. As objects, books possess paramount symbolic value. Simultaneously, however, they are constantly on the verge of disappearing in favor of the imagined story world encoded in the words on their printed pages. Bruno Latour, the most outspoken advocate of the agency of objects, has continuously insisted that scholars and scientists have to make every attempt to unearth the hidden networks of influence that intertwine humans with their animate and inanimate environment. The emerging practices of textual materialism constitute an answer to Latour's challenge.

In this chapter, I return to the pragmatic and material definition of the book as a secondary medium outlined earlier. The strategic differentiation between media of storage and reproduction on the one hand, and technologies of production on the other, allows us to reread the most influential early media theorist Marshall McLuhan as a pioneer of textual materialism. Where Luhmann counts media as one environmental factor among many, McLuhan saw in them the prime component for an understanding of modern society. McLuhan's contributions to a materialist aesthetic of the book have long been overshadowed by the reception of his writings on electronic technologies. His influential work *The Gutenberg Galaxy* (1962) begins with a short preface that proclaims the printed, typeset book as an inefficient vehicle for his thoughts.[13] Yet, as open as McLuhan was to appearances on television and as much as he was embraced by pop culture, advertising, and the counterculture, the fact remains that the author who denigrates book reading as print-induced hypnosis transported his lasting contributions through the medium of the book. This paradox runs like a coherent subtext through The Gutenberg Galaxy.

As a proponent of simultaneity and embodied, multisensory experience, McLuhan rebelled against the standard format of the academic monograph consisting of a beginning, middle, and end strung together by a unifying thesis. The only viable method for historical inquiry, according to the short preface of The Gutenberg Galaxy, is the associative arrangement of facts, figures, and arguments in loose order. McLuhan rationalizes the disorderly format of The Gutenberg Galaxy as a means to an end: the aim is to achieve a genuine critical assessment of historical processes through a medium that is largely unsuitable for such an undertaking. Wherever possible, McLuhan thus tries to counteract conventions and expectations connected to the material form and ordering of a scholarly book—as when he encourages the reader in his preface to turn to the concluding chapter first.

Among historians of print, McLuhan's idiosyncrasies met with resistance. In her magisterial The Printing Press as an Agent of Change, Elizabeth L. Eisenstein explicitly refers to The Gutenberg Galaxy as an inspiration for her own work, yet she cannot help—as so many other critics since—to fault McLuhan for his methodology: "The author has solved his difficulties by the simple (albeit inelegant) device of dispensing with chronological sequence and historical context altogether" (40). She nevertheless credits him for "pointing to a large number of significant issues that cry out for historical investigation" (41). Beyond this, McLuhan's enduring relevance to print culture studies lies in his fusion of scholarship and practice. The Gutenberg Galaxy not only consciously employs the structure of the codex, it also foregrounds the material appearance of typography. In a passage on the visual style of manuscripts, McLuhan remarks, "[I]f reading aloud favours synesthesia and tactility, so did the ancient and medieval manuscript" (83). He points out that printed books have used Gothic lettering to achieve the same effect of tactility. The Renaissance revival of Roman letterforms, however, disperses this tactility through its "much less textural and more highly visual lettering which is called 'Roman' and which is the lettering we find in ordinary print, as on this page" (83). In a peculiar recursive operation, the latter sentence is an example in which the medium of the book does not counteract or limit the informational content; rather, the sentence would contain a false statement if we encountered it in any form other than in Roman type on a printed page.

McLuhan disrupts even more bibliographical conventions. In the standard University of Toronto Press edition of The Gutenberg Galaxy, only the uneven pages are numbered. As if to compensate for the lack of pagination on the verso pages, the printed numerals on the recto sides are remarkably large. Further adding to these unconventional features, the book lacks proper chapters. In their stead, it contains dozens of small sections introduced by large-print, bold headlines that incorporate the essence of the following section in a reduced, quotable maxim. A dingbat in the form of a rounded asterisk precedes each first sentence of the mini-chapters. Critics have taken this format to signify a bridge between medieval and electronic cultures. Janine Marchessault holds that it "resembles in its form not only the audile-tactile and mosaic qualities of the medieval manuscript, but it would be perfectly adaptable to new electronic forms of hypertext" (119). This interpretation accords great value to McLuhan's intention as voiced in the text. Based on the actual reading experience of The Gutenberg Galaxy, it appears doubtful whether this book simply consists of content that could be transferred to another medial form without friction.[14]

Until 2011, The Gutenberg Galaxy proved resistant to any transfer to other formats for a new edition. It had been reprinted numerous times since 1962, but the printing plates still had the same layout as in the first edition. Ostensibly, the conversion process for this embodied artifact proved to be so work-intensive that the publisher waited for the centennial of McLuhan's birth to undertake a newly typeset reedition. The metamedial reference to Roman typography imposed strict limits on the book designers at the University of Toronto Press. The back cover of the anniversary edition boasts that the "new interior design updates *The Gutenberg Galaxy* for twenty-first-century readers, while honouring the innovative, avant-garde spirit of the original." McLuhan's headlines, in this edition, appear in a sleek sans-serif typeface, further removing its typography from the expressive Textura scripts that the author cherished. Yet, for the body text, the editors had to employ a Roman font, otherwise they would have had to change McLuhan's words. *The Medium Is the Massage*, McLuhan's experimental collaboration with the designer Quentin Fiore, uses similar metamedial strategies as *The Gutenberg Galaxy*. The most obvious instance occurs on page 34–35, where two facing white pages depict two thumbs entering the book from the left and right side. These thumbs approximate the position where readers would likely hold the volume. Through this design, readers are forced to consider not just what is depicted in the image; they are also compelled to contemplate the presence of the medium in their hands. This creative tethering to a set format in a specific shape stabilized reprintings of *The Medium Is the Massage* and several of McLuhan's other books by Gingko Press in the early 2000s, as well as during the centennial in 2011.[15] It is a peculiar ironic twist in McLuhan's legacy that a small, independent publishing house with a distinct dedication to fine printing, facsimiles, and typography would acquire the worldwide rights to republish McLuhan.

While McLuhan's major books criticize the format of the book and build a case for electric orality, they still rely on their medium to a great degree. In his aversion to typographic representations, he speaks as a critic of design, not of media. As such, McLuhan's creative subversion of printed paper works best on printed paper. This dialectical dynamic blends well with Luhmann's understanding of internal criticism. He holds that intra-systemic operations of difference do not compromise a system's autopoiesis. Quite the contrary: "Every communication invites protest. As soon as something specific is offered for acceptance, one can also negate it. The system is not structurally bound to acceptance, not even to a preference for acceptance" (*Social* 173). On a different level, this dynamic holds for the continuing existence of books as well. Fierce criticism in book-form, even directed at the medium itself, helps to ensure the stability of the medium, perhaps more than complacent redundancy would. If "the medium is the message," then the bibliographic form of *The Gutenberg Galaxy* trumps its subversive content.

Despite McLuhan's struggle with the medium of the book, his work may serve as a reminder of the importance of medial materialities, not only on the level of each individual book or TV screen, but on a larger social scale. His provocations are methodical, resulting in insights that contradict conventional wisdom to a hyperbolic degree. While heaping insults on letterpress printing, he remains a man of the letter. Long stretches of his writings praise the work of experimental writers including T.S. Eliot, James Joyce, Stéphane Mallarmé, and Ezra Pound. Throughout the *Gutenberg Galaxy*, McLuhan depicts Joyce as a writer who understood the effects of the printed book well and used ingenious methods to innovate within it. In *Understanding Media*, he mourns the lack of attention devoted to the "effects of print on human sensibility," insisting that only artists have been able to escape the general blindness: "Indirect comment on the effects of the printed book is available in abundance in the work of Rabelais, Cervantes, Montaigne, Swift, Pope, and Joyce. They used typography to create new art forms" (187). The charge of technological determinism that is often leveled against McLuhan has to be qualified when it comes to the domain of art. Here, the media theorist shows himself to be much more lenient concerning the supposed dominance of medium over message.

McLuhan's stature in literary and media studies is currently on the rise, owing partially to the work of Friedrich A. Kittler, whose *Discourse Networks 1800/1900* reconceived literature as a cultural storage medium and provided the groundwork for Gumbrecht's post-hermeneutic program. Against the unidirectional historiography of McLuhan, Kittler perceives the predominant media technologies of an era as entwined with institutions and practices. The intellectual heritage of McLuhan and Kittler asks us to clarify the phenomenological differences between screen reading and paper reading, to probe beyond the similar surface visuality of e-book and print book to the respective production chains and institutional networks that need to be in place for the unlikely product to end up in the reader's hands. Reading does not take place in a transmedial sphere filled with endless neutral content. The emergent communicative domain of literature is bound to hard facts, such as the flows of capital between graphic designers and database administrators, bookbinders, and hard disk manufacturers, or struggling publishing houses and oligopolistic Internet corporations. What does it entail, then, to bring these contexts to the table when analyzing a literary text?

In connection with contemporary literature, N. Katherine Hayles was one of the first scholars who attempted to erect a materialist hermeneutics at the boundary between electronic writing and print. Her conceptual trilogy of monographs—consisting of *How We Became Posthuman*, *Writing Machines*, and *My Mother Was a Computer*—includes suggestive theories of electronic and digital textuality, always tied to the underlying technical and material conditions. Furthermore, Hayles engages with the medial aspects of literature and advocates a specific interpretive practice, albeit—as we shall see—with a distinct angle derived from her interest in electronic communications. Hayles's central contribution to the field of textual materialism is her media theory of the computer. Her analysis debunks the popular idea of disembodied information as a "powerful dream," consequential but nonetheless false (*How We Became* 13). Hayles draws the veil on the supposed free play of visuality on the computer screen and encounters the unsightly, but no less material "electronic polarities on disks" (31). All visual surface effects are built like an inverted pyramid upon these initial polarities. One unique feature of the long-distance coding string between the material code and the visual display is that at crucial points in the chain, changes may be introduced—for example changing the font of a 1,000-page Word document from Arial to Times New Roman—that instantly radiate back through the chain to alter the appearance and the underlying code.

The intuitive notion to liken the mediality of a printed page to the representation of a printed page on a screen—after all they look alike—

thus proves to be fundamentally misleading. Even though a given block of electronic text may appear in collated, unified form on the screen, there is no such corresponding unity in the storage medium. Here, the text is dispersed across files, programs, and hardware, leading Hayles to suggest that it would be "more accurate to call an electronic text a *process* than an object" (*My Mother* 101). Electronic texts reside nowhere in particular in this ensemble, yet they need the whole physical-procedural apparatus to work smoothly in order to be displayed. Facing the materialities of computation, Hayles concludes, we need to find a new notion of textuality "that is not dematerialized and that does depend on the substrate in which it is instantiated" (102). While I would underwrite much of Hayles's argument, not all of these steps are necessary in every single reading of literary works in the form of a printed book. But as we have seen in the introduction, the fundamental categorical difference between printed text and text on a screen rests on much deeper divergences than just visual quality. Fixity, permanence, and embodied spatiality are the medial properties that characterize the book as a secondary medium.[16] Flexibility, mutability, but also the precarious reliance on complex machineries and coding operations typify the electronic text as a tertiary medium.

The differential phenomenological qualities that separate screen and paper as carrier media are on display in Hayles's volume *Writing Machines*. This monograph is an instructive case study for the ways in which scholarly writing has an aesthetic bearing on contemporary print culture. The accompanying Web site of the MIT Mediawork Pamphlets series, in which *Writing Machines* was published, lists McLuhan's *The Medium Is the Massage* as an inspiration for the experimental combination of scholarly writing and visual design ("About the Series"). Beyond its theoretical contents, *Writing Machines* is a book that itself practices metamediality. The book, designed by Anne Burdick, imitates the visual features of hypertext and Web pages in multiple ways. Thin lines that resemble barcodes flow from the cover onto every page. Inside the book, one may browse through the pages to see how the barcodes slowly move from the book's edge to cover almost half the page. Burdick's design encourages physical interaction to a high degree. Furthermore, important keywords are highlighted to resemble clickable hyperlinks. A large number of images and screenshots emulates the multimodal look of a Web site environment. Despite all these gestures toward hypertext, the eminent feature of the book is its self-reflexive presentation of bibliographic attributes. The right edges of all the pages are imprinted with small black lines that coalesce into writing when the reader thumbs and bends them to the side. The book's fore-edge reveals the words "WRITING" and "MACHINES" as one bends the book either upward or downward. Typography is also used to subtly underscore the structure of the text. As Burdick explains in the appendix, two fonts were used to differentiate the book's autobiographical sections from its scholarly parts—the former are set in Cree Sans, the latter in Egyptienne. Burdick also created a blend of these typefaces for the concluding remarks. Similar to *The Gutenberg Galaxy*, Hayles's *Writing Machines* employs bibliographic strategies even as its main interest lies in electronic communication.

Within the text proper, Hayles introduces several critical terms so as to instantiate a materialist form of literary criticism, among them "technotext" and "media-specific analysis." Reconceptualizing print, computers, telegraphy, and other tools as "inscription technologies," Hayles holds that a literary work may employ certain creative methods that hearken back to its production, mobilizing "reflexive loops between its imaginative world and the material apparatus embodying that creation as a physical presence" (*Writing* 25). Building on this definition, Hayles then merges two strands of thought that should better be addressed separately:

> Literary works that strengthen, foreground, and thematize the connections between themselves as material artifacts and the imaginative realm of verbal/semiotic signifiers they instantiate open a window on the larger connections that unite literature as a verbal art to its material forms. To name such works, I propose "technotexts," a term that connects the technology that produces the texts to the texts' verbal constructions. (*Writing* 25–26)

In my view, there is a non sequitur in the logical connection between the first and the second sentence. First, the focus is on the link that a work might establish between the language-based content and the material artifact. In a printed book, all of this would occur in the interaction between reader and artifact. As Pross insisted by differentiating secondary and tertiary media, readers do not need the production technology in this interchange. The printing machine and the author's word processor have no direct causal relation to the experiential scenario of reading. In a figurative sense, the text may indeed refer to its production technologies. However, this is by far not the only form in which language can thematize its medial environment. In her basic premises, Hayles is very close to the notion of metamediality proposed here, but her concept is narrower in that it articulates the process solely through the lens of technology.

To integrate the idea of the technotext into a broader scholarly program, Hayles introduces the concept of "media-specific analysis" or MSA. She holds that MSA forms the end result of a process in which literary criticism sheds the assumptions specific to print, which have dominated the field ever since its inception. Many factors long ignored by academics need to be reintroduced into critical discourse, which would entail an extension of the critical toolbox: "Understanding literature as the interplay between form, content, and medium, MSA insists that texts must always be embodied to exist in the world. The materiality of those embodiments interacts dynamically with linguistic, rhetorical, and literary practices to create the effects we call literature" (*Writing* 31). Overall, MSA appears as a sound critical approach that synthesizes many of the interdisciplinary pursuits and conversations now occurring in media studies, literary sociology, and the history of the book.[17] Yet, Hayles's analytical practice only partially fulfills the promise of this bold disciplinary outline. MSA falls prey to what I would term the "technological fallacy," inherited from the Kittlerian focus on writing-down systems.

The English translations of Kittler's works have somewhat obscured the fact that writing tools hold the prime position in Kittlerian media theory. His main work, *Discourse Networks*, bears the original title *Aufschreibesysteme*, which can be literally translated as "writing-down systems."[18] Kittler's basic reasoning is that technologies and storage apparatuses determine the way the author thinks; accordingly the author's predetermined thoughts are reflected in the literary work. Thus, to understand the meaning of a literary work truly, one has to illuminate the discourse network, or better the inscription system from which it derives. In his influential *Gramophone, Film, Typewriter*, Kittler employs a biographical approach and uses letters and other correspondences, as well as nonfictional or philosophical essays as sources from which to resurrect an image of the respective author's psychic state at the time of composition. The literary work itself is thus demoted to the last element of the chain; it merely fulfills what is already entailed in the psycho-technological realm of the author.

Analogous to the "intentional fallacy" theorized by William K. Wimsatt and Monroe C. Beardsley, the logical leap of the "technological fallacy" short-circuits the author's influence with the literary work. Adopting the Kittlerian method, Hayles often reads autobiographical accounts against the fictional works themselves to find the personal comments of the authors realized within their novels. Longer parts of her interpretation of *House of Leaves* in *Writing Machines* deal with a personal interview she conducted with Mark Z. Danielewski and another interview published in *Critique*.[19] All of the information she is thereby able to include is helpful for an understanding of the book's genesis. It is truly fascinating that Danielewski typed the book as a continuous text, sketched out the intricate visual design entirely in pencil, and ended up digitally laying out the whole book himself at the Pantheon offices (Hayles, *Writing* 124–28). But Hayles's perspective focuses so intently on authors and their writing tools that the finalized artifact and the actual scene of reading often disappear from view. In Hayles's more recent writings, this tendency has become more pronounced, as I show in my readings of Danielewski's work in Chapter 3. Ultimately, Haylesian media-specific analysis gives too much value to the author/technology-complex and leaves the literary work as a mere trace of the creative processes at the nexus of writer and machine. Since Hayles's scientific and technological expertise overrides her interest in the materiality of the book, I choose to instead align my approach with the hermeneutic methodology of close reading.[20] Nevertheless, Haylesian MSA is a provocative contribution to the evolving field of textual materialism. To counterbalance its technological bias, the following section engages with the field of book history, whose perspective on the embodied artifact has developed from a wholly different disciplinary context.

## ¶ Book (and) History

In literary and cultural studies, the emerging academic discourse of textual materialism still holds a marginal position. However, the relevance of the medial aspects of texts was never neglected in other branches of literary criticism, especially when conceived within the larger framework of philology. Here, textual criticism and bibliography have little investment in the meaning of literary artifacts and all the more in the technical details of book production and the material features of individual books. Robert Darnton holds that post–World War II developments in the theory and methodology of literary and cultural studies pushed bibliography to the sidelines: "From the New Criticism of the 1940s to the deconstruction of the 1960s and the new historicism of the 1980s, the study of texts became increasingly detached from their embodiment in books. Bibliography began to look like an arcane discipline that might have uses for editing Shakespeare but little relevance for understanding modern literature" (*Case* 135). In the classical understanding of textual criticism as an ancillary discipline to the humanities, the field's extent stops at the threshold of literary criticism, for which it supplies authoritative, critical editions of primary texts. Literary critics are supposed to take the baton and use critical editions for their work. This longstanding agreement within the field was only challenged from the 1980s onward, when a number of textual critics began to trespass on unfamiliar territory. Two of the most prominent detractors from the bibliographic consensus were Donald F. McKenzie and Jerome McGann, both of whom claimed that in the interest of a more complete understanding of literature, neither literary nor textual critics could afford to ignore their respective theories.

During his bibliographical studies, McKenzie increasingly came to doubt positivist understandings of authorial intention and the historical study of the materialities of book production that dominated the field over the course of much of the twentieth century. In his influential 1981 essay "Typography and Meaning," he summarizes his central arguments and calls for a new appreciation of the meaningful aspects of bibliography in the interpretation of literary texts. Using the example of William Congreve's collected *Works* from 1710, he points out that the entirety of the published work figures within the process of signification. Its expressive materiality makes it impossible, he contends, "to divorce the substance of the text on the one hand from the physical form of its presentation on the other" (200). The totality of bibliographic factors such as typography, page design, paper, and book format, McKenzie argues, guides the reader's experience of the work. They are not simply marginal addenda; their form is inextricably bound up with the semantic contents of Congreve's plays. The book itself is an expressive means. Although it met with considerable criticism, McKenzie's "Typography and Meaning" and his ensuing publications influenced a circle of researchers who went on to form the nucleus of the emerging field "book history," among them the historians Robert Darnton and Roger Chartier.

Both Darnton and Chartier have published extensively on French cultural history with a specific focus on the history of books and printing technologies. Despite their predominant investment in French *histoire du livre*, their programmatic work is also foundational for Anglo-American book history. Darnton aimed to systematize the field's main concerns in his "communications circuit," which maps the field of book history along the route of a book from author to reader ("What Is" 12). Darnton's underlying idea of circularity pervades a great deal of book-historical scholarship, even while some researchers criticize his scheme for conceptual shortcomings.[21] To map the altered logistics and economics of our emerging digital communications circuit, Darnton's model would need to be radically modified: instead of printers, the digital circuit now features soft- and hardware makers, as well as digital designers; suppliers bring in aluminum, glass, and rare-earth materials instead of paper and ink; shippers and booksellers now include telecommunications providers such as AT&T and the electronic marketplaces of Amazon, Apple, and Google.

A modified, differential model of the communications circuit allows critics to stress the divergent dynamics of book culture in the present, as recently undertaken by Ted Striphas in *The Late Age of Print*. Striphas's account, however, mostly parses the evolution of book culture with regard to economics and daily usage routines. For the field of literary studies, Jerome McGann has developed some of the most helpful and adaptable book historical tools. In *The Textual Condition* (1991) McGann reformulates textual criticism not as an addendum to literary criticism, but as an integral part. The end result, according to McGann, would be a "materialist hermeneutics" (15) that seriously interrogates "symbolic exchanges," i.e. acts of writing and reading, as "material negotations" (3). Here, McGann shares many affinities with Hayles. The unique strength of his approach, however, lies in its insistence on the bibliographical study of printed matter. With reference to Gérard Genette's influential *Paratexts*, McGann introduces a pair of analytical terms that guide his analysis. He distinguishes immaterial, language-based "linguistic codes" from material "bibliographic codes," with the latter term usefully grouping all aspects that carry meaning in a book, but are not part of the language-based content.[22] Instead of approaching these aspects as peripheral to the work itself, McGann understands a literary work as a "double helix of perceptual codes," an amalgam in which both material and immaterial features interact to generate aesthetic experiences (*Textual* 77). Elucidating these layers of meaning involves conducting close readings of the different editions with a specific eye toward the nexus between text and medium.

Building on the formative work of McKenzie, Darnton, and McGann, recent studies in the field have begun to tackle more directly the peculiarities of literary book and print culture. Especially the essay collections

*Reading Books* (1996) by Michele Moylan and Lane Stiles and *Illuminating Letters* (2001) by Paul C. Gutjahr and Megan L. Benton are indicative in this regard. In their historical scope, however, these studies only rarely venture into the second half of the twentieth century. Yet the career of the material book in fiction did not simply terminate when the codex lost its monopoly on data transmission. Even in the altered media ecology of the present, bibliographic forms of literature have not broken with the past. Instead, today's book fictions continue, refashion, and reinvent the creative techniques and aesthetic programs of earlier periods.

## ¶ Enduring Modernisms, Enduring Codices

Most readings of Dave Eggers, Mark Z. Danielewski, and Jonathan Safran Foer situate these authors as proponents of either a late postmodernism or an emergent post-postmodernism.[23] However, the current flurry of innovative book fictions also underscores the lasting influence of a modernist sensibility, as described by Jerome McGann and other book historians. With recourse to James Joyce's *Ulysses*, McGann holds that "many of the key works of the modernist movement in literature, especially the work produced before 1930, heavily exploit the signifying power of documentary and bibliographical materials" (*Textual* 79). Building on McGann's overview, Johanna Drucker's *The Visible Word* (1994) thoroughly grounds modernist avant-garde writing in printing technologies and book formats. In her study, Drucker—herself a practicing book artist—describes the bond between literature and the book as much more precarious than does McGann. Drucker formulates a perspective on avant-garde textual artworks of the early twentieth century that does justice to the medial investment of a great number of individual artists engaged in Futurism, Vorticism, Dada, or Cubism.

A crucial figure who paved the way for the modernists' interest in the book as an aesthetic object was the late-nineteenth-century British author and printer William Morris. At the epicenter of the arts-and-crafts movement in Britain, Morris attempted to redefine the business of printing as a craft. In the shadow of several revivals—of Gothic print style, of medievalism in bookmaking, of ornamental work in books—

Morris founded his own printing house, the Kelmscott Press, in 1891 (Peterson xii–xiii). Against the commodified and often ill-designed Victorian book, he promoted increased attention to the aesthetic aspects of printing. The Kelmscott Press went on to produce dozens of literary works with its custom set of fonts on specially selected materials, the apex of its achievement being the 1896 edition of Chaucer's works. Morris's retreat into arts-and-crafts aesthetics was just one strategy used by printers to react to the technologization of their trade and the explosion in the number of books in circulation. Willa Z. Silverman has recently shown that the author and publisher Octave Uzanne stood at the center of a fin-de-siècle cult of deluxe book collecting in France. In opposition to Morris, Uzanne and his fellow bibliophiles embraced new photomechanical processes, chemically treated paper, and mechanical press equipment for their potential in fine printing. At a time when the Linotype and wood-pulp paper democratized the public sphere and flooded the Atlantic world with print, Uzanne saw the expensive, lavishly illustrated editions of French classics as a prime agent of social distinction, geared to "advance an elitist aesthetic of the book" (Silverman 22). With Uzanne as an exemplary case, we can see how the social relevance of technologies of inscription pale in comparison to the material artifact—at least with regard to secondary media. "Rather than merely coexisting in opposition to one another," Silverman holds, "the sectors of commercial and fine book production were in fact closely interrelated, with technology serving as an essential link between them" (23). Whereas the technology has a relatively neutral function in this matrix—it can produce pulp magazines just as well as collector's editions—the printed artifact actively assigns meaning, value, and social status through its circulation.

In its various facets, the renewed interest in printing practices in the late nineteenth century spilled over into emerging modernisms in the arts. As Drucker argues, Morris's engagement with the medium of the book proved to be seminal: "[I]n spite of its *retardataire* stylistics and conservative promotion of anachronistic methods of production, Morris's work served to sensitize the eyes of the late nineteenth-century public to the visual appearance of the page as a significant feature of literary production" (*Visible* 93). While avant-garde authors felt the need to overcome the flowery look and the faux-medieval aesthetics of Morrisean fine printing, they shared an underlying sense of urgency in their exploration of the printed book. In their attempts to break with conventions—to "make it new" in Ezra Pound's famous aphorism—literary modernists also tried to reinvent the book. According to McGann, Pound holds not only a pivotal position in modernist literary history, but also in modernist book history: "Were one to write that history, Ezra Pound would appear once again the crucial point of departure" (*Black* 76). The author took to heart many of Morris's maxims about the production of a printed work of art and himself became an expert in bookmaking with a lifelong interest in the production process of his volumes (*Black* 79). As such, Ezra Pound stands as the prototype of the medial writer who extends the range of his creative practice from language outward to the carrier medium of the book. Such authorial involvement in the printed product is increasingly relevant for contemporary literature, as I show in later chapters. Suffice it to say here that American literature currently sees a renewed interest in bookmaking and printing. As is obvious in the examples of Morris, Uzanne, and Pound, however, this twenty-first-century phenomenon is not without precedent.

The work of Drucker and McGann highlights another aspect that connects the modernist literary scene in Europe and the United States to the present: the little magazine. Since the mid-nineteenth century, such small publishing ventures arose with certain regularity. They proved to be the perfect breeding ground for experiments with book production and typography: "Editorial and design responsibility for such publications generally resided with the sole editor, and the informality of collaborations which gave the works form was frequently the result of ongoing social contact as much as any institutionalized editorial board or policy" (Drucker, *Visible* 103). Without this half-commercial, half-improvised form of reproduction, Futurism, Dadaism, and many other artistic "-isms" of the period would have been unthinkable. The small-scale production circle countered the mass medium of the press and the renowned literary quarterlies with a focus on connoisseurship and in-group mentality.[24]

The participants in these intimate social circles were often personally acquainted, since writers and readers intermingled at social events. Instead of dividing labor, these magazines saw publishers that simultaneously curated, edited, designed, and contributed to their publications. "[I]n production and, to a more qualified degree, in reception," writes Drucker, "these works formed a social sphere whose members might often be at odds over aesthetic particulars, but were bonded through their separation from the more traditional, conservative, or contemporary bourgeois realms from which they sought to distinguish themselves" (Visible 104). Aside from serving as an outlet for literary prose and poetry, little magazines were also a prime conduit for social distinction. Magazines like Poetry, The Masses, or The Little Review attempted to steer their sociocultural reception through paratexts, much like the contemporary literary quarterly McSweeney's does now, as I show in the next chapter.

Beyond the enduring relevance of modernism, the lessons we can draw from book historical scholarship extend to the endurance of paper-based communication over the longue durée. The history of the book has been full of revolutions, both large and small, but it has also seen remarkably long periods of stability during which individual systems of production, distribution, and reception were firmly in place and altered little. Print historian Frederick G. Kilgour accordingly framed the development of the book as a history of "punctuated equilibria," referencing the influential concept in evolutionary science coined by Stephen Jay Gould and Niles Eldredge (4). The properties of the codex have remained remarkably stable throughout the centuries, leading some scholars to reconsider the historical impact of Gutenberg's printing press.[25] Offset printing, "the most important printing innovation to gain maturity in the twentieth century" (Kilgour 133), ultimately ended the predominance of the movable type apparatus and still stands as the mechanical base of current book production. This new technology, however, was only able to wield its full power when word processing and digital typography broke out of printing houses into the workplace, and finally the home. When Apple and IBM entered the market with the first computers for private use in 1981 and 1984, they started a process that would facilitate the typesetting and design of books considerably. Also in the mid-1980s, a number of software products emerged that laid the foundation for a new printing production process. Adobe PostScript made letters and images compatible across a range of computers and printers; the TrueType system for digital typography introduced scalable vector graphics for enhanced printing output; Aldus PageMaker and QuarkXPress brought page layout functionality to personal computers at an affordable price (Mosley 103). Currently, most people who write either in a professional or private context will probably have dabbled with desktop publishing programs like Word or Publisher from Microsoft, or with Adobe's InDesign.

From the perspective of literary studies, these developments have significant effects on the way media texts circulate. In publishing, evolving computer technology combined with modern printing machines drastically lowered the costs of book production. It became feasible for a large number of small presses to publish book projects that turn small profits, if any. Not only has it become easier to publish a standard book; the advance of publishing software has also brought with it the annihilation of technical limits on the production of visually enhanced texts. Page designers are no longer simply setting type, which is essentially the same thing Gutenberg did in the fifteenth century. With growing computing power, many are now designing type instead of just setting it. Typography can thus be custom made for a specific edition of a book—as we have seen in Hayles's *Writing Machines*—raising the potential for intertwining the discursive components in complex ways with the bibliographic artifact. Also, the new design possibilities have redefined the way in which text is presented between the two covers of a book. Borders, charts, graphs, and pictures casually mingle with typography in digital files, and offset printing diminishes the production difference between a letter and a picture. Furthermore, even the physical arrangement of pages can easily be manipulated.

Bibliographical inquiry has not suddenly become obsolete just because many commentators have pronounced the death of the book. On the contrary, in certain segments American literature has reached unprecedented levels of bibliographic expressivity in its full embrace of bibliographic codes that—due to high incremental costs—could not be purposefully employed by writers prior to desktop publishing and offset printing. James Mosley accordingly sees a host of revolutions and upheavals in production technology, yet remarkable stability in the end product: "The printed book as an object has not changed radically since its introduction in the fifteenth century . . . Indeed, it is generally agreed that—although the appearance of offset lithography is subtly different from that of letterpress printing—digital types and typesetting have on the whole enhanced the look of printing without altering it noticeably" (11). Looking at any number of media critics from Kittler, to Hayles, and to Bolter, this view of book production in the digital age seems far from "generally agreed." Yet Mosley's sober, functionalist view of production technology as subordinate to the final product of the book provides a healthy antidote to technological determinism and inter-medial utopianism. In the hands of book historians, revolution turns into evolution. All in all, the field of book history is still exploring its disciplinary form while simultaneously pushing into the mainstream of literary studies. The exact descriptive practices of book historians should appeal to literary critics schooled in thorough considerations of linguistic content. This methodology has its merits not only for "old books," but also for contemporary literature, where an increasing num-ber of mass-produced literary texts now employ calculated book design to direct the reading experience. Given the sheer complexity of appara-tuses, software codes, and processes of computation and production, the continuing emergence of books as artworks still—and maybe more than before—deserves attention.

## ¶ The Metamedium as Social Text

The material covered in this chapter allows for a more nuanced and ex-tended definition of metamediality, along with a more precise outlook on its social function. I understand it as a form of artistic self-reference that systematically mirrors, addresses, or interrogates the material properties of its medium. Literary metamediality draws attention to the status of texts as medial artifacts and examines the relationship between the text and its carrier medium, such as the printed book. In linking discourse and medium, metamediality reduces complexity by stabilizing a specific sensory experience of a literary work. Simultaneously, it fosters an increasingly complex, embodied mode of reading, which appreciates the entire artifact as an integrated work of art. Metamedial forms of expression thus qualify as elements of an evolving semantics within contemporary literature that attempts to rationalize the hypercomplex media environment constituted by the diversified channels through which texts circulate.[26]

Departing from this understanding, the central aim behind the readings in the following chapters is to (re)establish connections between printed words and their embodied form. To explore the metamedial process means to embed narrative or paratexts into the specific material shape in which they were (and are) circulated in society. If texts can initiate what Gumbrecht calls "presence effects" (Production 107), the exact textual and medial ensemble that triggers these effects needs to be interrogated. In all this, the form of textual materialism advocated here is not to be understood as a throwback to the intrinsic method of the New Criticism.[27] Interpreting the materiality of texts should not produce readings cut off from the cultural realm. Instead, as Johanna Drucker argues, the external features of designed artifacts constitute a prime locus in which cultures encounter and describe themselves: "Durability, scale, reflectiveness, richness and density of saturation and color, tactile and visual pleasure—all of these factor in—not as transcendent and historically independent universals, but as aspects whose historical and cultural specificity cannot be divorced from their substantial properties" (Visible, 45). To close read media, even on the microscale of individual printed-and-bound artifacts, always already means investigating culture. This methodological perspective correlates with the New Historicist notion of "cultural work," i.e. the way in which texts not merely represent reality but actively shape it. The medium, to a greater or lesser degree, contributes to the overall meaning of the literary text and therefore influences the cultural work that the artifact performs. Long before Drucker, Donald F. McKenzie had already postulated that the study of material texts always has a social dimension and had called for a "sociology of texts" that would embrace the entire field (200). Such a sociology of texts, however, is in dire need of a theory of the social. It is in this domain, as suggested over the course of this chapter, that the systems theory of Niklas Luhmann pays rich dividends, as this theory is premised less on the human subject and individual agency and more on communicative practices and institutions.

As an analytical method, medial close reading treats the literary text as a staging ground of the social. It holds the potential to complicate, or rather activate, the dichotomy between text and context, between art and the social. Bruno Latour's work in Actor-Network-Theory—in itself less a theory than a programmatic outline for practices—articulates a similar impulse to unearth activities of objects and artifacts, instead of merely looking for social explanations above and beyond them. With recourse to Plato's cave allegory, Latour has lamented that "all the objects people have learned to cherish have been replaced by puppets projecting social shadows which are supposed to be the only 'true reality' that is 'behind' the appreciation of the work of art" (236). Choosing material books—rather than authors or readers—as entry points into contemporary print culture allows us to reconstruct the inflow and outflow of agencies. Printed artifacts come about through associations (among writers, printers, publishers, etc.), but once produced and sold, they freely create new associations as they circulate (among readers, critics, other writers, etc.).

The challenge, then, is to trace these associations and connecting communications through the material archive. Such tracing is difficult with novels, which usually present themselves as singular occurrences. Thus, instead of giving center stage to the novel as the dominant genre of contemporary literary expression, the following chapter engages with the serial format of the literary magazine. As we have seen, small literary magazines constitute a field in which social connections, group identities, and bookmaking coalesce into unlikely and unstable hubs of literary production. The evolution of the McSweeney's publishing house provides a suggestive index of the coevolution of literature and its medial and institutional environment. In its serialized output and evolving aesthetic program, McSweeney's speaks to the irritations and innovations that digitization has triggered across the communications circuit of American literature.

## 2. A Bookish Institution: The McSweeney's Universe

IN HIS STANDARD SURVEY OF THE American magazine scene, Edward E. Chielens defines little magazines as publications "founded by an individual or small group, usually with a small, precarious budget, in order to publish new writers or a new school of literature not accepted by the large commercial publications" (vii). By his own account, Dave Eggers curated the first issue of *McSweeney's Quarterly Concern* in 1998 with a similar motivation: "I began wondering if it were possible to start a new journal, assembled from . . . articles not fit for other magazines—a quarterly of orphaned stories" ("Introduction," viii). Many modernist little magazines were avant-garde publications aiming to push the envelope in the realm of experimental and refined literature. Ezra Pound's fluctuating allegiances with various British and American periodicals exemplify the conflicted, but awesomely productive search for a truly autonomous site of cultural production. Against this, Eggers does not claim to provide an outlet for avant-gardist literature. While he laments the small number of journals publishing unconventional fiction and nonfiction, his initial concern was for "literary humor" (viii). He concedes, however, that as the journal's popularity grew, contributors increasingly composed pieces specifically for publication in *McSweeney's*.

Dubbed an "informal collective" (Nicol 102), a literary "coterie" (Burn), or "a key barometer of the literary climate, especially among the young and hip" (McGrath), the McSweeney's Universe has had a perceptible influence on the American literary scene, particularly after the charismatic founder Dave Eggers became a literary celebrity.[1] Eggers's public persona at times overshadows his individual works to an extent where reviews of his books as well as scholarly essays concern themselves more with the author than with his texts. In the first monograph on Eggers, Caroline D. Hamilton devotes much space to the external discourses surrounding Eggers's celebrity status and presents sociological arguments about the McSweeney's readership.[2] Although Eggers is an important actor, his communicative sway pales when compared to the hundreds of thousands of printed copies that bear his name and circulate throughout the world. However immense his public profile in the U.S. literary scene may be, Dave Eggers's early works—from the initial issues of *McSweeney's* through his memoir and his first novel— significantly transcend his personal realm. In this chapter, I read them as symptomatic artifacts in which the American literary system adapts to its changing environment. At the same time, the McSweeney's Universe has in itself become a microsystem in which associations and networks between writers and styles accumulate and evolve.[3]

The publication date of the quarterly's first issue roughly coincides with the introduction of e-book readers to the mainstream U.S. market. Having developed within a fully digitized environment from its very inception, McSweeney's stands as an exemplary institution of print culture in the digital era. The serial publication *McSweeney's* can monitor its own reception and comment on it in subsequent issues. The current issue of the literary journal is therefore always an important connecting communication to the previous numbers. The McSweeney's Universe functions autopoietically on a very small scale, as it processes the evolution of public discourse and media technologies according to the logic of its own communicative system. For Eggers and his wide network of associates, digitization was never a challenge to, but always an integral component of, contemporary book culture. In fact, many readers will have first encountered McSweeney's as a humor site on the Web, a branch of the firm that still operates under the whimsical title "Timothy McSweeney's Internet Tendency."

The larger presence of McSweeney's surpasses the printed pages of the journal. In the early years, the McSweeney's coterie of writers performed numerous idiosyncratic public events. For the first few issues, Eggers would regularly organize release parties with impromptu invitations posted to the McSweeney's Web site. For issue two, about 600 people gathered in a shoddy venue in Chinatown, where boxes full of freshly printed copies were sold. In 1999 some interns and associates of the journal opened a "McSweeney's Store" in Brooklyn, which offered "Small Rubber Cubes, Lumberjack Supply, Customized Trophies, Rodeo Supply, Pewter Cast Bird Feet . . . [and] Books by the Page" (The Editors of McSweeney's 16). The store's aim was to accurately arrange and sell the most outlandish products alongside McSweeney's publications, which thus appeared like random items in a store full of strange objects. The youthful fanfare of these happenings—Eggers and his friends were mostly in their twenties at the time—reveals an embodied ethos of literary interaction. Release parties, book signings, and public readings form a part of contemporary print culture that hardly enters scholarly accounts. The literary work remains at the center in this network of practices, yet not as the immaterial story it relates. The aesthetic experience for partygoers or store patrons extends to their lived experience with and through the book. As the eccentric McSweeney's Store shows, texts become social texts in the cluttered staging ground of material culture.

During the period from 1998 to 2010, Eggers and his staff produced thirty-six issues of McSweeney's Quarterly Concern, which form the archive that the following readings are based on. On one level, McSweeney's merely serves as a channel that allows various forms of writing to enter the literary marketplace: the company publishes several periodicals and has its own imprint of books, with about forty fiction titles in print by the end of 2010. From the perspective of textual materialism and book history, however, McSweeney's publications figure as embodied arti-facts that contain self-descriptions and running metacommentary on literature and bookmaking in digital society.

## ¶ From Paperback to Hardcover:
### Launching *McSweeney's Quarterly Concern*

Prior to the massive success of his memoir *A Heartbreaking Work of Stag-gering Genius* (2000), Dave Eggers established a unique literary format in the first five issues of his quarterly. *McSweeney's* 1, 2, and 3 share a similar, recognizable design. Beyond this, each issue gravitates toward a specific bibliographic theme: the first reflects on typography and page layout, the second subverts the sequential ordering of pages, and the third invades the margins of the physical book. Issues four and five then initiate the serial trademark of *McSweeney's*. Since their publication, the exterior form of every subsequent issue has been completely different from the preceding one. The first batch of issues also introduced paratextual spaces as essential components of the journal, in which the editors reflect on the mechanics and economics of book production. These seri-alized artifacts are crystallizing points for a coterie of writers, a growing fan base, and an emergent semantics of contemporary bookmaking.

As with any serial product, the first number forms a crucial corner-stone since it creates the basic norms, recurring features, and com-mon themes that form the connective tissue for the series as a whole. *McSweeney's* 1 is a paperback volume 7 × 9.5 inches in size and about 140 pages thick. Bearing just one miniature line drawing, the minimal-ist typographic cover with its center-justified headlines underscores Eggers's preference for classical book fonts (see fig. 1). It references the typographic title pages that were common prior to bookbinding mechanization and the introduction of the dust jacket in the late nine-teenth century.[4] For all textual components of *McSweeney's*, Dave Eggers

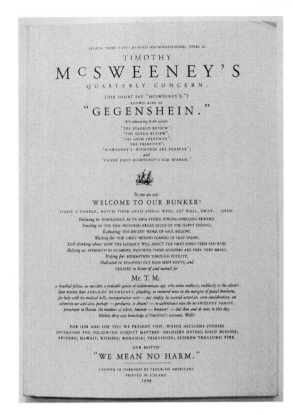

Fig. 1. Cover of *McSweeney's 1* (1998). Courtesy of McSweeney's Publishing. Photograph by Alexander Starre.

uses Garamond 3, a 1930s Old Style typeface by the American designers Morris Fuller Benton and Thomas Maitland Cleland. This choice of a standard font, which is still in use to the present day, is in itself highly suggestive. In the introduction to the anthology *The Best of McSweeney's* (2004), Eggers casually explains that he picked the font "because it looked good in so many permutations—italics, small caps, all caps, tracked out, justified or not" ("Introduction" vii). As a classic book typeface, Garamond inevitably lends a traditional, nostalgic air to the new publication. Thus, even before reading a single word, McSweeney's audiences experience a number of connotations based on its graphic design.

What is more, the Garamond font has a special place in the history of printing. Despite their name, Old Style typefaces (also called "Old Face" or "Garalde") originally signaled a major innovation in type design. Early printers from around 1500 mainly used two type families: the Gutenbergian Blackletter and the Italian Humanist types. Both of them imitated the scribal traditions of their regional cultures, thus firmly embodying preprint traditions. Garamond strayed from the manuscript aesthetics of these two fonts and pioneered a visual style specifically suited for the technology of letterpress printing. As Tova Rabinowitz explains, this shift came about as readers accepted printed books in their own right and publishers slowly strayed from the convention to imitate handwriting in movable type (91). Much like how later typographers developed Times New Roman for newspapers, the creators of Old Style typefaces perceived the printed book as the target medium for their work. Accordingly, contemporary graphic designers rarely use Garamond on Web sites, screen displays, or in other contexts that call for a sleek visual style. The cover of *McSweeney's* 1 contains abundant self-reflexive humor, for example, when it gives eight alternate titles for the new literary journal. The polished form of its typeface, however, is at odds with the discursive content of the page. Instead of reinforcing the nostalgic grandeur suggested by the typography, the tone is satirical and informal throughout, with the editorial voice of *McSweeney's* directly addressing the reader: "*To you we say*: Welcome to our bunker!"[5]

The extensive use of paratextual space continues on the copyright page of the first issue. Here, Eggers discloses his financial calculations. He explains that the circulation of 2,500 copies cost exactly $4,109 in printing and $1,400 in shipping. After giving away a portion to promote the journal, he hopes to sell about 1,500 copies for eight dollars apiece, leaving a profit of roughly $2,000. Extending these disclosures into the domain of manufacturing, Eggers mentions the nation of Iceland, "where this was most assuredly printed" (*McSweeney's* 1, 2).[6] This bit of information has to be specifically marked as true to ensure that readers will not decode it as a hoax. Through the simple pronoun "this," Eggers achieves an anchoring of words to page—a place deixis—that creates a feedback loop between reading experience and medium. In his pioneering, late-nineteenth-century work on semiotics, Charles Sanders Peirce pointed to the special cognitive operation initiated by a deictic pronoun. As an "index," such a pronoun asks the reader to "establish a real connection between his mind and the object" (Peirce 14). While a "real connection" between mind and matter has been all but debunked by cognitive science and systems theory, Peirce still accurately notes the potential of indexical expressions to make subjects aware of their material surroundings.

With its detailed production minutiae, the journal attempts to counteract the loss of aura that Walter Benjamin famously diagnosed with regard to the mechanically reproducible artwork. The material appeal of this simple paperback magazine profits considerably from the fact that it was printed at Oddi Printing in Reykjavík, a location far removed from New York. The aesthetic theory underlying Benjamin's influential "Work of Art" essay largely excludes verbal art, and focuses instead on visual forms of representation. Within the essay, this is a logical decision as Benjamin's argument rests on the tension between a unique original and its copies. Rethinking the individual book as an artwork, however, we can reverse Benjamin's argument. About the original work of art, Benjamin writes: "In even the most perfect reproduction, *one* thing is lacking: the here and now of the work of art—its unique existence in a particular place. It is this unique existence—and nothing else—that bears the mark of the history to which the work has been subject" (21). Once the differentiation between original and copy collapses into a type/token relationship, as it does with the book, Benjamin's place-bound aestheticism does apply to the mass-produced artifact. In a functional sense, the book possesses personal and historical properties similar to a painting or a sculpture, so that we may attribute para-original status to each copy of a book. The axiological terms "authenticity" and "aura" are inadequate tools to describe the processes set in motion by the *McSweeney's* paratexts. Yet in his emphasis on the artifactual status of the book, Eggers certainly evokes the key themes of Benjamin's influential essay.

The combination of direct reader address and deictic localization recurs in a final component of the copyright page. Having established the cost projections of issue one, Eggers writes, "This journal was typeset using a small group of fonts that you already have on your computer, with software you already own" (*McSweeney's* 1, 2). The editor directly references the state of desktop publishing hard- and software at the end of the 1990s. The implied reader of this passage—an urban dweller either in New York or in another large city with an independent book store that carries *McSweeney's*—supposedly possesses the necessary tools to write, typeset, and publish a similar artifact. With this small note, *McSweeney's* purports a bookmaking philosophy far from a nostalgic return to letterpress composition, fine printing, or handbinding. The magazine embraces the tools of the digital age, yet—and this is the main twist—not as media, but as technologies. The computer, as it surfaces here, possesses the capacity to make the book a better artistic medium. Simultaneously a bibliophile and an advocate for innovative production technologies, Eggers effectively continues the publishing lineage of the French book lover Octave Uzanne. Where Uzanne was a self-confident elitist, however, Eggers tries to avoid this label through his paratextual rhetoric of democratic empowerment.

In its internal organization, *McSweeney's* 1 establishes a rough template for future issues. The table of contents precedes a section with letters to the editor, followed by individual stories and essays. Here, readers perceive the signature *McSweeney's* page design for the first time. A thin line frames every page, encompassing the body text and indicating the space for the page numbers and the running headlines of each piece. On the one hand, this layout appears dilettantish and unfinished, as if the guiding lines of the design software had mistakenly been reproduced in the final product. On the other hand, this design increases the metamedial potential of each *McSweeney's* page. These pages invite reflection on their borders and on the creative space that is inherently limited to the dimensions of the book. With the designer's margins and tools exposed, readers become involved in the process of experiencing each *McSweeney's* page *as* page. Only with issue thirty-nine (2011) was this page design quietly phased out; the look of *McSweeney's* now approaches conventional book layout.

The front cover of the second issue (1999) serially builds upon the first one (see fig. 2). The design takes up virtually all elements of the first cover, from the alternative title to the "Printed in Iceland" notice. Yet, the cover incorporates more pictorial elements by adding simple tables, dial charts, and line drawings. The large, horizontal table in the upper half of the cover contains the most relevant information— the names of the contributors—in the smallest font size. In the usual off-hand manner, the box advertises "big-name writers"; several lines down, we read, "Did you get the joke about the big name writers set in very small type?" The cover page also intensifies the double coding of typography as decorative element and semantic signifier. In the lower corners, two blocks of text provide visual symmetry to the page. The

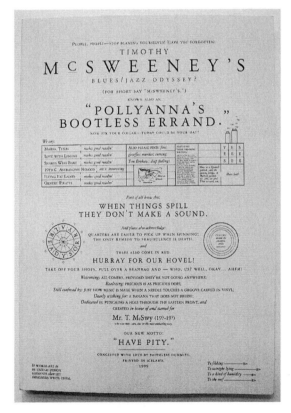

Fig. 2. Cover of McSweeney's 2 (1999). Courtesy of McSweeney's Publishing. Photograph by Alexander Starre.

left-hand snippet reflects on its degraded status as design element: "If words are to be used as design elements then let designers write them."

The issue's copyright page sprawls over three full pages, with an embedded short story taking up a good portion the text. The narrative starts at the point where Eggers explains the logistics of subscribing. Here, an anonymous "McSweeney's representative" enters, who collects all subscription requests that arrive in the mail at "the McSweeney's compound." With this representative, Eggers ridicules his own fetish for the printed objects stockpiled at his apartment, each of them "heavy and smooth, looking and feeling so good in bunches like that, like gold bars maybe, only white, white, *white*" (*McSweeney's* 2, 2). In the following, the representative addresses all envelopes by hand and even jots brief, customized notes into the individual copies. The interaction of human with paper takes on mythical proportions, yet the satirical tone subverts the grandiose rhetoric. Toward the end of the brief story, the narrator gets sidetracked as he recounts how the representative picks up a set of custom-made stamps from a stationery shop:

> He wanted desperately to try them out...*Stamp stamp stamp!* But he resisted, he resisted long enough to make it home—the last block a blur (he must have sprinted)—and once home and up the stairs to his bedroom, he stamped easily fifty envelopes, all at once, a mad orgy of stamping, the ink—self-inking!—covering liberally, evenly, wonderfully—though only, careful, careful! if stamped while on a flat, flat, sturdy surface (the carpet would not do). (3)

The figural narration is reminiscent of the frantic voice of Poe's murderer in "The Tell-Tale Heart." While certainly satiric, this hyperbolic, eroticized portrait of ink and paper still indicates profound pleasure with bibliographic detail, not least through its excessive length and detail.

Sarah Brouillette holds that in passages like this, Eggers relies on an "ethic of disclosure" that preempts criticism by confronting issues of composition and editing directly. She holds that the author hereby attempts to find "a safe position from which to create textual products within a field that still denounces wide-spread success and vilifies commercial interest." Brouillette frames her argument with Pierre Bourdieu's theory of the literary field, in which distinction from commercial market interests creates spheres of interaction that mirror this very market in their circulation of cultural capital. Her insights go a long way toward explaining the curious attention to financial details in many of Eggers's publications. Still, paratextual metamediality as performed by the story of the *McSweeney's* representative also functions on an intratextual level to renegotiate the act of reading as an embodied activity. The preemption of criticism does not primarily create a "safe position" for Dave Eggers—he is merely an authorial persona for all but a small part of the *McSweeney's* readership. The quaint portrait of Eggers's paper-loving avatar instead subverts the embrace of screens as superior media in mainstream American culture. Specifically addressing a young readership, Eggers's paratexts try to ventriloquize a self-conscious audience wavering among literary reading, consumerism, and book collecting.

Beyond the anxiety of selling out, Eggers's self-mocking paratexts speak to a larger dynamic in American postwar literature. As McGurl argues, contemporary authors often exhibit "a dialectic of shame and pride, self-hatred and self-esteem" (284). Faced with unprecedented social and geographic mobility, authors now participate in hyper-complex networks of criticism, scholarship, and taste that "provide an infinite array of chances for failure" (284). The combination of shame and pride of course figures strongly throughout literary history, perhaps best exemplified in the timeworn rhetorical strategy of the "humility topos," which Benjamin Franklin used to great effect in his *Autobiography*. For the modern subject, the act of communicating through a mass medium is indeed a risky undertaking, threatening to upset the author's public prestige as well as her sense of selfhood. In this process, the "pride of publication, which externalizes the self as printed text" (McGurl 312) is inevitably linked to the anxiety of negative feedback from the reading public. Shame and pride durably inscribe their traces on the pages of the first *McSweeney's* issues. Behind every piece of self-flagellation lurks a trace of the fundamental pleasure associated with the craft and skill enshrined in the final artifact. Facing confinement in the endless re-cursion of self-consciousness, the authorial voices of McSweeney's feed off of the irreducible there-ness of their creations.

McSweeney's 2 contains a range of content similar to the first issue. Humorous pieces still form the majority, although there is a notable tendency toward longer, more carefully edited texts. The concentrated, immersive reading of these extended pieces is interrupted at several points by Todd Pruzan's fragmented story "Hooper's Bathhouse." This interactive text recalls the popular "Choose Your Own Adventure" series published by Bantam in the 1970s. This genre features the uncommon perspective of second-person narration, so as to entice young readers to envision themselves as protagonists. Pruzan's story opens the issue and sprawls across the entire volume, nudged in between several other pieces. Following the snippets of the story, readers navigate back and forth through the journal. Not surprisingly, however, "Hooper's Bath-house" is a satire as well. Depending on the paths the reader takes, the protagonist and his friends either end up going back home, smoking marijuana with some older boys, or getting slaughtered by pirates.

In Pruzan's story, issue two engages with the sequential ordering of a bound volume. In Writing Space, Jay David Bolter identifies nonlinear interactive fictions as a "revolt against the assumption of our literate culture that we should read and write linearly" (151). Bolter's chapter on "Interactive Fictions" rests on a teleological, even typological, narrative in which the writings of Sterne, Joyce, and Borges prefigured electron-ically mediated hypertext. This historiography of literary form arises from Bolter's theory of "remediation" and thus inherently favors new media, which are capable of visually representing older media. On par with postmodern epistemology, he seems to suggest that interactive fictions question the ability of linear narratives to adequately render con-temporary experience and knowledge. For the straightforward humor pieces in McSweeney's, this would be an exaggerated reading. Standing on the shoulders of their metafictional predecessors, McSweeney's writers no longer have a general interest in tearing down the conventions of linear writing and printing. As such, Pruzan's interactive story carries little reflexive potential in its whimsical prose. Eggers instead uses "Hooper's Bathhouse" as a designer's exercise that imbues the act of turning pages with meaning. Ironically debunking the illusion of the fictional world, the story seems to obliterate itself. What remains beneath this failed act of communication is the basic medial practice of book culture: flipping sheets of paper. Like an aesthetic ground-clearing, issue two writes itself into the very stuff of which it is made.

Having grown to almost 300 pages, McSweeney's 3 (1999) completes a trilogy of white paperbacks. Where the first issue placed considerable emphasis on typography and the second on sequential ordering, issue three attempts to push its contents into every corner of the codex. The cover now bears more pictorial elements but remains focused on text. Brief references to the production process sprawl all across the cover's borders and segments. The snippets include short statements such as "Nothing need happen here," "Count the imperfections. They are many, they are ravishing," and "This area was blank for the longest time." In these comments, the editors contemplate the expanse of the physical page and the potential ways of filling it with meaningful content. Another fragment claims, "Editing for space is too easy to be moral." While this statement criticizes the common practice to trim or enlarge text in order to make it fit into predefined spaces, it also resonates with the peculiar McSweeney's style. Through localized text that inhabits its container, Eggers attempts to show that he "edits for place," not for space. A concentric image with nestled boxes and circles takes up the center of the cover. Resembling a movable wheel chart or volvelle, this design element references a long historical lineage going back to early modern astronomical and navigational books. The third issue propels its contents outward, with the spine containing the miniature story "Projected but Not Improbable Transcript of Author's Parents' Marriage's End, 1971" by David Foster Wallace. Through the placement of this piece, Eggers reinforces a bibliographic aesthetics that has no division between text and paratext.

The invasion of space that is conventionally left empty continues throughout the issue. Next to a gatefold that contains a collage by

Lawrence Weschler, an otherwise blank page carries some minuscule print in the fold between the two pages. It reads: "Interesting fact: When you want to have a gatefold fold to the left, you are told, by Bjorn, your project supervisor at Oddi Printing, that if you would like to have it fold out to the left, then you must also have this extra page, on which we are now chatting . . . So we have this page" (*McSweeney's* 3, 224–25). This tiny piece of text is set so close to the fold of the book, the so-called gutter, that readers have to bend the book and move up close. The deictic markers "behind" and "in front" clearly localize this discursive fragment in space next to an image and on the opposite side of a paper leaf that contains an essay by Weschler. Such transgressions lay bare the book design and production conventions. Readers are thus constantly drawn into a productive process of making and breaking boundaries. Such paratextual transgressions are nevertheless still reliant on the overall closure provided by the printed-and-bound artifact. The very wholeness of the book lends significance to the experiments performed within it. By analogy, we may say that the systems-theoretical mechanism of operational closure and intrinsic openness operates on the microlevel of the individual issue.

Aside from these renegotiations of physical boundaries, *McSweeney's* 3 also continues Eggers's preoccupation with fonts. The last page of the volume features a "Note about the Type," referencing the tradition of such explanatory addenda at major publishing firms like Knopf or Scribner. At first glance, the note looks like a small postscript with trivia about the designer of the typeface, its historical classification, and its visual impact. As soon as one starts reading, though, the witty *McSweeney's* humor sets in. With regard to Garamond, Eggers's editorial voice admits: "No one, including the author, knows anything about its history or creator" ("Note" 288). After this declaration, a paratextual mini-narrative nevertheless imagines Garamond as a paranoid man going through marital trouble and artistic crises.[7] In the first part of the narrative, Garamond suspects that his wife, Genevieve, is having an affair with "Palatino," the sixteenth-century calligraphy artist who served as namesake for Hermann Zapf's font of the same name. Yet, following his extensive deliberations, a different tone enters the story. The narrator recounts how Garamond perceives his work as a typographer:

> He wanted things to happen with his type on the page. He wanted the words he put on the page to not only be different, in terms of serif and line, he wanted them to look like something from another world or time. He wanted to reinvent, start over from scratch. But it was impossible. He was trapped within a cage built over thousands of years, by millions of people, and now all he could do was polish its bars, add a coat of paint. That he could not reinvent language completely was the most frustrating thing. ("Note" 207)

Garamond becomes the personification of typography as a whole. His artistic impulse far transcends the idea of representing a predefined language with effective typographic signs. Speaking through Garamond, Eggers voices his qualms about the "crystal goblet" theory of typography, as further discussed in Chapter 3, which judges a font by its capacity to make language easily readable but render itself invisible. He attempts to ensure that readers do not perceive the typographic extravagance of McSweeney's merely as an inconsequential surface effect.

McSweeney's 3 also depicts how metamedial effects stem not only from design, but also from narrative prose. In John Warner's magical-realist short story "The Circus Elephants Look Sad Because They Are," the protagonist, James, returns to his home after a day full of strange incidents. He encounters his unnamed wife sitting amid a heap of stray books on the floor. She blames James for not having checked on the books during the night, as she heard them screaming loudly from the shelf. The books supposedly threatened to kill themselves because James kept ignoring them. A number of them made good on their threats and attempted suicide. The whole scene resembles a massacre, while his wife attempts to help: "She lifts the book as if it were a broken bird and closes it, wincing at the slight crackling noise from the damaged spine. She caresses the cover with her fingertips before gently wrapping the book in toilet paper" (35). James joins the effort to clean up: "That night, most of the night, on hands and knees, James scrubs the floor where his wife points out the inky smears that have leaked from the books that had, in no uncertain terms the night previous, told her that those who had not been already choked off by dust, planned to hurl themselves from the bookshelf to the floor and their deaths" (35). Warner clearly points to the moral of this odd fable at the end, when James lifts his wife up from the floor. She admonishes him to be careful and not drop her to the floor like the suicidal volumes from their shelf. The status of the anthropomorphic books rises to the same level as the wife's. As family members, the bound volumes require as much attention as humans.

Even while irony pervades the story via its inflated, mock-somber tone, Warner aligns himself with the bibliographic interests of *McSweeney's*. This miniature short story employs the device of medial mise en abyme as developed at more length in the next chapter. By replicating its material medium within the diegesis, the text encourages readers to reflect on medial embodiment. The metamedial effect of Warner's story critically hinges on the interplay between the fictional motif of books, the paratexts of the *McSweeney's* issue, and the physical form of the printed artifact. In addition, the serial framework of *McSweeney's* calibrates and focuses the reader's perception. If one were to take any of these factors away, for example by reprinting the story in a literature anthology or by reading it on a Kindle, such recursive effects would likely fade.

Issue four, published in 2000, decisively breaks with the uniform book design of its predecessors. Instead of the white-paperback format, the issue comes in a cardboard box that accommodates fourteen slim octavo booklets. Replacing the accustomed typographic design, the cover of the box features a single drawing of a red-breasted robin with human arms and wooden feet. To go along with these changes, *McSweeney's 4* selects cover design as its predominant theme. A separate booklet titled "Notes and Background" contains the extensive paratextual comments and copyright pages. In it, Dave Eggers delves into an extended discussion of book covers. Through his hyperactive editorial voice, he sums up the common industry practices in this area, which rarely leave room for authors to influence the external design of their books ("Notes" viii). After taking stock in this way, Eggers calls for more authorial control over the publishing process. As this issue coincided with the publication of *A Heartbreaking Work of Staggering Genius*, he points to his first-hand experience when stating that he "asked for and received full control" over the design of his memoir (viii). He amends his ostentatious declaration of authorial independence with "The Author's and Book Enjoyer's Bill of Rights."

The first article in this section reflects the McSweeney's attitude toward the technology of bookmaking, claiming that new software has given authors access to book design, so that "no author should accept a limited role due to his or her presumed visual ignorance, and no publishers shall put forth such a notion" ("Notes" ix). Desktop publishing and digitization, Eggers suggests, can benefit authors in their struggle for control over their work. The thirty-one articles of the "Bill of Rights" accentuate the autonomy of the literary system, especially in relation to the market. Eggers directly targets the "sales force," which should have as little say in designing books as possible (ix). In pedantic detail, he lists particular design elements he despises. These include images depicting "tangled sheets in any context, arrangements of half-empty bottles . . . women sniffing flowers" and typographic embellishments such as "silver or reflective raised letters" ("Notes" x). All of these elements are common in mass-market segments such as thrillers, crime fiction, or romance novels. As such, Eggers erects boundaries between different—sometimes gendered, virtually always classed—groups of readers and genres. It would be justified to charge Eggers with elitism, but this would not fully explain the communicative function of such assertions. If we think about art as a system that needs communication to distinguish between itself and its environment in order to continue its autopoiesis, such divisive rhetoric serves a vital purpose. It provides the discursive glue needed to shape in-groups of readers who thereby develop a sense of identity and belonging.

As if to reinforce these declarations, another booklet in the box contains the scholarly essay "Paperback Nabokov" in which Paul Maliszewski recounts Vladimir Nabokov's extraordinary attention to the details of cover design, as witnessed for example in his collaboration with Milton

Glaser for the design of his novel Pnin. On a more fundamental level, "Paperback Nabokov" leads to a suggestive hypothesis on canonization processes. Maliszewski holds that the current "literary publication" of Nabokov's books merely reflects the author's increasingly canonized status (19). Approaching this phenomenon from the angle of textual materialism, bibliographic codes not only echo but actively modify the cultural work any edition of Lolita performs. Seth Lerer recently proposed to conceive of canonization as a two-sided process consisting of both normative valuation and physical archival, in which the "artifactual nature of the book has made the canonizing of the literary work into an act of space management" (232). The availability of Nabokov's works as "large-format Vintage paperbacks" (Maliszewski 19) designed to grace bookshelves facilitates social distinction and recursively reinforces canonization. The twenty-five-cent paperback communicates disposability, while the twenty-five-dollar clothbound book conveys a sense of preciousness. In a medial sense, one could thus claim, books canonize themselves.

As part of McSweeney's 4, Maliszewski's "Paperback Nabokov" has considerable material significance. For one, Eggers's paratexts mention that the author himself was responsible for picking the cover illustration, a set of postage stamps depicting Lolita covers from several decades. This custom cover emphasizes that Nabokov's hard-won involvement in design comes easy for Maliszewski. Other booklets include very personal covers directly connected to the author or the author's family. As such, George Saunders and Rick Moody select photographs they took themselves. Lydia Davis and Denis Johnson use illustrations drawn by their sons. Dave Eggers here cultivates a visual rhetoric of intimacy: "Does the son-cover please us? It absolutely does. Do we prefer this cover, brimming with character and back-story as it is, over a cover executed by a designer who is a stranger to the author, and perhaps has not even read the work being illustrated? We do" ("Notes" vi). The desired effect relies on localization. Such cover designs imbue the mass-produced booklets with the aura of travel photographs and children's drawings.

Eggers's remarks about the printing process at Oddi in Iceland extend this metamedial rhetoric of localization. For these early issues, the journal's founder would personally oversee the final production stages in Reykjavík. In the paratexts of issue four, Eggers consequently includes a section that reads like a journal entry:

[A]s of this writing, we are still looking for the right box. We wanted a sturdy box for all this stuff, and told Bjossi, the project manager, about our sturdy book need, and Bjossi has responded by offering three boxes thus far, but the cardboard for each has been much too thin. No way would they have held up. So he has pledged to keep looking; an hour from now, at 8:30 a.m., we will drive over and hope for the best, see what he's got. We will be here until it's right (we're at the Radisson, room 431), because the right box is everything. ("Notes" xii)

The deictic, place-bound style of this passage infuses the box itself with significance. Almost by force, these lines channel the reader's attention toward the materiality of its container. They provide a glimpse at the timeframe when everything was still undecided, when the final box had not been found, and when the unlikeliness of the whole artifact was still plainly visible. Through such object-centered paratexts, Dave Eggers showcases the amount of work and the localized circumstances that brought about the existence of the artifact. The early issues of *McSweeney's* systematically stake out spaces—copyright pages, book spines, folds and creases—in which metamedial communication can make the agency of objects visible. Within art-specific communication processes, the medium must enter the accounts of readers and authors in order to remain a functional entity. In and through its serial artifacts, *McSweeney's* searches for innovative tricks to accentuate its embodied textuality.

While the first four issues of *McSweeney's* experiment with their materiality, they still represent conventional bibliographic formats of the American literary magazine. With few exceptions, such magazines are produced either in the folded, spine-less form of a booklet or in sturdier paperback volumes. With issue five (2000), Eggers and his staff opted for a hardcover binding for the first time. Distinctly straying from the conventional style of a literary journal, the magazine thus materially entered the domain of the print book, at the same time that the McSweeney's publishing house began to put out stand-alone monographs. In addition to incorporating the hardcover format, Eggers also produced multiple versions of the issue, combining three covers with three alternative dust jackets.

Overall, this issue includes nine paratextual copyright pages, devoting much space to the economic minutiae of publishing. For one, Eggers reprints a full cost estimate sent by Oddi Printing that lists all the specifications and the overall price for the print run of 20,000 copies (*McSweeney's* 5, 10). He explains in the paratexts that each issue costs about $3 to manufacture and ship. Based on this amount, he wonders why the majority of books in the U.S. tends to be "cheaply made" when it seems economically feasible to produce "high-quality hardcover editions of just about everything" (11). The low overhead costs figure decisively in these calculations, as Eggers points out later in the text (12). The McSweeney's business model prohibits paid staff, large offices, advertising, and cash payments to the contributors. Nevertheless, Eggers embraces the cash flows of the capitalist marketplace to realize book projects that are both mass produced and well made, thus beating the media conglomerates at their own economic game. In fact, even the most experimental issues of *McSweeney's* sell for less than a standard hardcover book in Germany, where the book market follows a fixed-price model.

In addition to the scattered remarks on pricing and printing, Eggers also embeds an extensive mission statement in the small print of the copyright pages. In the context of the debate on digitization, Eggers holds that "the direction we should be going is obvious, and is in some ways the opposite of the way most people are talking about going" (*McSweeney's* 5, 12). In a nutshell, the McSweeney's publishing model rests on the following rationale:

> In short we are talking about smaller and leaner operations that use the available resources and speed and flexibility of the market (i.e. the web and other consumer-driven methods), to enable us

to make not cheaper and cruder print-on-demand books or icky, cold, robotic (electronic) books, but better books, perfect and permanent hardcover books, to do so in an [sic] fiscally sound way, and to do so not just for old time's sake, but because it makes sense and gives us, us people with fingers and eyes, what we want and what we've always wanted: beautiful things, beautiful things in our hands—to be surrounded by little heavy papery beautiful things. (McSweeney's 5, 12)

It seems counterintuitive to print such a programmatic statement in a place as easily overlooked as the copyright page. Yet, by the fifth issue, subscribers had been well prepared to regard these paratextual elements as an essential component of the *Quarterly Concern*. Despite his romanticized portrait of bibliophilia, Eggers does not mourn the lost craftsmanship of manual bookmaking and typesetting. Rather, his tone is utopian as he stresses the potentials of authorial empowerment. He also constantly points to prior modes of book production as complicated, difficult, and expensive. While these publications may evoke nostalgia in some readers, the computer appears here as more of an enabling tool for better books than a threat to reading.

Neither, however, does Eggers praise the possibilities of web design and screen reading. Digital hard- and software are mere "resources" to produce printed books—resources that have become ever more accessible and affordable. Internet sites, search technologies, and online retailers help customers gain access to printed products on the fringe of literary publishing. *McSweeney's* then treats all of these gadgets as technological tools, not as artistic media. The same holds, as we have seen, for the McSweeney's Web site, which serves as a supplement to the bibliographic output. In the early years of McSweeney's, Eggers used the Web site in a way that supplemented the printed texts by providing additional production notes, lists of errata, and personal comments on the reception of the individual works. In this hierarchical order, the question of aesthetic value only matters with regard to the embodied artistic medium ("beautiful things, beautiful things"). Brouillette dismisses the mini-manifesto as pure play, pointing to its focus on the beauty of books as "profoundly aestheticizing" and its failure to offer any connection to "the larger world of capital and commodity production." If we observe McSweeney's from the standpoint of (symbolic) economics, as Brouillette does, such metamedial features do appear insignificant. But as Brouillette herself points out, the separation between text and paratext, between artwork and commercial framing, collapses entirely. From her perspective, this means that all of Dave Eggers's works can be decoded as commercial products in a capitalistic matrix. By the same token, I would argue, collapsing paratexts and artwork also opens up the formerly commercial sections of a book to aesthetic criticism.

Vis-à-vis the public discourse on the future of the book, the key phrases of the hardcover manifesto describe the book as a medium that is "permanent" and that can be "kept until one dies" (McSweeney's 5, 12). Eggers thus stresses the material and functional differences between book mediality and screen mediality. While each of them has its specific qualities, he obviously fears that commentators and critics discursively negate those of the printed book. He rhetorically imbues the archival quality of books with artistic potential counteracting Kevin Kelly's idea that books function better if they are freed from their carrier medium. The textual-material interactions of McSweeney's are fixed in time and place; they cannot freely circulate throughout digital channels without losing vital parts of their aesthetic and social significance. If the autopoiesis of literature relies on the experience of texts and if this experience includes interaction with a specific artifact, then the collectability and archival nature of such materials is not just a matter of consumerism—it is a matter of cultural endurance.

### ¶ Memoirist, Novelist, Publisher: Dave Eggers's Early Work

The year 2000 marked a turning point both in Dave Eggers's career and in the evolution of McSweeney's. After Eggers's first magazine project, Might, folded in 1997, Eggers briefly worked on the Esquire staff before committing himself fully to his memoir, A Heartbreaking Work of Staggering Genius. In the period between his resignation at Esquire in late 1998 and the publication of the memoir in 2000, he edited the first issues of

*McSweeney's* while finalizing the book manuscript. The memoir entered the McSweeney's Universe after the journal's first issues had been published.[8] As such, it also forms a crucial reference point for later works of his publishing house. Furthermore, the proceeds from the book allowed Eggers to expand the scope of McSweeney's, hire new staff, and start a book imprint. In 2001, the firm already put out five books, two of them novels. Eggers's decision to self-publish his first novel *You Shall Know Our Velocity* with McSweeney's, instead of selling it off to a major publisher, sparked a small debate in online journals, newspapers, and book reviews as to whether this was an act of subversive resistance to corporate publishing or simply an ingenious strategy to profit more directly. In any case, these books simultaneously established Eggers as a major author and ensured McSweeney's a wider audience and a stronger financial footing. Both works fuse questions of authenticity, literary perspective, and cultural memory with their bibliographic form.

In approaching *A Heartbreaking Work*, we face a bibliographical challenge: the choice of a specific edition. The book came out in the United States in three distinct versions: first, the 2000 Simon and Schuster hardcover; second, the 2001 Vintage paperback; and third, that same paperback edition with an additional section attached in tête-bêche binding[9] that has been titled *Mistakes We Knew We Were Making*. Parts of the American Vintage printing have this latter format; overseas, the British Picador edition uses it as well. This unconventional binding arrangement allows the designer to give the book two front covers. The variations between the different editions are not simply byproducts that occur within routine revision and correction processes. In Eggers's memoir, these variants instead have a clear aesthetic function and deliberately disrupt scholarly protocols.

For one, the Vintage tête-bêche binding complicates professional formatting guidelines, as set down for example in APA, Chicago, or MLA style guides. These guides have established the widespread typographic convention of distinguishing between titles in italics and those in quotation marks. Frequent readers of academic texts will have naturalized this convention and will automatically draw the correct conclusion regarding the title treatment. Formatting the appendix of Eggers's paperback edition as Mistakes would imply that it is a complete, independent work. If positioned as a supplementary piece, the format of the title as "Mistakes" would instead signal that the text is part of the larger publication. The extensive appendix to A Heartbreaking Work resists both of these established categories of classification. On the one hand, the respective length of the sections—437-page memoir, forty-eight-page appendix—suggests that the additional text is merely a part or a paratext of the larger book, like a preface or an introduction. On the other hand, the bibliographic codes of the book point in a different direction, as the appendix has its own cover, title page, and copyright page. Giving precedence to the aesthetic self-description of the text, I will reproduce the title in italics because Mistakes strongly asserts the section's independence in this manner. As we have seen, the memoir interrupts the seamless integration into a discursive classification system. Eggers thus challenges the "putting-into-discourse of printed artifacts," to slightly modify a phrase by Mark B.N. Hansen.[10] The literary work stages a bibliographic breakdown in order to assert itself as an object.

Mistakes also raises the question of reliability, for which textual scholars often use authorial intentions as a guideline. According to Jerome McGann, traditional bibliographic methodologies have long required the editors of critical editions to expunge textual corruptions "in order to reveal, as purely as possible, the original artist's creative intention" (Textual 73). As McGann states, the less author-centered "eclectic approach" propagated by Fredson Bowers and G. Thomas Tanselle aims to unearth a reliable text by distinguishing substantive parts of the work which may emerge from the interaction of author, editor, and publisher, from so-called "accidentals" (73). For contemporary literature, manuscripts and copy texts are ever less relevant, as authors compose and correct their works digitally. Also, printer's mistakes and censorship issues figure little in the American publishing industry. Yet, as Eggers's book shows, textual variants may be intentional additions once authors decide that their work should exist in divergent forms.

It is difficult to ascertain whether Eggers's paratextual assertions of having received "complete" or "total" control over the design process are factually correct. Nevertheless, these statements construct a strong authorial persona who commands the reading experience. By repeatedly pointing to the bibliographic codes of the book and by assuring the reader that they are substantive parts, not printing accidentals, Eggers's narrative voice increases the probability that readers will experience *A Heartbreaking Work* simultaneously as text and as book.[11]

As readers of *McSweeney's* will have anticipated, the memoir's copyright page undermines paratextual conventions. Eggers designed it in a way that camouflages the unconventional content in the established layout of such a page. Since contemporary copyright pages often accommodate relatively large amounts of legal information, unsuspecting readers might pass over this segment of *A Heartbreaking Work*. The text starts with plain legal specifications, before a distinct narrative voice takes over that informs the reader of the corporate infrastructure of Vintage Books, Random House, and Bertelsmann AG. After the notice "Manufactured in the United States of America," the text again veers into personal territory: "Height: 5′11″; Weight: 175; Eyes: blue; Hair: brown; Hands: chubbier than one would expect; Allergies: only to dander; Place on the sexual-orientation scale, with 1 being perfectly straight, and 10 being perfectly gay: [chart with a circled '3']." In the confluence of these data sets, Eggers conveys his poetological understanding of the book as a work of art.

His memoirs, painfully personal as they are, figure beyond the coherent autobiographical narrative. They are also a material representation of his embodied self. Just as Eggers's body is a site that stores memories in the interplay between gray matter and consciousness, the material book externalizes mediated versions of these memories. The playful metamedial reflexivity of the early *McSweeney's* issues morphs into a more urgent, recursive interrogation of the artistic medium. The life-giving and life-preserving quality of books has been a topos ever since the Renaissance, reverberating through Shakespeare's sonnets as well as Milton's *Areopagitica*.[12] By reapplying this topos from writing to design, the analogy between book and body aims beyond witty self-reference. Eggers claims that the final artifact possesses a more visceral connection to its author because he designed it himself. This familiar proximity was already on display in the customized cover designs of *McSweeney's* 4, where the writers chose personal photos and illustrations. The lived experience of reading the book therefore may reveal aspects of the artist's character, such as his compulsive attention to detail or his anxious playfulness, in a multimodal form that transcends the verbal level.

The memoir continues with an extended paratextual apparatus stretching across forty-five pages. In sections such as "Rules and Suggestions for Enjoyment of This Book" or the "Incomplete Guide to Symbols and Metaphors," Eggers aims for reflexivity that intrinsically deconstructs itself. Similarly, he uses the paperback appendix to comment on the metamedial level of his work. Flipping the Vintage edition around to read the appendix, readers encounter a second copyright page. It reprints all legal items alongside two longer sections of text. In the first section, Eggers confronts accusations of bibliographic gimmickry, asserting his wish to "use spaces like this and to work within them, for no other reason than it entertains him and a small coterie of readers" (*Mistakes* 2). Citing entertainment as motive, this passage wants to preserve the playfulness of the text while preventing a purely ironic decoding.[13] As such, Eggers appears chronically afraid of readers who dismiss the entire narrative on the basis of its formal and bibliographic experiments. While the author attests to writing in the margins simply because he pleases, he explains the tête-bêche binding somewhat differently:

> Further, the fact that this paperback version starts from both sides, and that a reader must turn it over, lengthwise, to read from one side or other, does not mean that it is frivolous or, in parlance, *too clever for its own good*. It simply means that this was the best way to approach the problem of this appendix, which does not start from where the book leaves off, but starts from another point, an opposite point. (*Mistakes* 2)

Eggers renegotiates the relationship between writing and design, arguing that literary authors do not merely mediate their experience in formless language. Beyond this, he praises the book as a material metaphor for the meanings it transports.[14] In the realm of autobiographical writing, self-reference and formal experimentation correlate to experience differently than in fiction.

Large portions of A Heartbreaking Work attempt to literally touch the reader and stage presence effects on and through its pages. In addition to the bibliographic codes, the memoir uses the narrative voice to replicate such effects within its diegesis. As such, the narrator's obsession with bodies figures as one of the most prominent plot elements. Eggers is drawn to accidents and death, providing thorough renderings of wounds and diseases. Furthermore, there are dozens of instances during which the narrator envisions his own violent death or that of his brother, Toph. Even more revealing than these death-related incidents are several escapist fantasies of erotic contact. One such episode occurs when Eggers spends a night with a group of his friends at a bar in San Francisco. After contemplating how unlikely it is to meet so many high school friends thousands of miles away from the home of his youth, his interior monologue runs astray:

How dare we be standing around, talking about nothing, not running in one huge mass of people, running at something, something huge, knocking it over? Why do we all bother coming out, gathering here in numbers like this, without starting fires, tearing things down? How dare we not lock the doors and replace the white bulbs with red and commence with the massive orgy, the joyous mingling of a thousand arms, legs, breasts? (134)

Beyond the celebration of promiscuity, this peculiar rhetoric underscores how Eggers's idea of embodied connections extends beyond sexual intercourse. Aside from frequent references to the narrator's erotic encounters, A Heartbreaking Work contains surprisingly little actual sex. While the book celebrates the communion of bodies, the bacchanalia of the author's fantasies never actually materialize.

In passages like these, readers can witness the literary rendering of a mind that attempts to break the border separating consciousness from its bodily environment. The narrator struggles to achieve a form of sublation during which his consciousness can merge with those of others through close physical contact. As quoted above, he dreams of a communal effort to run at "something huge, knocking it over." In the end, all of these attempts end in failure. This outcome would hardly surprise systems theorists who maintain that the complex, evanescent processes of consciousness or communication are operationally closed. The mind simply cannot break out of its embodied shell; cognition and embodiment are both closely intertwined and shut off from each other. Likewise, bodies cannot "merge" with other bodies; they do not even interact directly with their environment, as Maturana and Varela posit in their biological theory of cognition. The incommensurability of touch invests this sensual dimension with a crucial affective influence. As John Durham Peters holds, "No real community endures without touch" (269).

Even while Eggers attempts to perform physical communion and communicate raw emotion, the narrator of A Heartbreaking Work knows that he is trapped in a narrative. Chapter VI relates a bizarre episode in which Dave Eggers attempts to become part of the cast of The Real World, the prototypical reality TV series broadcast by MTV in the 1990s. He does manage to enter the final casting, during which a producer named Laura conducts an extensive interview with him. The chapter presents this interview as a transcript from a video recording, the textual form thus authenticating the content. Yet, after a number of questions the narrator deliberately destroys the reality effect by merging the voice of interviewer and interviewee, admitting that the chapter is nothing but a "catchall for a bunch of anecdotes that would be too awkward to force together otherwise" (197). Exposing the two characters and their mutual conversation as imagined constructs, this passage shatters the ontological boundary between the diegetic levels of communication. The interview continues for several pages after readers are aware it is a transcript of Eggers's interrogation of himself. The section's anecdotes on death and despair converge in a final raving monologue, during which Eggers implores Laura to cast him for the show.

While it fails to solve the aporia of art versus life on the narrative level, Eggers's manic narrative leaves correlative traces in the lived experience of readers as a metamedial artifact. The transcript of Eggers's MTV interview contains a key metaphor for the whole memoir that illustrates the theory of the book that both Dave Eggers and McSweeney's endorse. Within the McSweeney's aesthetics, the book figures as a social artifact, an entity serving to create networks or imagined communities of spatially disconnected individuals. In the interview, Eggers explains his idea of the "lattice," the central image that provides solace after the death of his parents: "The lattice is the connective tissue. The lattice is everyone else, the lattice is my people, collective youth, people like me, hearts ripe, brains aglow... I see us as one, as a vast matrix, an army, a whole, each one of us responsible to one another, because no one else is" (211). The lattice provides a concrete symbol for the ephemeral idea of a network. Eggers extends this idea to his friends and associates at *Might* magazine and to all its subscribers. At the time, this description also applied to the interpersonal networks surrounding *McSweeney's Quarterly Concern*.

Further along, Eggers proclaims, "Let me be the lattice, the center of the lattice. Let me be the conduit" (237). If we equate the narrator with the empirical author Dave Eggers, this statement reads like preposterous hubris. Yet, the narrative promptly ridicules these transcendental flights of fancy. After the dramatic conclusion of the interview, the subsequent chapter begins: "Fuck it. Stupid show" (240). The narrator satirizes and disclaims much of the rhetorical bravado of the previous section. Still, this narrative shift does not eradicate the import of the lattice. Eggers theorizes a communication system that provides orientation and solace to the individual who partakes in it. As seen above, the person Dave Eggers falls short of his aim to become the ultimate conduit. In the face of this, he needs a surrogate agent to fill in as conduit. Overall, the assemblage of semiotic and bibliographic codes suggests that the printed artifact itself is the only viable candidate for this position. *A Heartbreaking Work* recounts Eggers's futile but manically creative quest to maximize his exposure to bodies, to extend his embodiment in a way that will let a large number of people partake in his existence. As we have seen in the paratexts of the first *McSweeney's* issues, the rhetorical, communal unity carries over—hyperbolically ironized, yet ultimately sincere—into the embrace of the codex book as a mass-produced art form that combines vast dispersal with concrete materiality. Implicitly, Eggers thus provides his own axiological media theory, in which the relative endurance and accessibility of what Pross calls "secondary media" convey a stronger communicative connection between sender and receiver than any electronic media of communication can.

In its struggle with the anxieties and insecurities of its genre, Bran Nicol holds, the memoir stages its own destruction and, ultimately, the destruction of the author (110–11). As a work of art, however, the book also accomplishes a constructive end: Through its self-description as a material artifact, it foregrounds the capability of books to function as communicative mediators. Even more, by presenting itself as a symbol of the author's presence, this text embraces book printing as a technology to extend the body into space. The book is a veritable "extension of man," though not in the kinesthetic, McLuhanite sense. It circulates as an autonomous work, separate from both its author and its reader; yet, it provides communicative triggers that may spark presence effects for either of the two. Encouraged by critical and commercial success, Dave Eggers's "lattice" of friends, acquaintances, and magazine subscribers slowly transforms into a microcosm of literary communication. As the circulation of *McSweeney's* rises, this network intersects in ever more places with the larger system of American literature.

Published by Simon and Schuster, *A Heartbreaking Work* only partially overlaps with the McSweeney's Universe. Eggers's second book, *You Shall Know Our Velocity* (2002), conversely, is a debut in two senses: for one, it is Eggers's first novel. Also, it is the first book in which he oversaw virtually every step in production, from composition, to layout, to printing. The novel can justifiably be read as a lightly concealed allegory of the author's rise to wealth and fame, with the protagonist, Will, as a fictional stand-in for Eggers himself. After all, the book's status as a follow-up to the autobiographical *Heartbreaking Work* suggests that many readers will make similar connections between the two works. Yet the novel also deserves to be read as just that: a novel—a fictional text that has an existence outside of its author's zone of influence.

Similar to the subsequent *McSweeney's* issues seven and eight, the covers of *You Shall Know Our Velocity* are left in raw condition, exposing a surface of bland book board. The external design foregrounds the simple components of a book and the craftsmanship needed to create it. Using a so-called half-and-half cover, the book has a cloth wrapping that only extends over the spine and a small portion of the front and back cover. On its surface, however, *Velocity* contains no other illustrations. Instead, Eggers incorporates the whole codex into the narrative. The novel begins in the upper left corner of the cardboard cover, in black Garamond letters, set in embossed all caps (see fig. 3). The cover does not credit Dave Eggers as author, its design thus matching the conventions of a fictional autobiography. The passage printed on the cover engages in subtle ways with its spatial placement:

Everything within takes place after Jack died and before my mom and I drowned in a burning ferry in the cool tannin-tinted Guaviare River, in east-central Colombia, with forty-two locals we hadn't yet met. It was a clear and eyeblue day, that day, as was the first day of this story, a few years ago in January, on Chicago's north side, in the opulent shadow of Wrigley and with the wind coming low and searching off the jagged half-frozen lake. I was inside, very warm, walking from door to door. (1)[15]

The indexical reference "Everything within" points to its own placement outside of the paper block that forms the book. Furthermore, these two words stake out the extent of the plot by indicating the amount of time covered in the pages to follow. While first-person narrator Will has not yet revealed his name, he alludes to the tragic event that initiates the plot, the death of his friend Jack from a car accident. Furthermore, he appears to be speaking from beyond the grave, a paradox that is not resolved in the first edition of the book. The last sentence on the cover creates an interesting feedback loop with the reading experience. When the narrator states that he is "inside," he presumably means inside his house. On another level this also indicates that the reader will need to flip the cover to re-encounter the narrator on the inside of the book itself. Once readers open the book, they find the regular body text continued on the front endpapers.

Fig. 3. Exterior Design of Dave Eggers, *You Shall Know Our Velocity* (San Francisco: McSweeney's, 2002). Courtesy of McSweeney's Publishing. Photograph by Harald Wenzel.

At heart, *Velocity* is a road novel accelerated by airplanes. Childhood friends Will and Hand embark on an outrageous quest to randomly distribute $32,000 in cash among needy people around the world. Both men are in their late twenties and come from Catholic, Polish American families. Will now lives in Chicago and Hand in St. Louis; both work in dead-end jobs. At his job with a construction company, Will had posed for a promotional picture. An ad agency unwittingly used this picture for a logo silhouette that adorns the products of a lightbulb company. This transaction earns Will a generous compensation payment, which coincides, however, with the tragic death of his friend Jack. Will tells the reader that he feels he has not earned the large amount of money: "So I'd been given $80,000 to screw in a lightbulb. There is almost no way to dress it up; that's what it was" (41). Will's large sum of money brings to mind Dave Eggers's proceeds from his first book. Will never seems to think about selfishly spending the money; to him, charity is the only viable use. The two friends travel from Chicago to Senegal, Morocco to the Baltics, before Hand heads home and Will attends a wedding in Mexico.

Aside from the central theme of charity, Velocity also confronts a more abstract problem: the storage and retrieval of memories. At the outset, Will warns the reader about his decrepit mental state. He claims to be traumatized by Jack's death and haunted by his memories of an incident at Jack's storage unit in Oconomowoc, a town outside of Milwaukee. When he tried to salvage his friend's personal effects from storage, two robbers attacked him and mauled his face, which still bears fresh scars. Will recounts this fight in short vignettes throughout the book, as abrupt flashbacks to the traumatic event frequently interrupt his narrative. To visualize his cognitive disarray, Will creates an extravagant allegory. He pictures himself sitting at a desk in the middle of a beautiful landscape. From this desk, he freely observes the world and records his observations. The desk sits on top of a submerged structure, a basement of memories ten stories deep. This building functions like a library, housing "a mixture of records, dossiers, quotations, historical documents, timelines, fragments, cultural studies—the most glorious and banal bloody memories" (30–31). Whenever he needs to call up elements from his memory, the library staff sends up the corresponding information. By choosing the allegory of the library for the invisible functions of his mind, Will presents himself as an adherent of embodied, bibliographic information. Despite the increasingly erratic performance of the librarians, he professes that he values the hierarchical structure of his memory archive and its "presence" (31). The imagined materiality of his memories, their embodiment in folders and books, soothes him.

Where Will shores up a library against his mental chaos, Hand embraces the data streams of the information age. He approaches people in a direct, unpretentious manner and freely relates inconsequential bits of trivia he picked up online, in documentaries, and in the news. Hand thus exemplifies the type of "hyper attention" that derives from the fast-paced browsing of different media stimuli.[16] The luggage that Will and Hand take on their journey symbolizes these differing character traits. Both restrict themselves to the bare minimum by only packing under-wear, spare shirts, and toiletries. On top of this, Hand brings "some discs, his Walkman, a handful of tapes for the rental cars, some State Department traveler advisories, and a sheaf of papers he'd printed from the Center for Disease Control website, almost entirely about ebola" (21). This collection of entertainment media and arbitrary printouts typifies Hand's careless attitude toward information.

Even though *Velocity* employs fewer metamedial devices than *A Heart-breaking Work*, the narrator manipulates the pages of the book with con-fidence and ease. Throughout the novel, about a dozen visual elements accompany the text. Color photographs illustrate parts of the journey, while several documents and papers appear as facsimiles. In each case, text and image flow together in a straightforward way as images are introduced and directly referenced in the text. During their stay in the Baltics, Will and Hand draw a treasure map that shows the way to a buried stack of money. Will reproduces the map on a full page, com-plete with burned edges, simply stating: "Here is the map" (309). This implicit mise en abyme—paper printed on paper—does not transcend the ontological diegetic divide; it does, however, lend the novel the air of a scrapbook. By documenting his travels in this way, Will creates a bibliographic representation of his internal library.

In the first hardcover edition of *Velocity*, the theme of memory and its medial representation figure less prominently than the extended discussions of money and ethics. This thematic focus changes in later editions. In 2003, a year after the first edition, McSweeney's published a small print run of a revised version of the book called *Sacrament*. The book's cover has roughly the same external design as the first edition. It still consists of a raw cardboard front cover, while the spine and entire back cover are wrapped in red cloth. The title of the book is printed in red ink, with the parenthetical addendum "known previously as *You Shall Know Our Velocity*." Dave Eggers's name is still absent from the title page. Instead, *Sacrament* adds a fictional editor onto the fictional autobiography: "Edited and with a new insertion by Frances 'Hand' Wisneiwski." Below this tagline, the silhouette logo of Will and the lightbulb is reproduced in black. The edition contains several small corrections and alterations, yet the biggest change is a fifty-page insert presumably written by Hand that bears the page numbers 251 through 300. Due to the small print run and the lack of reprintings, this edition sparked the interest of book collectors.[17] The McSweeney's Web site offered a digital file of Hand's "Interruption" as a free download for a limited time in 2003. Just as the Vintage paperback of *A Heartbreaking Work* was not only an edition, *Sacrament* expands upon *Velocity* and should likewise be considered a separate work.[18] Notably, none of the critical studies published to this date acknowledges the existence of *Sacrament*. Thus, the novel foregrounds how the cultural work and the historicity of texts—both key tenets of New Historicist scholarship—are reliant on their physical appearance and archival availability.

Turning to the content of the inserted "Interruption," we find Hand explaining how he rented a small house on the coast of New Zealand to work on this additional section, three years after Will died in Colombia (Eggers, *Sacrament* 252). To remedy Will's errata and lies, he promises to tell the reader exactly which parts are fabricated and how the actual events occurred. When he professes not to be rewriting Will's text but merely "illuminating this manuscript" (254), Hand frames his alterations as embellishments in a medieval book that will make the final product all the more beautiful. Illuminated manuscripts from the Middle Ages used red ink to highlight and accentuate parts of the text, a practice called "rubrication." The red ink used for the cover design and the borders of Hand's "Interruption" visually reference these conventions. Hand mirrors the structure of Will's account by writing one journal entry for each day that he spends revising the manuscript, resulting in eight sections. Unlike Will, Hand addresses the reader directly and knows the status of the text as a mass-produced book. He also considers publishing issues, for example when he voices his hopes that the publishers will insert his pages where he would prefer them to appear—"between Will's Sunday and Monday" (255). Readers can confirm that the publishers of *Sacrament* and the later Vintage edition granted him this wish.

Eggers has Hand explain the seeming paradox of the narrative voice that speaks from beyond the grave. In the only footnote of his section, Hand writes:

> Though the text as printed before and after my interlude is as Will wrote it, there's no way, of course, he could have written that first page, being no longer with us, and therefore not close to a word processor. His manuscript was sent to the publisher before his second departure, for South America, and after his death there, they shopped the task of writing a neat opening paragraph to a writer of semi-fictions with a tendency toward the clever setup. The result speaks for itself. (268)

On this submerged level of communication, the reader (re-)encounters Dave Eggers, as a second-rate hack contracted by the publishing house to write a catchy opening. Hand despises this author of "semi-fictions," a clear allusion to *A Heartbreaking Work*. This metaleptic play between author and character adds an external layer to the editorial fiction of *Sacrament*.

Hand then exposes three blatant lies that pertain to crucial elements of the original book. First, Hand claims, Will was never in a fight with two robbers at Jack's storage unit. Accordingly, the scabs and scars on his face that shocked people wherever they went are also fictitious. Second, Will also invented the character of Jack and his death in a car accident. Without these two incidents, the tragic foundations of the plot collapse, as Hand acknowledges: "It's a comfort, a small one, that at least you few people who will read my comments will know that there were always just two of us, and our motivations were self-made and without tragic source" (269). Will's third and final ruse is the claim that his mother was still alive at the time of his writing and afterward drowned together with him. Hand claims that Will's mother had died years before in the aftermath of a medical procedure. Through its small print-run and its randomized dispersal in the paperback reprint, *Sacrament* enacts its fictional editor's conviction that only "few people" will read his version. The mass-market paperback versions now sold by Vintage and Penguin do not include Hand's alterations, so regular buyers hardly have the chance to read the alternative story that he purports.

Hand has no definite explanation for why his friend added so much fabricated matter to his story. Although giving some credit to the sincere parts of the story, Hand professes that he dislikes the shape Will gave to the plot. In a way, the reader also witnesses a staged debate between Dave Eggers and the critical literary public. This is especially obvious when Hand addresses the problem of nonfictional writing in a more general sense:

> I realize how difficult the world makes it for those who want to lead and talk about unusual lives in a candid way, in a first-person way. I understand that to sublimate a life in fictions, to spread the ashes of one's life over a number of stories and books, is considerably better-accepted, and protects one greatly from certain perils—notably, the rousing of the anger or scorn of all the bitches of the world (more often male than female). (281)

Eggers enacts the extradiegetic dialogue between author and public through Hand as an embedded narratorial vehicle. Still, the fictional framework of the work as a whole runs counter to a purely biographical reading.

Publication and distribution cut the bond between author and work, while they inaugurate a peculiar connection between medium and text that lasts as long as copies of a book are in circulation or enter personal or public archives. As literary works, *Velocity* and *Sacrament* communicate through books and as books. As suggested above, Will visualizes his memory as a vast library in which physical documents store his past. If we extend this image into the reader's sphere, *Velocity* represents an extension of Will's memory, a physical presence that remains after its fictive author has disappeared. The raw cardboard that protects the pages of the book underscores this archival condition. The material vehicle wants to be stored and kept, not admired for its visual excellence.

Sacrament considerably expands the novel's topos of storage. In Velocity, Jack's storage unit at Oconomowoc forms the backdrop for the disputed brawl. This room full of things houses Jack's material legacy. Just as Hand's section in Sacrament mirrors the structure of Will's book, it also reiterates many of its central motives. After his friend's death, Hand therefore visits another storage unit in which Will has stowed away his belongings.[19] Strangely, he attests, the piles of possessions cause him more grief than the funeral. After crying for a short while, Hand catalogues the objects Will stored in his room, among them boxes of bathroom supplies, posters, lamps, and a number of books (265). These things seem randomly assembled, yet as a cumulative presence they appear to haunt Hand. Several objects trigger specific memories, so that Hand feels as if Will himself lingered in this place. On the whole, Hand is torn between his emotional attachment and the impulse to throw away and burn everything. Finally, Hand muses, "Memory, perhaps, should have no physical shape" (264). This vision of shapeless, immaterial memory echoes utopian hopes for freely circulating, digital information. Still, Hand finds some common ground with Will's vision of embodied memory in his "Interruption." While Hand distrusts the literary book as a storage medium, he instead reenchants the codex as the token of symbolic gift exchange.

The key to this rather unexpected metaphysical turn lies in an episode that Will allegedly left out of his account. Hand relates how he and Will, during a layover at the airport in Copenhagen, walk into the airport chapel. With a mass in progress, they listen to the priest explaining the sacrament of the Eucharist as the "external, social demonstration of how we feel within" (287). This obviously strikes a chord with Hand, who immediately begins to ponder the significance of their journey according to this worldly interpretation of the Christian sacrament. He holds that their attempt to disperse cash to people along their way has certain ritualistic qualities, so that the value of the charitable act lies not in the commercial worth of the currency but in the social act of exchange. In his last longer journal entry, Hand then transfers this theory onto the book itself: "I think the book as a whole is a sacrament of sorts, a physical representation, of too many things otherwise ephemeral—a social demonstration of a partly unknowable internal state, a messy combination of Twain's shapeless string of absurdities, and something like that state of secular grace I was talking about earlier. Maybe all books are sacraments" (296–97). The ultimate paragraphs of Hand's "Interruption" hereby return to the metamedial questions raised in Eggers's *Heartbreaking Work*. The narrator produces a number of alternative descriptions of the book, yet the most striking of these is the "social demonstration" of an "internal state." In such a conception, Will's book and Hand's addendum communicate through their outward appearance. These designed artifacts figure in the overall construction of the narrator's perspective. Embedded in a piece of fiction, Hand's theory extends the idea of narratorial credibility from the discursive to the medial level. As a textual simulation of a mind, the fictional autobiography may profit if the author consciously attends to its outward form. Aside from "telling" the story in the mode of language, the literary writer may also "show" the story to the reader in the design of the book. A heightened degree of reader involvement, often postulated for the carefully crafted writing style of "showing," is perhaps at work in this context as well.

As Eggers self-consciously extends the characterization of a personalized narrator to the shape of the text, he attempts to supplement the literary illusion with a tactile component. With the device of the fictional editor, he asks his readers to decode *Velocity* and *Sacrament* as creations of their narrators. More than emblems of their author's investment in social justice, *Velocity* and *Sacrament* act as self-contained bibliographic artifacts that perform cultural work through their spatial dispersal. *Velocity* encapsulates the exuberant, manic-depressive flights of its narrator as an archival, mass-produced tragedy. *Sacrament* is a derivative work that couches its companion text in the sober, disillusioned voice of a fictional editor. While *Sacrament* deconstructs the authentic façade of its predecessor, it simultaneously reconstructs the medium of the book. Ultimately, Hand seems to claim that the hypocritical fabrications within *Velocity* are outweighed by the book's capacity as an embodied remainder (and reminder) of Will's existence.

## ¶ A Decade of Book Design

Feeding off the success of Eggers's *A Heartbreaking Work* and his subsequent books, the McSweeney's venture further expanded throughout the past decade. McSweeney's has become a veritable cultural hub, publishing two art-related periodicals aside from *McSweeney's Quarterly Concern*. The literary review *The Believer*, edited by Vendela Vida, Heidi Julavits, and Ed Park, started in 2003 and contains criticism, essays, and interviews in its nine issues per year. The second periodical, *Wholphin*, collects fictional and documentary short films on DVD. *Wholphin*, edited by Brent Hoff, premiered in 2005 but was discontinued in 2012 after fifteen issues. McSweeney's initiated two more periodicals in 2011, the sports magazine *Grantland* and the food journal *Lucky Peach*. As we have seen, the first five issues of *McSweeney's* staked out a serial space of material textuality and provided ample self-descriptions of writing and reading as embodied social practices. In his memoir and his debut novel, Dave Eggers then attempted to refocus postmodernist self-reference on issues of authenticity and archival forms of memory. As to the quarterly's further evolution, this section focuses on three recurring themes that inform the magazine within and across its diverse contributions, paratexts, and material forms. First, *McSweeney's* experiments with digital and analog dissemination media while reinforcing the primacy of the printed artifact. Second, the magazine remains open to writing styles and forms of representation rarely found in literary journals. Third, in its most experimental issues, *McSweeney's* disrupts publication practices and cultural protocols of bookmaking.

Several themed issues of *McSweeney's* incorporate nonbibliographic medial artifacts, such as *McSweeney's* 6 (2001), which inaugurated the magazine's interaction with other carrier media. Following on the heels of the first hardcover issue, issue six features a large selection of photographs, drawings, and other art pieces that appear alongside

A BOOKISH INSTITUTION

the texts. As the copyright pages explain, Lawrence Weschler originally planned to curate a complete issue devoted to visual art (8). This concept then merged with the idea to include an audio CD with a musical score performed by the alternative rock band They Might Be Giants. The outer form of the book underscores its visual art theme. Bound in an oblong format with cloth covering, the pages provide broad spaces to accommodate the full-color reproductions of visual art. The heavy paper stock with a cream finish sets itself apart from the simple white stock used in the earlier issues. While the paratexts heavily advertise the quality of the music on the CD, the general framing of the recorded medium suggests that it has a supplementary function. Even though many of the songs do contain lyrics, the reading or viewing of the printed piece takes precedence. In most cases, the vocals of the songs divert the attention, so that one needs to listen and read separately to appreciate either text or music. While issue six exhibits genuine interest in the intermedial exchanges among music, visual art, and writing, issue eleven (2003) openly parodies the medium of the DVD. The main section of the DVD called "Deleted Scenes" contains clips in which nine contributors to the issue read from their respective short stories published in the book. The second section, "Extra-Deleted Scenes," includes more short films such as a scene from a theater play by Denis Johnson and a spoof of the MTV show *Cribs*, in which Jonathan Ames presents his Brooklyn apartment to the viewers. The hyperbolic third section presents "Behind the Scenes of the Deleted Scenes and Extra-Deleted Scenes," a making-of documentary of the production process. For this making-of film, the disc features an alternative version with a director's commentary by Francis Ford Coppola, who supposedly improvised his comments while viewing a muted version of the clip (The Editors of McSweeney's 93–95).

The ambient effect of the alternative rock CD and the metasatire of the DVD embellish the journal as intermedial supplements. Issue seventeen (2005) leaves behind the notion of the unified codex altogether. Up to this issue, *McSweeney's* employed creative forms that were more or less consistent with the standard bibliographic unit of the book. In issue seventeen, the journal inhabits a wholly different medial shape. Posing as a stack of mail, the issue addresses a specific segment of its production and reception environment. It recursively interacts with its distribution chain, an often overlooked segment of Darnton's "communications circuit." As Adams and Barker point out, distribution is not merely about transporting a given parcel from point A to point B: "It is a densely woven network about which we still know comparatively little" (58). The new phenomenon of online bookselling intensified the invisibility of distribution from the consumer, with books now miraculously turning up at the doorstep a day after ordering. Yet, this seamless consumer experience relies on an intricate backbone of technologies, logistics, and labor.

As we have seen in the first *McSweeney's* issues, the paratextual minutiae concerning the economics and logistics of each issue prominently list the figures for shipping and handling. For a small journal that collaborates with an Icelandic printer, transportation and distribution are central concerns, as the editor and his assistants need to monitor, or even organize, each issue's mailing. The everyday activities at the McSweeney's headquarters inspired issue seventeen, Eggers explains: "[B]ecause we had been sending our issues through the mail for so long, it seemed natural that eventually we'd experiment with the very form of mail" (The Editors of McSweeney's 163). The issue consists of eight individual parcels held together by a rubber band, confronting readers with objects that resemble the printed ephemera of everyday communication. This stack of mail results in an intense alienation effect in which the material existence of such pieces of stationery and mail wrappings becomes itself the object of aesthetic experience. *McSweeney's* 17 generates such mundane presence effects as stretching a rubber band, tearing a letter that is sealed shut, and groping through oversized advertisements, which collectively feed into the multimodal reading process of *McSweeney's*. Sorting through the items, readers find two standard letter envelopes, one large manila envelope, two magazines, and two advertising flyers. Aside from the advertisements, all pieces carry the standard inscriptions of postal items, including a street address, imitations of postal stamps, and subscriber data. Each is addressed to the fictional Sgt. Maria Vasquez in Arlington, Virginia. As such, the issue creates a material fiction; it asks the reader to temporarily accept the ontological status of the pile of mail. I propose to call this metatextual fiction the "medial diegesis." The superimposed sphere of the medial diegesis extends the literary illusion, otherwise bracketed within a liminal paratextual frame, outward into space.

The delivery of the issue disrupted postal routines, as the street address given on the envelopes belonged to the parents of managing editor Eli Horowitz, who recalls that hundreds of pieces stemming from issue seventeen eventually turned up at his parents' house: "I guess the bundle would split apart along the way, and then all those letters and catalogs and magazines would join the mailstream and get delivered like actual mail. Despite the fact that none of it had actual postage" (The Editors of McSweeney's 169). The mail-themed issue exposes the material infrastructure of the U.S. Postal Service, a ubiquitous network often taken for granted but increasingly threatened by economic strictures. In his canonical novel *The Crying of Lot 49*, Thomas Pynchon already used the postal system as an extended metaphor for the entropic and possibly subversive dispersal of information. To Oedipa Maas, a paranoid fantasy like the underground Tristero mail system seems entirely plausible. In the present, the postal system stands apart from other communication networks not simply because it transports information but because it transports things. The placement or displacement of mail items— including books and literary journals—becomes noteworthy in itself once digital alternatives for this delivery method arise.

In a second instance of medial mimicry, issue thirty-three (2009) took on the form of a large, quality newspaper. In this issue, however, the impulse behind the innovative form takes on a more urgent, less playful tone. The issue assertively positions itself as a materialized statement in current debates on the future of newspapers. As strong as the Web's influence on other medial forms has been, it hit the American newspaper earliest and hardest. The prospects for large city newspapers with a national readership have grown dire over the past years. In this scenario, *McSweeney's* 33 appeared as a broadsheet measuring 15 × 22 inches. Purposely selecting the largest standardized newspaper size, Eggers and his staff probe the possibilities of the material medium of the newspaper. A standalone section titled "Information Pamphlet" contains the characteristic editorial paratexts. Eggers here provides an exact economic stat sheet, which reiterates many arguments voiced in earlier issues. He specifically addresses the correlation of falling profits for large conglomerates and easier market access for small ventures: "The point we were trying to prove was that if a group of newspaper-lovers—say a group of journalists laid off from a daily paper—wished to start their own daily, they might be able to do so without a huge capital outlay" ("Information Pamphlet"). This passage can be read side-by-side with the proclamation from issue five about the economic feasibility of hardcover books. Once again, *McSweeney's* adopts a rhetoric of empowerment that suggests that the new digital and Web-driven technologies can be used not only by large multimedia companies but also by small-scale operations.

The "Pamphlet" also advocates medium-specific design that fully inhabits the final carrier medium and its material properties: "We went into this knowing that print has to look different than the internet. With shrinking editorial holes in many newspapers, more and more the look of a paper mimics that of the Web. But the large size of newspapers, and the increased affordability of full color, presents great opportunities" ("Information Pamphlet"). The front page of the paper embodies this design philosophy. It does not compartmentalize its space into columns and sections to include articles and small teasers for special features inside. Below the masthead, drawn by cartoonist Daniel Clowes, a single photograph instead takes up the entire front page with a scenic view of the San Francisco–Oakland Bay Bridge construction site. Even when readers open the paper, none of the navigational aids so typical to the contemporary newspaper appear. By omitting these design elements, the *Panorama* offers itself to a different implied readership—one that is to treat the whole of the paper as a unified artifact, not just as a collection of articles that have been collated in the most efficient and fastest form. The inside pages of the broadsheet sections clearly mark the paper as a McSweeney's publication. The signature frames and borders, so common to Eggers's design style, accompany and differentiate the individual articles. Generally, newspapers use borderlines and frames to set off individual pieces on the page. Eggers, however, continues to mark each page with a thick outer frame. So even while individual items are set off using further lines, the overall frame reinforces the unity of the page as a perceptual whole. As far as typography is concerned, the *Panorama* transfers its Old Style–look to newsprint by employing Sabon, Jan Tschichold's postwar reworking of Garamond designs. The modernist type designer intended Sabon as a flexible font that would work well across the ensemble of typesetting machines manufactured by the Monotype and Linotype companies (Lawson 151).

A telling piece in the *Panorama* measures the environmental impact of digitized data transmission against its distribution on printed paper. Nicholson Baker's "Can a Paper Mill Save a Forest?" openly addresses the material it is printed on. Baker reports in depth on the two paper mills in the town of Jay, Maine, one of which closed down in 2009. He cites communications researcher Don Carli, whose Institute for Sustainable Communication conducts studies on the environmental impact of electronic communications. Carli argues that paper-based communication does not necessarily entail a bigger carbon footprint than the seemingly clean delivery of texts through online services. To Carli, the whole equation varies depending on sustainable forest management and the use of renewable energy. What usually escapes public notice is the immense amount of energy needed to power the data centers that form the backbone of the Internet. As long as the United States generates electricity from coal, however, the massive energy demand of computers, servers, and display devices results in significant environmental damage. Carli states, "So when we start thinking about transforming more and more of our communication to digital media . . . we really do have to be asking, 'Where will the electrons come from?'" (qtd. in N. Baker, "Can a Paper Mill" 2). With his report, Baker attempts to provide glances at the vastly different material infrastructures needed to produce analog and digital newspapers. The novelist is of course hardly a neutral reporter in this context. Where his *McSweeney's* article employs a subdued authorial voice, his earlier book *Double Fold* (2001) was a fierce, polemical attack on libraries and their preservation policies. Baker's book is closely interwoven with the *San Francisco Panorama*, as it lays out an archival ethics built on the twentieth-century preservation history of American newspapers in public libraries. His self-reflexive perspective on the mediality of the newspaper speaks to the investment of *McSweeney's* both in aesthetics and ethics.

The metamedial potential of McSweeney's print products complicates simple dichotomies of literary text and social context. In many readings, a given text functions like a veil that the critic has to draw away carefully so as to reveal the "real" social issues and struggles it conceals. The dynamic frameworks of Latour and Luhmann, however, allow us to understand literary texts as more than aesthetic utterances in a sea of social contexts and practices. As constitutive elements of a communication system, literary texts do not stand against the social, they produce a specific form of the social. Social action therefore may be, but does not have to be something nonliterary. During a historical period that renegotiates the medial basis of social communication, McSweeney's books force the materialities of communication into plain view. In the present case, the *San Francisco Panorama* attempts to show its readers what the materiality of a newspaper can mean for the reading experience, as opposed to the computational images on the screens of laptops or e-readers. With Baker, one could claim that the new technologies encourage the destruction of physical books and newspapers, while demanding an increasing supply of electricity. Thus, the ethical stakes of media change in the information age also reside in the media themselves, not just in external social interests.

A second cluster of themed issues contains another recurring theme in *McSweeney's*: unconventional writing styles and marginal genres. Throughout, Eggers and his coeditors use the serialized journal to place fringe material within an established frame of literary communication. Negotiating the "literariness" of various writing forms, the journal links up cultural valorization with medial embodiment. With postmodern-ism, Luhmann argues, self-descriptions of art have assimilated the idea of negating art.[20] Surveying the various forms in which artists react to the postwar proclamations of "anything goes," Luhmann holds that contexts and containers serve an important function: "Most recent modern art experiments with eliminating any art-internal signals. As a result art depends all the more on frames and external signals to in-dicate that an object not recognizable as art is nonetheless meant to be seen as art" (Art 295). He further contends that evaluative questions of quality only emerge within these frames when observers decide to de-code something as art. Having achieved some stability and recognition as an institution of American literary culture, McSweeney's began to test the feasibility of literary communication for writing forms that seem to fall outside the domain of high art. The earliest incarnation of this was issue thirteen (2004), a comprehensive anthology of North American comics collated by cartoonist Chris Ware. In two interrelated essays, I have elsewhere explored the anthology's aesthetic dimensions and its impact on canonization.[21] As guest editor, Ware produced a 270-page hardcover book with golden engravings, covered in a dust jacket that folds out to a newspaper-sized full-color poster. With Ware at the fore-front, many cartoonists now attempt to insert their work into a literary context by using the physical book as their emancipatory tool.

Similar mechanisms inform two further issues devoted to pulp fic-tion and extinct genres. The paperback issue ten (2002) mimics the look and feel of a pulp fiction magazine. To achieve this effect, the editors deviated from standard McSweeney's style, using typography that is "as awkward and overenthusiastic as were many of those magazines" (McSweeney's 10, 4). While Garamond remains the body font, McSweeney's 10 uses various other typefaces for the headlines and running titles. The bulbous letterings use heavy slab serifs whose decorative excess breaks with the subdued typography of prior McSweeney's issues. The issue is typeset in a two-column format, typical for pulp magazines. Through-out the book, the reader finds reprints of advertisements taken from the original pages of 1930s and 40s serials. All of these stem from the private collection of guest editor Michael Chabon. For *McSweeney's* 10, Chabon contracted twenty writers to submit short stories that follow a coherent plot pattern and fall into the generic categories of pulp writing. The issue includes stories by Neil Gaiman, Nick Hornby, Stephen King, Michael Crichton, Elmore Leonard, and Dave Eggers. In the introduction, Chabon writes that during the heyday of the magazine short story, authors such as Henry James, Edith Wharton, William Faulkner, or John Cheever enjoyed greater latitude to publish gripping genre pieces alongside their more polished pieces.

Like Ware's comics issue, Chabon's pulp compendium evokes the link between media and canonization. Before "pulp" morphed into a generic denomination for lurid and sensationalist fiction, it was a quintessentially metamedial term. A pulp magazine simply denoted a periodical printed on wood pulp paper. Late in the nineteenth century, Western paper manufacturers shifted the material base of their trade from old rags—which were converted into rag paper—to plant fibers (Müller 251–62). While paper quality and durability declined in this process, the use of wood pulp drastically decreased the price of paper. Pulp fiction was thus economically cheap before audiences thought of it as intellectually cheap. For David M. Earle, the coevolving value system of paper and fiction shows a "multilayered prejudice regarding the *form* of literature," begging the question "why certain media and formats have lended themselves to canonization while others have been kept out of the archives" (20). Today, the nascent e-book trade repeats these entangled ordering processes. Since 2007, for example, the best-seller lists of the *New York Times* distinguish among "trade" paperbacks, "mass-market" paperbacks, and e-books. The last two items mostly contain thrillers, romances, and crime fiction. The "trade" category, however, distinguishes itself both materially and quality-wise. As Elsa Dixler explains in an article that accompanied the redesign of the NYT best-seller lists, a trade book is both "taller and wider" and "considerably more expensive." Beyond this, Dixler claims that trade paperbacks contain "the novels that reading groups choose and college professors teach." As indicated by the overhaul of the *New York Times* best-seller list, resilient medial ordering mechanisms still matter despite the efforts of postmodern artists and scholars to cross the borders of high and low.

Issue ten set a template that Eggers followed in several further issues, as he contracted guest editors and authors to write in the form of specific genres or under certain constraints.[22] McSweeney's 31 (2009), to single out one of these, contains a selection of "neglected or deceased literary forms," as its copyright page informs the reader. The collection of extinct styles extends as far back as the Socratic dialogue, with other notable forms including the ancient Chinese anecdote called "biji," the Icelandic saga, and the consuetudinary, a record of the daily occurrences in monasteries. The materiality of the issue underscores its interest in timeworn artifacts. The oversized volume (8.5 × 11.5 inches) is bound in a thick hardcover that bears a gilded wave stamp. The page design combines the medieval practice of red rubrication with clean, spacious Garamond typography. The columns of body text in this issue crowd the gutter of the book, much like William Morris recommended in his 1893 essay "Printing" (64). In the large quarto format, visual unity thus extends beyond the individual page to the full two-page spread.

All textual forms in the issue originate in preelectronic times. Therefore, their historical genesis is inherently bound up with past writing and publishing technologies, as well as with the medium of the book and the manuscript. McSweeney's 31 thus encapsulates what I have earlier termed the literary dialectic of digitization. Digitized publishing simultaneously threatens book mediality and enables artists to perfectly emulate and adapt older forms. Through several strategies, the individual contributors engage with the historical mediality of their genre. Douglas Coupland, writing in the Chinese biji form, presents a postmodern media narrative centered on the filming of a Survivor season on a Pacific island. In pictorial inserts, Coupland depicts the technological tools of modern travel and entertainment. The pages of the story he titled "Survivor" include screenshots of Google Maps and YouTube (43, 49), hyperlinks (49), listings of TV satellites (48), and information copied and pasted from Wikipedia (55, 57). This multimodal ensemble creates a striking contrast between the neat, Morrisean page design and the digital data sprawl.

Shelley Jackson, on the other hand, welcomes the bibliographic form of the quarto book in her uncanny adaptation of a monastery rulebook, or "consuetudinary." The piece is somewhat of a surprise, as critics have primarily praised Jackson for her work in hypertext. Her hypertext novel *Patchwork Girl* (1995) weaves her own writing together with source material from Mary Shelley's *Frankenstein* and texts by L. Frank Baum, Jacques Derrida, and others. *Patchwork Girl* received distinct acclaim in hypertext studies, first and foremost by Jackson's mentor, George P. Landow, who sees her work as the harbinger of a new "digital information regime" (241). Jackson herself, however, refuses to be seen exclusively as a hypertext author. In her essay "Stitch Bitch," published in the critical volume *Rethinking Media Change*, Jackson rejects the label hypertext and replaces it with "non-linear writing," which, she argues, can occur in several medial forms (242). Her vision for the future of electronic textuality and book publishing is one of coevolution: "I hope the flexibility of electronic media means they evolve many different conventions, a sort of articulation of the possibilities, rather than a narrowing. (Let books take inspiration from them and evolve as well)" (241). Throughout her work, Jackson employs computers in their twofold function as media and technologies.

Medial embodiment is a core theme of *Patchwork Girl*, as Hayles succinctly argues: "*Patchwork Girl* could be *only* an electronic text because the trace of the computer interface, penetrating deeply into its signifying structures, does more than mark the visible surface of the text; it becomes incorporated into the textual body" (*My Mother* 161). While media-dependent, this narrative strategy is not restricted to one medium. After *Patchwork Girl*, Jackson radicalized her idea of embodied narrative in the art project *Skin*, in which a story consisting of 2,095 words takes shape as single-word tattoos on the bodies of volunteers. Jackson's electronic fiction constitutes a prototypical form of metamedial writing on the computer. One could also imagine media-specific fictions that impose their physical presence on new display technologies such as the iPad or Kindle on which they are delivered. However, the rapid obsolescence of each one of these devices along with the transferable design standards of digital markup languages still often forestall localized electronic writing.

Jackson's "Consuetudinary of the Word Church" falls in line with the embodied artworks of *Patchwork Girl* and *Skin*. The hybrid, semiautobiographical text describes the statutes and regulations of the "Word Church," a fictional school founded by Shelley Jackson herself that instructs each student to become a psychic medium for the voices of the deceased. Preceding the text proper, her introduction sketches a fictional history of the manuscript:

> The original of this text, laboriously handwritten on thirty-seven pages of an otherwise empty notebook and starting, by accident or design, at its intended end (thus the words COMPOSITION BOOK appear on the back cover, upside down), was until now the sole existing copy, since the SJVS [Shelley Jackson Vocational School] never chose to set it into type, out of simple negligence or a superstitious conviction that to do so would only remove it further from its source. (133)

In a critical edition of manuscript text, such notes on the textual condition are quite commonly procured by textual scholars who have prepared transcriptions based on the original. In a fictional text, however, such a bibliographical abstract loses its referential function. It is no longer a paratext, but part of the diegetic illusion generated by Jackson—an elaborate editorial fiction. We might call such an extensive rendering of a document's look and feel "bibliographic ekphrasis," a book-centered form of traditional ekphrasis aiming to evoke, in J.A. Cuddon's words, "an image in the mind's eye as intense as if the described object were actually before the reader" (252). By opening her text with the ekphrastic rendering of a manuscript, Jackson conjures an original embodiment for the ensuing text. Readers are thus primed to keep their grasp on the material text while letting their mind enter the "Consuetudinary."

Within the fictional world, a character called the Founder supposedly received the founding creed of her church in a revelation after a prolonged period of isolation. At her church, this authorial persona teaches the doctrine that the "land of the dead is made of language" (132) and that therefore acts of speaking and writing channel voices from beyond the grave. The entire "Consuetudinary" obsessively details the physiology of the mouth, with specific emphasis on the bodily fluids it secretes. Set around the turn of the twentieth century, the story references the spiritualist extravagances of the day, most notably in the form of ectoplasm that the Founder produced from her mouth. John Durham Peters sees the idea of ectoplasm as a peculiar outgrowth of the sprawling differentiation within the media ecology of the late nineteenth century, embodying the (still unrealized) dream of teleporting material information from one place to another (98). The central section of Jackson's "Consuetudinary" chronicles an eighteen-part induction process, during which disciples must reenact key stations of the author's life. The first twelve stations are concerned with operations of the mouth, mimicking the language acquisition process of a child. The thirteenth section, bearing the title "She read," describes the Founder's first encounters with books. Reading comes to her as a first experience with the dead, as she finds paper to bear "the imprint of the thoughts and desires of someone long gone" (142). She rhetorically asks, "What is a book?" without providing an answer. Instead of putting the book's materiality into discourse, Jackson thereby leaves readers with the presence effect of a physical book.

The central part of the story sketches a materialist conception of human world appropriation. Remarkably, the section titled "She read" is not about reading at all—it is about eating books: "It is worth adding that the young Founder, chronically out of pocket and thus deprived of chewing gum, had a habit, deprecated by the Cheesehill librarian, of chewing on corners neatly torn off the pages of books. Unquestionably the eating of books, full as much as the reading of them, primed her for the passage of spirits" (142–43). For Gumbrecht, eating is the most visceral method of engaging with the environment, "the most direct way of becoming one with the things of the world in their tangible presence" (Production 87). Shelley Jackson's body-centered fiction thus forms an aesthetic antidote to the cultural denigration of eating as a basic epistemological practice. To mimic her own paper eating, the Founder suggests an exercise to her students, in which they first construct "twenty-six miniature books, one for each letter of the alphabet," before swallowing them in daily succession (Jackson, "Consuetudinary" 143). Jackson literalizes what it means to metaphorically "devour" or "consume" a book. In her multimedia oeuvre, readers and writers always figure as embodied beings who encounter texts by colliding with medial objects.

On the whole, the McSweeney's project of rejuvenating extinct genres and placing popular ones into a literary frame relies heavily on the mediality of the journal. Literariness in the modern era, as Luhmann holds, has increasingly been associated with the notion of "interestingness" (Art 87–88), used to great effect for example in the critical writings of Henry James. The interesting quality of a literary text, however, also rests on the procedural passage of books through the market-bound communications circuit. In order to remain interesting, individual texts and genres need to become available in new editions in regular intervals. Luhmann sees this continuous process of innovation at work on the level of textuality—new texts foster the autopoiesis of the literary system (Theory 175–76). The general reading public and the institutions of literary criticism typically access texts in relatively fresh material forms. Depending on their canonical status, older texts either descend into obscurity or are absorbed into permanent archives. Such storage sites do not foster connecting communications in the way that contemporary reeditions or rewritings do. The same holds for translations into foreign languages, which often coincide with thorough reappraisals of the original work. The introduction of e-books likewise instilled a sense of newness to a vast archive of public domain texts.

In its thematic issues, McSweeney's offers itself as a materialized testing ground for genres on the threshold of the literary—either in a temporal or in an evaluative sense.[23] It caters to cultural protocols attached to the medium of the book, which still appear to function in the face of digitization. As McSweeney's reframes old and new material

119

into coherent, finite artifacts, it opens up channels of communication in which newspaper comics, fables, and consuetudinaries appear both as new and as permanent. Evaluation and revaluation of such texts may follow different paths when the newsprint of the comic strip does not imply instant obsolescence or when the form of an ancient Scandinavian saga pleases contemporary eyes.

A final cluster of *McSweeney's* issues includes highly experimental book sculptures. In the progression of the series, *McSweeney's 16* (2005) was the first to decisively stray from the codex form. It is a book-like contrivance that can be folded outward three times to reveal four plastic pockets pasted onto cardboard covers. These pockets contain, by order of opening, a comb, the regular paperback journal, a novella by Ann Beattie, and a deck of cards with an interactive story by Robert Coover. The latter piece shows how Coover, who had experimented with electronic hypertext in the 1990s, uses the ludic carrier medium of playing cards as a conduit for printed hypertext. Building on the nursery rhyme about the Queen of Hearts—as familiar from Lewis Carroll's *Alice's Adventures in Wonderland*—the farcical story "Heart Suit" recounts the pursuit of the unknown perpetrator who stole the King of Hearts's favorite home-baked tarts. Coover is not the first author to experiment with narrative bits parceled out across several pieces of paper. In 1962, the French avant-gardist Marc Saporta published *Composition No. 1*, a somber narrative dispersed across 150 loose-leaf, unnumbered pages. In the introduction to the 1963 English edition, Saporta instructed the reader "to shuffle these pages like a deck of cards, to cut, if he likes, with his left hand, as at a fortune teller's" (qtd. in Bolter 148).[24]

Somewhat surprisingly, issue sixteen lacks the usual explanatory paratexts. Apart from a few remarks on submissions and a correction for the prior issue, the staff provides no information regarding the production process and the material form of the issue. All fifteen issues, which had appeared up to this point, had addressed these concerns at some length. Many of these issues, while experimenting with bindings and layout, still adhered to the standard book format. Subscribers and long-term readers probably looked for guidance concerning the strange shape of issue sixteen on the copyright page—only to find out that there is none. Lacking explicit metacommentary, readers have to rely on their hermeneutic skills to make sense of the issue's form and content. At this point, the cumulative serial memory of the individual reader has likely advanced to a stage at which Eggers's explicit paratextual commentary is on the verge of becoming repetitive. *McSweeney's* readers are now conditioned to experience the journal as an entangled double helix of text and medium. From this angle, the comb inserted in the first flap of the issue functions less as a symbol—a metaphoric element that points somewhere else—than as an embodied emblem that continuously points back to its material existence. The comb carries the name "Timothy" in a cursive, silvery engraving. Referencing the eponymous Timothy McSweeney, this strange object embodies the aesthetics of the entire journal. Yet again, *McSweeney's* asks its readers to look at objects, not through them, and perceive them as irreducible things.

In his essay "Thing Theory," Bill Brown formulates a suggestive distinction between things and objects. Brown claims that we only take actual notice of objects when they lose their habitualized meaning and assert their "thingness," for example when they stop working for us (4). The "Timothy-comb" demonstrates this exact moment in which an object becomes a thing. As the first component that readers encounter when flipping open the issue, the comb exposes the unlikeliness of its placement in a literary journal. Like a Duchampian ready-made, the comb invades the space of literary communication. It stops short, however, of pretending to be art. It merely attunes the visual and tactile senses of the reader to the mediality of literature. The comb, in short, does not communicate combing. It communicates the thingness of the comb. Through objects like these, *McSweeney's* has obviously found a new answer to the serial dilemma that Umberto Eco described as the precarious balance between innovation and repetition ("Interpreting" 96–100). The serial anticipation of the *McSweeney's* reader rests just as much on the magazine's innovative form as on its content.

Published only months after the foldable "comb issue," *McSweeney's* 19 (2006) again strays from the codex format. At first sight, the issue reuses the storage concept of the box familiar to readers from issue four. Whereas the design and the individual contents of *McSweeney's* 4 openly presented themselves as literary objects—complete with titles, author names, and a table of contents—issue nineteen is more in line with the "junk mail issue" as it imitates nonliterary primary documents. As exterior container, Dave Eggers employs a cigar box, made from sturdy cardboard and illustrated by the artist Michael Kupperman. The visual design calls up iconic images of warfare: on the lid, an army admiral uses binoculars to locate a fighter jet in the sky; four inserted images depict tanks with their gun pointed straight at the reader; around the edges of the box, drawings of missiles, gas masks, and a mushroom cloud recall Cold War iconography. Inside the box, the reader finds fourteen printed items, including such diverse ephemera as small pocket books, promotional leaflets, letters, and photographs. In addition, a paperback book with several short stories and a novella by T.C. Boyle lie at the bottom of the box.

The ephemeral objects in the cigar box feature paper and design that achieves remarkable mimicry. The reprint of a British information leaflet from 1939 advertises "Some Things You Should Know If War Should Come." The folded leaflet is printed on tinted paper stock and graphically renders the creases and defects of the 70-year-old original document. The fine-grained print job and the lack of margins create an effect akin to trompe l'oeil painting. If the reader folds the paper of this reprinted leaflet, the resulting creases will be hard to differentiate from the creases already printed onto it. The same holds for a series of letters from 1911 concerning one Nelson Squires, who was incarcerated on charges of "living in carnal intercourse with a negro woman." The re-produced correspondence uses several paper sizes, such as small scraps of ruled paper, on which Nelson scrawled his lines from prison with a pencil. An original miniature card with air-raid instructions is reprinted on paper that has the quality and size to endure in someone's wallet. A black-and-white image depicting a group of children in costumes bears the rounded edges typical of mid-twentieth-century photo prints.

Through several items containing military information, the issue implicitly references its immediate historical context. In 2006, American forces were embroiled in both the Iraq War and the military operations in Afghanistan. Public support of the Bush administration had declined significantly due to the scenes of torture at Abu Ghraib prison and the ongoing civil war in Iraq. By reprinting ephemeral leftovers from the disordered cultural archive, *McSweeney's* 19 uncovers historical connections and political ironies. A "Pocket Guide to the Middle East" from 1957 gathers facts and trivia for military personnel in Iraq, Israel, Saudi Arabia, or Syria. Providing a snapshot of the late 1950s, the pocket book contains seemingly innocent prose that has a bitter ring to it when read in 2006: "Whatever their station in life, you'll find Iraqis hospitable, generous, cheerful, and friendly. Make them your friends" ("Pocket Guide" 46). Promotional and educational flyers and leaflets for the U.S. forces from World War I and II, as well as an advertisement for Civil War veterans all exhibit the militaristic rhetoric of the day. Two records from the present mingle with the historical documents: the first is a letter by Donald Rumsfeld addressing leaks of classified information; the second is a photocopy of a dental exam given to George W. Bush by Air Force medical staff in 1973.

Through these carefully arranged artifacts, the issue erects an extended medial diegesis that comprises both the historical documents and the narratives collected in the paperback book. While the reprinted materials make a claim for historical authenticity, the whole arrangement nevertheless asks readers to suspend their disbelief and to buy into the aesthetic illusion of the cigar box. The issue pretends to be a box of collected ephemera that someone might have stashed away in their home. Readers thus invade the private space of an imagined collector of ephemera, a scenario similar to the pile of mail addressed to Sgt. Maria Vasquez. I return to the concept of the medial diegesis—meaning the creation of books and book-like objects that are themselves part of the aesthetic illusion—in my discussion of the novels of Mark Z. Danielewski, Reif Larsen, and Salvador Plascencia below.

Eggers and his coeditors attempted to create absolute facsimiles—not just visual reproductions—of selected ephemeral pieces. Eggers recounts that this effort began with an abolitionist newsletter he bought at an antiquarian book fair: "There's something about a primary document that soaks you in a period or frame of mind better than something secondary or filtered" (The Editors of McSweeney's 186). *McSweeney's* 19 engages with the disordered, sprawling archive of printed ephemera that stretches across antiquarian book stores, flea markets, and private collections. The initial bibliographical phase of the creative process then gave way to a second stage, which relied heavily on digital communication and design technologies. Via eBay, the *McSweeney's* staff collected a large amount of ephemera. Using scanning and image processing software, the staff then converted these ephemera into digital files. At the printer TWP in Singapore, machines and workers manufactured the final print objects using the information encoded in digital files (The Editors of McSweeney's 186). In this constellation, one can glimpse the effect of digitization and globalized commerce on book publishing. The uneven distribution of income rates across the world allows the industrialized nations to outsource the manufacture of cars and textiles, but also of affordable books. To say that *McSweeney's* refutes digitization would therefore be a gross oversimplification. Even if the magazine's inspirations originate in book culture and their final products return to the same sphere, the processes occurring between these two analog spheres are primarily digital.

### ¶ The Humanitarian Book?

As Dave Eggers's popularity has grown with each of his books, so has *McSweeney's* gradually attained influential status in the publishing world.[25] In 2005, Eggers was included in the TIME 100, the TIME magazine's list of the world's most influential people. From 2002 onward, Dave Eggers's writing career moved in a new direction. With his nonfiction books *What Is the What?* (2006) and *Zeitoun* (2009), Eggers set in writing the stories of the Sudanese refugee Valentino Achak Deng and of Abdulrahman Zeitoun, a Syrian American victim of hurricane Katrina. Even though *What Is the What* is subtitled "a novel," both books are documentary in so far as they try to accurately relay two narratives of

adversity. The books were produced in hardcover editions by McSweeney's, allowing Eggers to channel the proceeds into special foundations
that he cofounded with the two men portrayed in the books. The two
most extensive accounts of Dave Eggers's career by Sarah Brouillette
and Caroline D. Hamilton claim a teleological development in which
Eggers moved from narcissistic, "literary" experiments to praiseworthy,
humanitarian philanthropy. Hamilton endorses the idea of ethical consumerism: "McSweeney's Books provides a model for the publishing industry that seizes the advantages of the capitalist system and harnesses
them to positive political ends. Global distribution chains can be used
to sell books whose profits are redirected into local, community projects
such as literacy centers, disaster relief, and human-rights causes" (94).
For both critics, the only viable form of ethical involvement happens
outside the realm of literature, somewhere in the diffuse sphere of politics and humanitarianism. In this scenario, books turn into "fair trade
goods," whose surplus value is that they put extra money in the hands
of poverty-stricken people (97). However, if we desist from normative
judgments and stop to locate "the social"—along with ideas like "social
justice"—outside of the literary, a different perspective reveals itself.

While it may figure as an agent in political and economic contexts,
McSweeney's exerts its prime influence as a literary institution. Even
Eggers's philanthropic pursuits are not primarily humanitarian or political: the 826 National writing and tutoring centers aim to improve
children's literacy and writing abilities; the ScholarMatch program provides financial aid to students who cannot afford college; the Valentino
Achak Deng Foundation builds schools and libraries in South Sudan. All
of these projects qualify as humanitarian, yet their objectives transcend
the human sphere. McSweeney's does not put food in people's mouth,
but books in their hands. By raising literacy rates, providing education,
and encouraging young writers, Eggers's nonprofits attempt to expand
the scope of the literary system and insure its long-term relevance. There
is nothing intrinsically good or bad about this self-centered scenario.
Similar to human individuals who shape society as agents in multiple
social systems (for example as jury members in a law court, as consum-

ers in the economy, and as voters in politics), books have at least a dual function as commodities and as communicational devices. It is tempting to use literary sociology as a master discourse in understanding the marketplace mechanics of contemporary cultural production; nevertheless, the literary field has an aesthetic interior whose functional logic cannot simply be debunked as a tangential side effect to cultural capital.

The McSweeney's aesthetics of book mediality are indicative of a general tendency in American literature. After all, literary journals can function as a testing ground for new forms of expression and they have—at least in the United States—often been the first step of young authors toward a writing career. The McSweeney's experiment that covers the entire first decade of the twenty-first century provides a rich archive that bears testimony to the coevolution of literary communication and mediality. With metamediality as its main formal feature, the bibliographic output of McSweeney's initiates a form of writing and designing books that reverberates through the American novel of the 2000s. Recent studies focusing on the role of literary communication within the contemporary media ecology have considered the novel at length, neglecting the more unwieldy domains of American literary print culture.[26] While my account of the McSweeney's Universe highlights seriality and connecting communications, the following readings cannot easily make such claims for connectivity and mutual influence. Nevertheless, recent studies have already positioned several of the individual novels discussed here alongside each other in an attempt to place them in literary-historical frameworks.[27] One could certainly hypothesize the emergence of a new postmodernist (sub)genre like "the metamedial novel," but I am more interested in the coevolution of American literature with the surrounding media ecology that has infused the various forms of metamediality in specific novels with new cultural functions. These functions play out in a communicative sphere in which the mediality of the novel as a work of art is renegotiated in complex and creative processes.

The following chapters bracket three authors who have received scant scholarly attention—Chip Kidd, Reif Larsen, and Salvador Plascencia—

with two of the most acclaimed and successful contemporary American novelists, Mark Z. Danielewski and Jonathan Safran Foer. All of these texts have found a sizeable audience among American readers, underscoring the importance of their authors for mainstream literary communication. While their techniques are often experimental, they do not address themselves to a specialized niche audience, as was the case with *McSweeney's* prior to Dave Eggers's breakthrough. Where the publishing house McSweeney's presents an exemplary case study of the literary communication circuit in early twenty-first-century U.S. culture, the following novels reach mass audiences as singular works of art. Yet, projected against the symptomatic history of McSweeney's Publishing, their exceptional and distinctive features fade to reveal an intricate set of intertextual and interpersonal connections. Altogether, they tell an open-ended history of the interplay between the novel and the book in the early age of digitization.

## 3. Mark Z. Danielewski's Complex Codices

TO ENCOUNTER THE BEST-SELLING NOVEL *House of Leaves* today means to come upon a different *House of Leaves* than in 2000, its
original year of publication. At the turn of the millennium, Mark Z.
Danielewski's book instantly became a much larger phenomenon than
just a text written by an author. In one way, *House of Leaves* is a node—the
central one—in a communication network that stretches across various
inscription surfaces and communication technologies.[1] The instant cult
status bestowed on the novel owes much to the exuberance of fans,
who used online message boards to post lengthy analytical essays, brief
comments on every particle of the plot, and schematic charts of formal
features. In a way, the sprawling ensemble of fan comments may be seen
as an emblem of the "active reader" whose constructive work has come
to eclipse the importance of the original text. However, there is hardly

any contemporary work of fiction that resonates in a more pointed manner with Niklas Luhmann's notion of compact communication as referenced in Chapter 1. Sprawling textuality occurs outside of the book, while the novel's own mechanics owe more to the perceptual limits of its material form. Even though its proximity to flexible digitality and networked communication is plainly obvious, *House of Leaves* orchestrates a hyper-stable and holistic poetics in which every single discursive and material fragment feeds into its status as an artwork. This chapter lays open Danielewski's novel both as text and book, showing that it qualifies as a master text of metamedial expression in digital print culture.

By becoming a bibliographically closed artwork, Danielewski's novel enables the openness of signification that Umberto Eco saw as the trademark of the avant-garde *opera aperta*. As opposed to electronic textuality, which divorces the storage and display of text, *House of Leaves* employs a vision of total design in which the presence of the book figures as much as its discursive content within the final communicative act. On the whole, it is hardly a new idea that a literary work is part of a communication network consisting of both interpersonal and intertextual conversation. Prior to the late twentieth century, such ephemeral art-related conversation took place in many forms: face-to-face conversations in homes, universities, and reading clubs, as well as written communication through letters. With the advent of networked communication technologies, these ephemeral forms have begun to migrate to online newsgroups and forums. Such derivative conversations have thereby become archivable and searchable, which may explain the increased scholarly attention devoted to such forms of communication outside of the field of anthropology. Scholars do not need to conduct fieldwork to observe these communicative interactions; the field now seems freely accessible on the computer screen. While it is remarkable that *House of Leaves* points outward to a wide array of artifacts and media, its truly unique quality lies in the finite bibliographic form.

According to N. Katherine Hayles, the most prolific Danielewski scholar, the novel is an example of what she terms "Work as Assemblage," meaning "cluster[s] of related texts that quote, comment upon, amplify, and otherwise intermediate one another" (*My Mother* 105).[2] Hayles employs Deleuze and Guattari's notion of rhizomatic structures en route to formulating a model for the multimedia Work as Assemblage (WaA). In this configuration, the literary text takes its place as part of a decentered, rhizomatic network in which further textual components are "branching out from one another in patterns of fractal complexity" (106). And more: "[T]he WaA derives its energy from its ability to mutate and transform as it grows and shrinks, converges and disperses according to the desires of the loosely formed collectives that create it. Moving fluidly among and across media, its components take forms distinctive to the media in which they flourish, so the specificities of media are essential to understanding its morphing configurations" (107). In a way, Hayles here remains true to her materialist theory of hermeneutics as outlined in *Writing Machines*. Yet by using the metaphor of the rhizome, she also decenters the novel in such a way that its place in the communication network becomes level with all others. With this step, Hayles overestimates the relevance of the communication that occurs in the authorized online forum and other sites elsewhere on the Web.

In the medial assemblage that makes up the extended spectacle of the text, the novel claims a superior position to all other intertexts. With the exception of the record *Haunted* (2000) by Danielewski's sister Poe, which may have a comparable communicative relevance to *House of Leaves*, the clearly derivative communication that occurs online coalesces around the compact communication of the novel. Instead of embodying the horizontal layout of a rhizomatic ensemble, the communicative world of *House of Leaves* erects a vertical hierarchy that begins and ends with the gravitational, centripetal attraction of the novel as a discursive-medial object. The unrivaled material and narrative complexity incorporated by a literary work transcends all derivative communications. According to Luhmann, such unlikely formal cohesion is a foundational feature of art: "[A]n artwork distinguishes itself by virtue of the *low probability of its emergence*. The work of art is an ostentatiously improbable occurrence" (*Art* 153). The process through which this remarkable novel entered the art system was indeed full of contingencies, which included the ten-year writing process, the slow-evolving fandom around the unfinished manuscript, the painstaking process of page design, and the enormous number of finalized copies printed and bound by the publisher, Pantheon. Finally, one can never be sure that a published novel will make an impact in the sites of art-related communication. Only when readers, critics, and scholars discursively value a text in sufficient numbers does it become fully active in the social system of art.

Such a systemic framing of the cultural work performed by Danielewski's novel allows us, I believe, to understand the exceptional productivity of the text as it sparked and continues to spark myriads of connecting communications. The astonishing extent of the derivative online conversations directly feeds off the bibliographic stability of the original text along with its metamedial narrative strategies. To this effect, Danielewski refashioned the bibliographic convention of the "edition" of a specific work, underscoring his concern with stability. The copyright page of Danielewski's book, in a form similar to Eggers's first works, is already part of the narrative. The legal copyright information at the top contains factual bibliographical data, including the ISBN numbers of both the hardcover and the paperback format. But a chart at the bottom of the page complicates matters. Under the heading "A Note On This Edition," the chart lists four different bibliographic variants: "Full Color," "2-Color," "Black & White," and "Incomplete." A blue box around one of the editions indicates the version of the copy at hand. Several scholars, including Hayles, have taken for granted that the novel did appear in these four forms.[3] At the moment of publication in 2000, however, only two of these editions existed, the "Black & White" and the "2-Color."[4] Until 2006, no "Incomplete" and no "Full Color" editions were in print.

For Hayles, the supposed existence of four editions underscores her theory of the assemblage and the rhizome. Consequently, she stresses that each of these editions is "significantly different from the others" (*My Mother* 105). Is this really the case, though? During the initial best-selling phase, almost every American reader of the text would have encountered *House of Leaves* in the blue "2-Color" version. As fans have meticulously chronicled online, this standard blue version was briefly accompanied by a red version around 2003.[5] As with the random dispersal of alternative versions of *You Shall Know Our Velocity* in the Vintage paperback, the publisher deliberately obscured these bibliographic variants under the same ISBN number. This playful, covert manipulation of editions peaked in a final flourish in 2006 when Pantheon released "The Remastered Full-Color Edition" of the book, again using the same ISBN number and excluding any indicator of the later publication date. Also, the adjective "remastered" underscores the claim of a previously extant full-color edition, which never existed. After the publication of this "Remastered" edition, Pantheon phased out production of the "2-color" versions, so that later readers will likely have purchased the color edition. Overall, the most influential editions of this text—by the sheer number of people who bought each—are the blue "2-color" and the "Remastered Full-Color," both of which form the basis of the following readings.

Putting copies of these two versions side by side, readers can immediately see that it is not the differences between the two that first meet the eye, as Hayles would have it. Even though six years separate the two printings, these two books look remarkably alike. Both have an unconventionally broad format (7 × 9 inches) and carry the same cover. The front flap has exactly the same promotional text; a second cover page—a photograph of a collage of items with narrative relevance— also remains the same. The first regular page features the same eleven promotional "blurbs" in both editions. The title page of the book carries the misleading note "2nd edition" in both books. On the copyright page, the "Note On This Edition" visually indicates the respective edition. Other alterations to the copyright page are so minute that they easily escape notice. Throughout the main text of the book, however, the only divergent aspects between the two editions are those explicitly listed in the "Note on This Edition" on the copyright page. Beyond this, the bulk of the novel remains exactly as it was in the beginning. Nothing is reset or corrected; layout features, footnote numerals, and appendices stay the same.

All of this happens for a good reason: through its narrative strategies, *House of Leaves* anchors itself in a specific material form, which—though mass-produced—has to remain as stable as possible in order to ensure its complete artistic signification. The novel appears to embrace its position as ordering device within a hyper-complex communication system. In essence, this strict emphasis on textual stability catalyzes and propels the online community's embrace of the book. Through the "repeatable materiality" of the book—a term coined by Foucault (*Archaeology* 114–15)—all of the Web site users have exactly the same material reference point when discussing *House of Leaves*. No substantially diverging versions of the book exist. No other American publishing house has picked up the rights and reformatted it to fit a different house style. All the fundamental bibliographic codes used in the novel remain as they were. With the stability of the book functioning as a play-enhancing constraint, readers are free to speculate about the narrative importance of any aspect in its design.[6] Pantheon presents none of these external features as falling under the domain of the publisher. Fonts, colors, and layout assert their significance alongside the textual content of the book. The very marginality of the few differences between the editions actually calls forth a type of forensic fandom that drives readers to purchase several editions and behave as amateur textual scholars in pursuit of a critical edition.[7]

*House of Leaves* streamlines the feedback loops linking authors, readers, and academics. In the main online forum, fans warmly greeted Hayles's 2002 article "Saving the Subject: Remediation in *House of Leaves.*" Many threads take up the critic's ideas and use them for additional readings. Furthermore, several students and even scholars appear to have posted inquiries on the forum, attempting to harness the fans' wisdom. Seasoned users often point such newcomers to Hayles's work. The more refined and extended argument of *Writing Machines*, conversely, had an impact not only within fan circles. During a 2007 book reading in Göttingen, Danielewski freely admitted that he read Hayles's work and approves of many of her ideas. Conversely, Hayles's *Writing Machines* emulates the typographic and bibliographic style of its literary predecessor, as mentioned earlier. The volume attempts to embody the methodology of media-specific analysis in its customized form and layout. To speak of Danielewski and Hayles as instances of "primary text" and "secondary text" therefore appears to be a gross oversimplification. Rather, the systemic impact of this experimental novel only emerges as a communicative event within the feedback mechanisms that connect several groups of agents. Media-specific analysis (MSA) may come to complement the narratological toolbox of literary studies. Within American literary culture in the early 2000s, however, MSA is also a product of coevolution between art and scholarship, built upon a singular novelistic object with massive public appeal. In sum, *House of Leaves* turns into a metamedium not merely through its material form as a book. It attains meaning only at the point where this metamediality is communicated, either in the quiet processes of private reading or in public exchanges based on these readings.

As many detailed studies of the specific forms and narrative devices of *House of Leaves* already exist, I will use the novel as a model text for a materialist interpretation focused on the phenomenon of metamediality. This novelistic *Gesamtkunstwerk* activates (at least) five metamedial dimensions of printed literature: external design; typography and visual elements; paratextual framing; diegetic reflexivity; medial mise en abyme and metalepsis. Some of these features are seldom integrated into scholarly readings of literary texts; others—such as textual forms and motifs—are commonplace. The complex codex of *House of Leaves* uses all these registers of medial signification in its quest to become the perfect narrative labyrinth. In following these five dimensions, my reading of *House of Leaves* starts at the outer edges of the novel and burrows inward through the diegetic levels into the center of Danielewski's fictional world. All attributes of metamediality introduced in this chapter return with varying frequency throughout my readings in this book. To be sure, none of these factors possesses the unique expressive force to initiate metamedial effects by itself. The basic idea of the hermeneutic circle holds true: the whole informs the part, while the parts inform the whole.

## ¶ External Design

Practitioners and textual scholars often describe a generic hardcover book with a number of standard technical terms: cover, spine, back cover, endpapers, fore-edge, etc. These outward forms have undergone centuries of evolution, standardization, and deviation. Bibliographers have traditionally explored such forms and conventions as historical objects. To foster the overall metamedial potential of a given text and thus to enter the arena of literary analysis, a given work must activate these medial building blocks. Within literary studies, Gérard Genette's *Paratexts* introduced a pioneering framework that accords significant value to these aspects. According to Genette, paratexts are all the meaningful elements that surround a literary text, but are not inherently part of it. Genette distinguishes between "peritextual" and "epitextual" elements, with the former being materially attached to the work, such as cover designs and title pages, and the latter circulating around it in the form of ads, interviews, or the like. He theorizes the material form of the book as a "publisher's peritext," which is "executed by the typesetter and printer but decided on by the publisher, possibly in consultation with the author" (*Paratexts* 16). In Genette's scheme, the publisher determines "the cover, the title page, and their appendages," as well as "the book's material construction (selection of format, of paper, of typeface, and so forth)" (16). This description appears reasonable only as long as the design of a specific book clearly designates these external areas as separate from the core of the artistic work. Recent American literature, however, increasingly brings forth texts that spill into their paratextual surroundings, bridging the arbitrary gaps between text and book, and between publisher's and author's peritext. Specially designed hard or soft covers, endpapers, flyleaves, title pages, imprints, and colophons offer themselves for interpretation and begin to function as bibliographic codes when they engage with the signification of the literary artwork.

The aesthetic illusion of *House of Leaves* in fact begins on the surface of its cover. The sole front cover that U.S. printings of the book have carried so far uses a simple typographic format with white type set against a black background, embellished with a small line drawing. At first glance, it is hard to make out that the black background contains the schematic map of a labyrinth. The outline of a labyrinth is printed in a glossy paper coating on the otherwise matte background. Feeling the cover of the book, readers experience a sensual impression of the diegetic labyrinth of *House of Leaves*. Its uncanny structure, the cover insinuates, transcends mere visual disorientation. While the typography inside the book obviously emulates a labyrinth, the materiality of the book embodies this underlying structure as well. The turning of strangely formatted pages and the spatial disorientation evoked by that formatting relies both on the tactile experience of the codex as on the visual qualities of the layout.

The exterior book design erects a complete medial diegesis. The cover has a front flap, a design feature that commonly contains a synopsis of the book's plot along with biographical information about the author. Cannily, *House of Leaves* taps into the cultural protocols that readers employ to make sense of a book. Browsing through the bookstore, someone unfamiliar with the hype surrounding the book might turn to the cover flap for an external, editorial perspective on its contents. Instead, the faux-promotional text validates the status of the novel as a primary document, which had supposedly circulated in excerpts on the Internet and among a devoted group of followers, among them "musicians, tattoo artists, programmers, strippers, environmentalists, and adrenaline junkies." This snippet of text already points toward the novel's character constellation. Johnny Truant, the fictional editor, works at a tattoo parlor and dates a stripper nicknamed Thumper. Whether the manuscript actually existed as a "badly bundled heap of paper" in the hands of Danielewski, as the passage claims, remains uncertain.[8] Yet, such a heap of paper will eventually surface in the diegetic confines of Johnny's story.

In its final lines, the jacket text reframes the object of the book as just one manifestation among others in which the novel exists: "Now, for the first time, this astonishing novel is made available in book form, complete with the original colored words, vertical footnotes, and newly added second and third appendices." Danielewski here subverts the

notion of an authentic, originary "work." According to this description, House of Leaves exists in many versions, with the final "book form"
supposedly being a complex mediation of earlier manifestations. The
ontological structure of the book enacts a hierarchical "mediation plot"
(Hayles, "Saving" 783) whose innermost layer is the filmic work of the
former photojournalist Will Navidson. The material of this film drives
the plot from the interpolated layers up to the top level, at which Johnny
Truant rearranges Zampanò's bits and pieces. To these levels, we need
to add the final materialized book, which attempts to surround all other
levels with an intricate medial diegesis. Part of the gothic pleasure in
reading House of Leaves lies in pretending that the individual copy has an
aura of authenticity that emanates from the form of the codex.

Facing the flap, a glossy photograph forms the first page of the book
proper and invites the reader to pause at the edge of the text. At first,
we see just a disheveled heap of items, most of which bear some kind
of writing. The picture shows a comic strip, a drawing of a staircase,
two tape measures, a compass, pills, stamps, a silver bullet, and several
scraps of paper with hand-written or typed notes. The ensuing introduction by Johnny Truant provides more information on these items.
The fictional editor here recounts how he scavenged the apartment of
Zampanò, the old man who had lived and died in the building where
Johnny's friend Lude lives. Zampanò, in his eighties, appears to have
died of natural causes, although claw marks on the wooden floor indicate a connection to the evanescent Minotaur who haunted Navidson's
house on Ash Tree Lane. Picking through his remains, Johnny and
Lude discover the container with Zampanò's notes on "The Navidson
Record," his semischolarly tract on the documentary film of the same
name. These notes are anything but orderly, as Johnny recounts:

As I discovered, there were reams and reams of it. Endless snarls
of words, sometimes twisting into meaning, sometimes into nothing at all, frequently breaking apart, always branching off into
other pieces I'd come across later—on old napkins, the tattered
edges of an envelope, once even on the back of a postage stamp;
everything and anything but empty; each fragment completely

covered with the creep of years and years of ink pronouncements; layered, crossed out, amended; handwritten, typed; legible, illegible; impenetrable, lucid; torn, stained, scotch taped; some bits crisp and clean, others faded, burnt or folded and refolded so many times the creases have obliterated whole passages of god knows what—sense? (xvii)

Skipping back to the photographic title page, readers can discover several of the pieces listed. With the character of Johnny Truant, Danielewski considerably extends the classical literary device of the fictional editor, as often used for example in the epistolary novels of German Romanticism. Johnny is not just an editor, but an amateur textual scholar scouring primary documents and explaining their material condition en route to a critical edition of the text. Though less erudite than Nabokov's Charles Kinbote in *Pale Fire*, Johnny works hard to restore the material unity of Zampanò's manuscript legacy. In hyperrealistic fashion, his scholarly apparatus includes photographic evidence of the editing process.

Johnny frames his catalogue of objects with several perplexing, metamedial remarks. He does not provide a thorough description of the container that holds Zampanò's notes, but merely talks of it as a "thing" (xviii). He also envisions the exact reading situation of an empirical reader of the Pantheon *House of Leaves*: "At least some of the horror I took away at four in the morning you now have before you, waiting for you a little like it waited for me that night, only without these few covering pages" (xvii). Situated on page seventeen of the introduction, Johnny's statement reflects on its spatial position preceding the text of "The Navidson Record." His introductory ramblings thus not only introduce the strange transcript that follows, they also physically cover it. Johnny insinuates that his own exposure to the raw material was more drastic than the reading experience of the tamed book can ever be. He then further reflects on the uncanny materiality of the storage trunk, whose "heaviness," "silence," and "stillness" unsettled him (xvii). In hindsight—this section is dated two years later than the events described—Johnny remembers the "resolute blackness" that seemed threatening all by itself, raising the possibility that this very blackness might murder him or even the reader (xvii). The blackness of the trunk of course resonates with the book's black cover. The exterior form of *House of Leaves* thus attempts to translate the materiality effect of a gothic trunk full of decaying paper.

Johnny's quest to bring the reader as close to his own reading experience as possible does not end with the ekphrastic evocation of blackness. He also tries to convince the reader to imitate his manner of reading. During the editing process, Johnny suffers from escalating panic attacks and hallucinations, which, he surmises, originate from his fixation on "The Navidson Record." In a literal sense, Johnny's close reading relies on being close to the papery surface of the text. The reader is invited to follow suit:

> To get a better idea try this: focus on these words, and whatever you do don't let your eyes wander past the perimeter of this page. Now imagine just beyond your peripheral vision, maybe behind you, maybe to the side of you, maybe even in front of you, but right where you can't see it, something is quietly closing in on you, so quiet in fact you can only hear it as silence. Find those pockets without sound. That's where it is. Right at this moment. But don't look. Keep your eyes here. (26–27)

Johnny employs several deictic expressions to lure the reader into this immersive experience of the book. The last word "here" has a twofold function: On the discursive level, it represents Johnny's speech, trying to guide the reader. On the visual level of the printed page, however, it directs the reader's wandering eyes to one location. The four letters become the visual focal point, not as representations of speech but as visible markings. Incidentally—or intentionally?—the word "here" crowds the gutter in the middle of the book, aiming the reader's eyes into the center instead of having them hover at the periphery. In this way, the embodied act of reading codepends on the placement of words and the form of the book. Overall, the book's visual design works in tandem with the narrative to ensure a complete bibliographic simulation. The typographic qualities of *House of Leaves* continue this aesthetics on almost every single page.

## ¶ Typography and Visual Elements

Beyond external formatting, book designers are also responsible for the selection and arrangement of type. Within literary and cultural studies, only very few disparate publications have so far addressed this topic.[9] Otherwise, these fields often subscribe to language-centered aesthetics, relegating physical or visual aspects to the status of mere accidentals within the reading process. Throughout the history of printing, we find similar conceptualizations of typography. In 1932, Beatrice Warde, famous typographic advocate and manager at the Monotype Corporation, formulated a consequential maxim concerning the role of typography in the production and dissemination of texts. She believed that the "mental eye," unlike the physical one, looks through type and not on it: "The type which, through any arbitrary warping of design or excess of 'color,' gets in the way of the mental picture to be conveyed, is a bad type" (Warde 113). The ideal typography, Warde surmised, is like a crystal goblet (109). In this scheme, the book is a pure tool—designed to let people use it, rather than doing something in and of itself. The imagined reader of such texts appreciates easy access and swift navigation.

In *Paratexts*, Gérard Genette cautiously strays from this philosophy of the codex as a tool. In his study, typography still firmly falls into the arena of the publisher; the author has little or no say in typesetting. Despite the ideal of transparency, Genette argues, literary scholars should accord some value to the black marks on the white page: "[N]o reader should be indifferent to the appropriateness of particular typographical choices, even if modern publishing tends to neutralize these choices by a perhaps irreversible tendency to standardization" (*Paratexts* 34). This hypothesis has not stood the test of time. Advances in soft- and hardware have provided authors with new tools to garner a more influential position in the typographic design process of their books. Johanna Drucker's work on typography provides a necessary corrective. Drucker exposes the naturalized conventions underlying typographic practice, distinguishing between two modes of typographic presentation: "marked" and "unmarked" texts. For literary texts, the norm came to be unmarked typography, a "single grey block of undisturbed text, seeming, in the graphic sense, to have appeared whole and complete" (Visible 95). The typographer's aims for serious literature are thus "to make the text as uniform, as neutral, as accessible and seamless as possible," so as to point not toward its own graphic splendor, but toward the supposed truth and beauty behind the text itself (95). This monopoly, Drucker writes, only came under attack with the Futurist and Dadaist movements, which were inspired by the ways in which commercial advertising used marked texts in order to reinforce their messages.

In the flood of disorienting texts that make up House of Leaves, the novel stresses the navigational function of its typography. In an early footnote, the fictional editors who prepare Johnny's version of the book for publication claim to have employed fonts to increase order: "In an effort to limit confusion, Mr. Truant's footnotes will appear in Courier font while Zampanò's will appear in Times" (4). This remark and other scattered annotations by the editors are set in yet another font, Bookman. Danielewski uses these fonts consciously, and by attributing them to the intentional choice of the editors, he invites speculation on their aesthetic import. As Jessica Pressman points out, "Zampanò's academic commentary appears in Times Roman, the font associated with newspapers and the Linotype; Truant's footnotes are in Courier, imitate a typewriter's inscription, and thematically identify him as the middle-man, the 'courier' of the manuscript; the terse notations from the Ed. are aptly presented in Bookman" ("House" 109–10). Pressman here interprets the significance of the fonts both by their visual features and by their telling names. The editors, in this regard, are quite literally "book-men" who turn the loose pages sent in by Johnny Truant into a coherent book.

With his suggestive graphic design, Mark Z. Danielewski has lead not only literary critics to interrogate the typography of House of Leaves. To a remarkable extent, such font-specific arguments proliferate in online fan forums. The official forum on the author's Web site devotes several threads exclusively to the novel's typography. One such thread bears the exclamatory title, "Pelafina is the author of House of Leaves!!!"

In the initial post, a forum user builds a narratological case for the argument that Johnny Truant's mother—on an intradiegetic level—actually authored the whole book and thus invented both Johnny Truant and Zampanò. Typography serves as the main exhibit: Mark Z. Danielewski uses Dante as his trademark font for his own name and the titles of his books.[10] Dante's strong serifs lend a unique iconicity to Danielewski's middle initial "Z." Claiming that Pelafina's letters are also set in Dante, the forum user speculates: "Doesn't this mean she is the author of the book? Wikipedia page [sic] on *House of Leaves* also mentions Pelafina's font being Dante and says that the font types are very important" ("Pelafina"). Within this thread, some users start amassing further evidence beyond the (false) Wikipedia information, much of which seems to support the proposed reading.

Many other fans disagree, pointing out that Pelafina's and Danielewski's respective fonts—albeit similar—are not actually the same. Through detailed analysis, especially of the more stylized letters such as "Q," "g," "a," and the ampersand sign "&," one can confirm that Pelafina's letters are set in Kennerley Old Style, originally designed by the American typographer Frederic W. Goudy (see fig. 4). Even though this evidence shatters the authorship theory developed in the discussion thread, Kennerley does render Pelafina's letters in a form that contributes significantly to her characterization. For one, the rich serifs infuse the text with an air of capriciousness, entirely fitting her manic psyche. Even more than this, the Kennerley character set features a distinctive

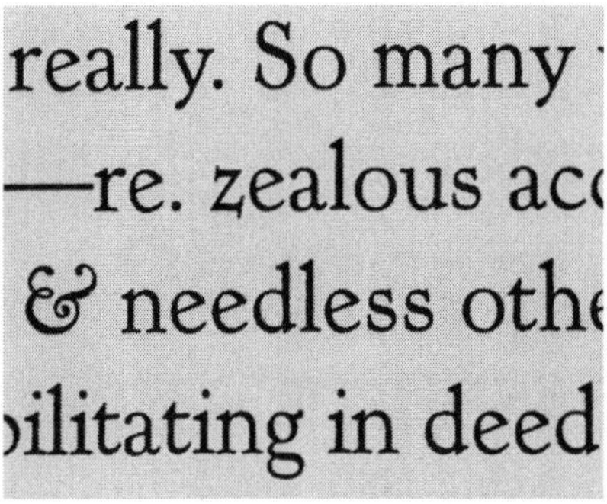

really. So many
—re. zealous ac(
& needless oth(
)ilitating in deed

Fig. 4. Detail from Mark Z. Danielewski, *House of Leaves: The Remastered Full-Color Edition* (New York: Pantheon, 2006), p. 621. Courtesy of Pantheon Books, an imprint of the Knopf Doubleday Publishing Group, a division of Random House LLC. Photograph by Alexander Starre.

letter "e," whose crossbar tilts upwards. All "e" letters in Pelafina's text thus appear instable, threatening to fall over at any point. This visual quality embodies the mood swings Johnny's mother undergoes in and between each letter. At this point, I do not intend to convey a master-theory to solve the mysteries created by *House of Leaves*. Its narrative fascination lies squarely in the fact that it constantly urges the reader down hermeneutic paths that prove to be convincing for a while, before other suggestive doors open onto different interpretive pathways. On one level, this effect explains the mass readership of the book, since the forensic pursuit of a final truth in a tangled web of significations is very rewarding—especially when hundreds of thousands of others share this cult experience. On another level, such reader involvement shows that the innovative potential of *House of Leaves* does not play itself out purely on a textual level. Rather, the book actively stages aspects of literary communication that usually do not meet the eye.

Contrary to the two prominent Danielewski scholars N. Katherine Hayles and Mark B.N. Hansen, I argue that *House of Leaves* performs cultural work on a *medial* level, not a media-technical one. The book opens up a communicative frame that engages text, medium, and their mutual feedback mechanisms. As Hayles and Hansen inquire into the dynamics of inscription that underlie Danielewski's oeuvre, both of them promote digital technologies as the central key for innovative contemporary literature. Their conceptual perspectives intertwine medium and technology and lead to conclusions such as the following: "So essential is digitality to contemporary processes of composition, storage, and production that print should properly be considered a particular form of output for digital files rather than a medium separate from digital instantiation" (Hayles, *Electronic* 159). Thus, notions of the "mark of the digital" (159) or the "digital topography" (Hansen, "Digital") overshadow the significance of the book as a secondary medium of storage and display. Hayles quotes Danielewski's comments on the digital production process at the beginning of a chain of reasoning, leading her to the conclusion that "digitality has become the textual condition of twenty-first-century literature" (*Electronic* 186). Taking up

Jerome McGann's notion of the "textual condition," Hayles issues this sweeping claim concerning the communication system of literature.

In McGann's understanding, the term "textual condition" refers to the concrete communication situation in which readers face a given text. This process unfolds via "material negotiations" between recipient and medium (*Textual* 3). To study these communicative acts that collectively constitute culture, McGann urges scholars to gather as much evidence as possible on the concrete textual condition of a literary work. For *House of Leaves* as it was read and received in the United States, such evidence is readily available. As explained above, the novel has been remarkably stable throughout its several print runs. The differences between the color printings deserve attention, but this recognition should not brush over the remarkable fact that Danielewski's work has retained virtually all of its bibliographic codes after a decade and a half of reprintings. Also, to return to Hayles, no official e-text of *House of Leaves* exists as of this writing. Amazon.com, which has millions of Kindle e-books, does not offer buyers an electronic copy of *House of Leaves*; owners of the iPad cannot purchase it in their iBooks application. Even if this changes in the future—and Pantheon indicates that it will—the litmus test for the textual condition cannot be the mere existence of a digital text. As McGann has proposed, a materialist hermeneutics pays heed both to the aesthetic form of an artifact and to aspects of its empirical distribution (*Textual* 15). Out of the sheer mass of books published in the new millennium, *House of Leaves* may be among the most ill-fitting pieces of evidence for a digital textual condition.

My case rests not just on the unavailability of the novel as an e-book. Much more than that, the novel employs such an array of metamedial devices specific to the book that it would be a wholly different artifact if studied as a digital text. For each specific text, we may attempt to reconstruct its "implied medium." Just as texts contain implicit information about their implied author and implied reader (as theorized by Wayne C. Booth and Wolfgang Iser, respectively), they increasingly provide clues about their preferred medium. The textual condition of twenty-first-century literature, then, still emerges on a case-by-case basis. Digitality is not its deterministic sovereign. If we examine the novel not in its relation to the digital machines that produce it, but to the physical book that contains it, the intertextual environment of *House of Leaves* changes radically. Instead of hypertexts and databases, the medial representation of an editorial fiction (*Herausgeberfiktion*) sets the book alongside the early epistolary novels of Samuel Richardson. Aside from his writing, Richardson also operated his own printing shop. In *Clarissa*, he employed his typographic expertise to manipulate the form of the fictional letters so as to approximate a manuscript. This has an especially striking effect in the letters the protagonist writes after her rape: sections of text in Clarissa's so-called "Mad Papers" are strewn around the page in a way that resembles Pelafina's letters from the mad house (S. Price 134). The aims behind this manipulation resemble the functional use of typography in Danielewski's horror novel: "Richardson's creation of the autograph manuscript in print is an effective compromise, in that it allows the author to write epistolary fiction which retains the credibility typically reserved for 'Original Manuscripts'" (135). The authenticating paper becomes the connective tissue for this strand of literary history.

Returning to the issue of typography, we can perceive how the book and the screen provide medial containers with specific attributes. With the book, the preliminary choice of fonts by the author and the editorial staff becomes finalized during the act of printing. For a specific work, these design choices do not entail an unchanged form throughout its existence. As can be seen in reissued works, such as anthologies or special series, literary texts are regularly given a different shape by new editors and artists. The 2010 edition of *Tristram Shandy* published by the British publishing start-up Visual Editions, for example, infuses the eighteenth-century book with a stunning visual design that uses glaring neon orange for many of Sterne's textual experiments. Yet, such refashionings become precarious when typography turns out to be an important device of the text, as in McLuhan's *Gutenberg Galaxy*. If typefaces transport meaning, they are indeed an organic part of a specific work. As Pelafina's font and the connecting communications it sparked in the fan forum indicate, many readers process the novel as a book, not only as a text. For the autopoiesis of literature, it hardly matters whether readers believe the claim that Pelafina wrote the book. The fact that typographic data is used as evidence within such interpretations at all is a fundamental communicative innovation.

Aside from the usage of fonts, the domain of typography also figures in *House of Leaves* with regard to coloring. Throughout the remastered edition, all instances of the word "house"—even the German homophone *Haus*—are printed in blue ink. Additionally, struck passages and the word "minotaur" appear in red. As an illustrative device, such coloring calls up the tradition of rubrication. We have already seen this practice referenced and employed in Dave Eggers's *Sacrament* and in *McSweeney's* 31. In the former, the technique alludes to a character whose rewriting of the text falls in line with the elaborative work of the medieval rubricator. *McSweeney's* uses rubrication as historical mimicry for their issue on extinct writing genres. In *House of Leaves*, the technique serves yet another function. As Martin Brick argues, the novel is an instance of anti-rubrication: "While medieval rubricators would have their readers deny the materiality of the text except for its ability to point toward an *authority* behind it, Danielewski desires the opposite. The text in its material sense—as pages printed with ink, arranged in a certain way, appearing a certain way to the eye—is ultimately all that can exist." Originally, rubrication aimed to provide the reader with interpretive tools that render the body text easier to fathom. As red ink in *House of Leaves* only intensifies the maze-like structure of the book, the printed colors lose all explanatory potential while retaining their unique bibliographic position.

Another experimental use of coloring occurs in chapter IX, the most labyrinthine chapter of the book, where on page 119 a blue box appears that encloses footnote #144. The footnote lists all the things that are *not* present in the endless rooms and hallways that Navidson's assistant Holloway Roberts traverses during his exploratory journey through the hidden inside of the house. Between pages 119 and 144, the blue box is present on every page, though every other page shows the image of the preceding one in a mirrored form. The resulting illusion is one of transparency: "Here the back of the page seems to open transparently onto the front, a notion that overruns the boundary between them and constructs the page as a leaky container rather than an unambiguous unit of print" (Hayles, *Writing* 123). The placement of the boxes corresponds to the traditional recto and verso denominations of the printed codex. The recto/front of a page displays the footnote's content in legible form, while the verso/back side carries its mirror image. Whereas Hayles is ready to claim that this visual element extends beyond the printed book, I would hold that it instead shifts the attention from the cultural construct of the page to the materiality of the sheet. We have become accustomed to regard each individual page of a book as a separate entity, but Danielewski refocuses our eyes to the physical substratum of that elusive page—the sheet. Where William Morris had urged book designers to emphasize the unity of the full recto-verso spread of a book, Danielewski conversely reminds the reader that texts are printed on the front and back of sheets—or leaves. As a basic unit, the sheet has more material coherence than the spread, for example when it is ripped out from the book. The bound codex of the novel embodies the material metaphor of the house of leaves—its structure of covers and glue literally houses the roughly 350 leaves of this book.

## ¶ Paratextual Framing

Whereas the last two sections addressed nonlinguistic design aspects, we now enter the domain of discourse. In *Paratexts*, Genette briefly comments on book formats, typefaces, and page design, but the bulk of his work is concerned with texts in the narrow sense: titles, epigraphs, dedications, and so forth. These verbal paratexts can be analyzed and interpreted with or without recourse to their position vis-à-vis the literary text proper. Paratexts may trigger metamedial effects by foregrounding the production process and the artifactual status of the fictional work. Title pages, prefaces, and even copyright pages may record certain facts about book design, typefaces, or even the economic costs of printing and distributing the book. As framing devices, paratexts can furthermore set up a fictional medial constellation, for example when claiming that the main text has been assembled from a recently discovered manuscript or from other printed ephemera. Even where fictional texts aim for mimetic realism, their reality effects can extend to the medium itself when they faithfully use the empirical pages as material icons—in the Peircean sense—for the fictional pages of a different document. The editorial fiction is one of the most common types of fictional prefatory matter, often explaining "the circumstances in which the pseudo-editor acquired possession of this text" (Genette, *Paratexts* 280). As a ploy for simulated authenticity, editorial fictions may describe the carrier medium of the "original" text in detailed form.

The strategy of collapsing the distinction between text and paratexts, as seen in the writings of Dave Eggers, comes full circle in Danielewski's novel. Where *A Heartbreaking Work* attributed its paratextual excursions to a speaking subject that corresponds with the empirical author, *House of Leaves* creates a total fiction that devours the publisher's peritext. The novel further appropriates all the elements of authorial communication that Genette lists: titles, dedications, epigraphs, prefaces. All of these features are present, but none of them exits the bounds of diegesis. The foreword (v) starts at the outermost narrative level of the editors. The epigraph "This is not for you" (ix), though it bears no signature, stems from Johnny Truant since it is set in Courier. Johnny's introduction itself (xi–xxiii) references the textual condition of the fictional artifact—in a way, it is an extended, biographically infused "Note on the Text" as commonly found in scholarly editions. Some unnumbered pages follow that contain a second enigmatic epigraph and a second title page indicating the beginning of Zampanò's unpublished manuscript "The Navidson Record." Only after these pseudo-authorial paratexts do we arrive at the bottom level of the narrative.

At the end of the book, the reader slowly reascends this narrative ladder. Johnny Truant has supposedly compiled the sections "Exhibits" (529–35) and "Appendix" (537–65), which contain diverse pieces collected or written by Zampanò with tangential relevance to "The Navidson Record." The anonymous editors claim responsibility for "Appendix II" (567–656), which reprints more photographs and records, including the "Pelican Poems" written either by Zampanò or by Johnny Truant, the "Whalestoe Letters" by Pelafina, as well as pictorial collages depicting scraps and pieces from Zampanò's storage trunk. Lastly, the editors supply "contrary evidence" in "Appendix III," including photographs and artwork that dispute several claims made by Johnny Truant. One such photograph shows a copy of *The Works of Hubert Howe Bancroft*, a book whose existence Johnny had denied in his introduction (xx).

The clear subdivision of paratextual levels, however, is constantly blurred throughout the novel. As such, one of the most heavily convoluted sections of footnotes in chapter XI sees the three voices of Zampanò, Johnny, and the editors converge to such an extent that readers have to doubt the neat separation of their communicative spheres (137–38). From early on, Johnny discredits himself as editor when he admits to altering pieces of Zampanò's manuscript to make his autobiographical footnotes more relevant to the text. Johnny directly addresses the reader about the instance in which he inserts a word into "The Navidson Record": "Now I'm sure you're wondering something. Is it just coincidence that this cold water predicament of mine also appears in this chapter? Not at all. Zampanò only wrote 'heater.' The word 'water' back there—I added that. Now there's an admission, eh?" (16). Johnny actually frames the whole text with a hostile attitude toward the reader, choosing "This is not for you" (ix) as his epigraph. The fictional paratexts of *House of Leaves* thus simultaneously reinforce and call into question the reliability of several document types.

## ¶ Diegetic Reflexivity

Crossing the threshold that separates the outside and inside of a text—Genette calls this border a "vestibule," a "boundary zone," or an "edge" (*Paratexts* 2)—we may find metamedial devices within the fictional world proper. Aside from the aspects listed in the previous chapters, such central domains of literary studies as characterization, setting, and motifs figure critically in the creation of metamedial effects. Recursive loops between text and medium work best when closely intertwined with the fictional world. As such, diegetic encounters with the medial form that holds the text are always implicitly reflexive. Examples of such encounters are characters who write, produce, or read books; settings such as book stores, libraries, or printing shops; motifs that interrogate writing processes or that bring into focus the larger media ecology of the computerized present and the book's place in it.

On this intradiegetic level of metamediality, *House of Leaves* provides an equally broad range of material. The three narrative voices of the book—the editors, Johnny Truant, and Zampanò—share a common preoccupation that forms the backbone of the entire plot: they all want to create a book. While for Zampanò, the scholarly treatise on *The Navidson Record* seemed to be a life-consuming task, Johnny Truant initially does not embrace the project fully. In one of his early footnotes, he explains, "To date, I've counted over two hundred rejection letters from various literary journals, publishing houses, even a few words of discouragement from prominent professors in east coast universities. No one wanted the old man's words—except me" (20). The reader therefore faces two narrator-characters, each of whom devotes long stretches of his narrative to comment on the production process of a book. While Zampanò's sections mediate this process in the distanced style of academic writing, Johnny's footnotes present the quest to publish as an existential pursuit to contain the horror of the house: "There's only one choice now: finish what Zampanò himself failed to finish. Re-inter this thing in a binding tomb. Make it only a book . . ." (327). On the intradiegetic level, *House of Leaves* is not just aesthetically bound to its medial carrier. The sturdy volume is also the only safe place to store the sprawling, dangerous textuality proliferating in and around the infamous house.

Zampanò's scholarly apparatus engages deeply with the media of film and photography, as well as with theories of architecture and trauma. Since his object of analysis is *The Navidson Record*, the old man invested considerable time and energy into researching these fields. As a blind man, Zampanò had to hire several research assistants, young college students who helped him locate sources and master difficult reading material. Johnny only possesses Zampanò's written notes and the various ephemera contained in his trunk. He meticulously records the textual condition of all these papers. Chapter XIII contains a fascinating take on the physical corruptions of the "original" manuscript in Johnny's hands. In this chapter, Zampanò addresses the ominous Minotaur which might lurk somewhere in the labyrinth on Ash Tree Lane. At one point, however, Zampanò seemed to have intentionally destroyed parts of the manuscript. Johnny explains, "Some kind of ash landed on the following pages, in some places burning away small holes, in other places eradicating large chunks of text. Rather than try to reconstruct what was destroyed I decided to just bracket the gaps—[]" (323). The following pages of "The Navidson Record" show considerable textual ellipses, all due to the material corruptions either intentionally inflicted or merely tolerated by Zampanò. Johnny's descriptions and the iconic representations of textual corruptions thus feed into an elaborate bibliographic ekphrasis.

The closer this section comes to the mythical creature of the Minotaur, the more effort the reader has to invest in filling the gaps left by the original manuscript. Aside from the burned holes, Zampanò has also crossed out individual words with his pen, which forces Johnny to invent another notation for passages that were "inked out" (328). He marks these with bold, capitalized letters "X." Later in the chapter Zampanò discusses the so-called "Holloway Tape," a record of Holloway's last moments inside the labyrinth. Out of sheer fright at the elusive creature that pursues him, he shoots himself in an isolated cavern. All of these events are recorded on film, as is the moment some minutes after his death when "[f]ingers of blackness" wipe out his body and a "terrible growl" is heard on the tape (338). Here and elsewhere, Zampanò tried to erase all commentary and footnotes on the Minotaur. However, "with a little bit of turpentine and a good old magnifying glass" (111), Johnny can recover most of it. These sections of the text are represented in struck-through lettering; in the full-color edition they appear in red. Reading these parts on paper entails a feedback loop between the medial surface and the narrative events. The presence of a medial artifact similar to intradiegetic documents intensifies the aesthetic illusion, as immersion into the plot and reflection on the substance coevolve. In these cases, the individual pages are material icons for Zampanò's notes; they form a medial surrogate for the fictional pages and can generate a tactile illusion of the elements depicted.

Confronted with all of these destructive marks of inscription, Johnny is at a loss to account for the exact nature of the instrument or technology that inflicted the small cutouts. He nevertheless fantasizes that the little holes result from an apocalyptic rain of "gray ash" that precedes the final "pyroclastic roar that will incinerate everything" (323). In miniature, Johnny encounters a central conundrum of textual criticism as he cannot link the physical marks on a document to its inscription technology. This scene functions as an allegory for the reader's potential attitude toward Danielewski's book. Intuitively, we know that the author has used several digital and non-digital inscription technologies while working on this book. Hayles accordingly claims that it is a perfect example of a technotext, an artifact that "interrogates the inscription technology that produces it" (*Writing* 25). A rigorous study of the complex composition history of this work would be needed to survey the full extent of technological aids and tools used by Danielewski throughout the ten years that he spent on the project. Of course, such research is hardly possible and not even practical, since it would have to rely heavily on the author's personal recollections. Danielewski's pencils and keyboards are just as remote from the readers of the book as the fountain pens of nineteenth-century novelists were from their contemporaneous audience. If the focus is on the narrative effect and the cultural work of *House of Leaves*, the material artifact and its narrative-medial intersections yield the most reliable conclusions about the reading experience. Printed books, magazines, or e-readers are frames of sensory experience a great deal more consequential than authorial inscription tools.

As narrative motifs, however, inscription instruments do figure prominently in the plot. Danielewski incessantly reflects on the dynamics of writing on surfaces. The two photographic collages in Appendix II, for example, depict the contents of the trunk, most likely interspersed with Johnny's own material (582–83). All scraps of paper are heavily marked up in various colors—one can make out the inked traces of black, green, red, and blue pens, yellow highlighters, as well as burned matches and red stains of unknown origin. Notably, the second collage includes the label of an inkwell, made by the German company Pelikan. This inkwell may be the material source for the "Pelican Poems," all of which were written in Europe with a pen of the same brand.

Further along in the chronology of Johnny Truant's story, the tattoo shop also serves as the setting for a central episode in which he encounters the Minotaur. While there are strong indicators that Johnny hallucinates the whole event, he still has the readers believe that a "long, bloody scratch" on his neck is physical evidence of the beast's claws (72). As he stumbles away from the vague predator, he spills a full platter of tattoo ink all over himself:

> I'm doused in black ink, my hands now completely covered, and see the floor is black, and—have you anticipated this or should I be more explicit?—jet on jet; for a blinding instant I have watched my hand vanish, in fact all of me has vanished, one hell of a disappearing act too, the already foreseen dissolution of self, lost without contrast, slipping into oblivion, until mid-gasp I catch sight of my reflection in the back of the tray, the ghost in the way: seems I'm not gone, not quite. My face has been splattered with purple, as have my arms, granting contrast, and thus defining me, marking me, and at least for the moment, preserving me. (72)

As Hayles notes, this section addresses the interplay of inscription and erasure, while also calling up the purple nail polish Johnny's mother had worn on the day she tried to strangle him (*Writing* 121–22). In his state of mounting paranoia, fueled by drug consumption, Johnny loses his grip on reality. Noticeably, his interpretation of the events in the tattoo shop echoes his medium of expression—writing with ink on paper. As such, his agency repeatedly seems to vanish and to be usurped by the textual artifacts that surround him. Johnny Truant does not write anymore—paper and ink write Johnny Truant.

A little earlier in this section, Johnny calls the whole incident an "omen," a foreshadowing of his future fate. Were he to die in the end, we would easily associate this act of metaphoric erasure with his death. As we see from the appendices and the explanatory notes of the Editors, Johnny after all survives the madness surrounding the collation of *House of Leaves* and sees its publication through. The fictional character merges with the material book at the moment of printing. The publication of *House of Leaves* in 2000 dissociates his character from the persona who wrote his notes, so that Johnny becomes a construct in the mind of each reader. However, the presence of the fictional editor does not entirely vanish; instead it is transposed into the physical artifact. Here, the most visible alteration of color in the 2006 edition introduces a final twist. The phrase "A Novel" on the bottom of the cover page, originally white, is now printed in purple. In the tattoo shop, the color purple saves the corporeal existence of Johnny Truant against the encroaching blackness. On the cover of *House of Leaves*, the purple marking symbolically links the body of the book with the body of its most dominant narrator/author persona. Dave Eggers likewise equates the physical form of his *Heartbreaking Work* with his body, thus claiming a profoundly authentic authorial presence. In *House of Leaves*, Mark Z. Danielewski erases all traces of his authorial persona to promote his book as the embodied representation of Johnny Truant. As such, the spilled-ink incident is not an omen of madness or erasure; it functions as an emblem for the inevitable transposition of corporeality from an individual body to a collective artifact.[11]

### ¶ Medial Mise en Abyme and Metalepsis

The most explicit variants within the spectrum of metamedial devices take the form of medial mise en abyme and metalepsis. Of this pair, mise en abyme arguably possesses less autoreferential potential than metalepsis. Werner Wolf defines mise en abyme as "a special relationship within an embedding structure, namely—with reference to the media—the 'mirroring' of parts or the totality of a framing or embedding higher level of a semiotic complex (text, work, performance) in a discernible unit located on an embedded, lower level" (56). Classical examples of mise en abyme are the play-within-a-play in Shakespeare's

*Hamlet* or interpolated stories in literary texts that resonate with aspects of the frame story. Due to its expansive notion of mediality as a "semiotic complex," Wolf's narratological concept assumes that any recourse to the embedding art form, i.e. painting, acting, storytelling, on a lower ontological level already promotes medial awareness. In the more narrow sense of "medium" used here, a medial mise en abyme only occurs whenever the artwork activates its own storage and reproduction medium. In printed literature, instances in which books occur in the fictional world constitute medial mises en abyme. For texts reproduced on a screen, this mirroring device would conversely entail fictional instances of screens.

I concur with Wolf insofar as I see no automatism between the autoreferential text and the reader's reflexive reaction. Mise-en-abymic structures are easily naturalized. Books—at least for now—still have a firm place in many people's lives, so their representation in literary texts often merely supports narrative realism. Readers need to actively decode a diegetic book as a reflexive comment that refers to the lifeworld in which they consume the book. Several work-intrinsic factors may facilitate such a reading, as Wolf outlines (58–60). A high frequency of mise-en-abymic structures may increase the likelihood that readers notice the recursive dynamics at work. The more books we find in the diegesis and the more we read about these books, the likelier it is that we will reflect on the act of reading a book. Also, paratextual framings may create a specific set of expectations in the reader by explicitly addressing medial questions, such as typesetting, bookmaking, or other issues concerning the manuscript.

Metalepsis—the paradoxical transgression of narrative boundaries—has even more autoreferential power in that it directly addresses the division between the empirical world and the fictional diegesis. Originally, the concept of narrative metalepsis was coined by Gérard Genette who used it to denote "any intrusion by the extradiegetic narrator or narratee into the diegetic universe" (*Narrative* 234). Narratologists now commonly distinguish between the rhetorical and the ontological variant of this device (Wolf 52–54). Authorial personae that pause to reflect on their options for continuing the plot without disturbing the stability of the narrative universe exemplify rhetorical metalepsis. Ontological metalepsis, conversely, triggers paradoxical effects and subverts borders that were thought to be stable. As the classic scenario of such "metaleptic contamination," Marie-Laure Ryan posits the motif of author and character meeting on the same ontological level (442). Medial metalepsis reaches beyond this discursive level of the text to the empirical reading situation. Metamedial transgressions of ontological boundaries pair off fictional characters or events with the book that readers hold in their hands. In the Introduction, we have already seen one of the most peculiar such instances in Danielewski's novel, during which Navidson reads and subsequently burns his copy of *House of Leaves*. Medial metalepsis rests on the duplication of such fictional objects on the real-life level of textual communication. In this manner, medial metalepsis reinforces borders while simultaneously subverting them: it strengthens the borderline between different media while undercutting narrative realism.

The stylistic devices of mise en abyme and metalepsis ensure that all elements accrued on the more peripheral levels of *House of Leaves* penetrate the very core of the narrative only to radiate back outward to the reader. The material text not only surfaces on the ontological level of the Navidson story, it also finds its way into Johnny's hands. If we rearrange the jumbled chronology of Johnny's diary, we can see that in March 1998, he finishes work on the main part of the text. He then hauls all material to a storage unit in Culver City and leaves for a cross-country road trip to Virginia to look for the fabled Navidson house (413). At this point, he already calls his work "the book" (413). During his road trip, he starts keeping a journal, the first entry of which dates from May 1, 1998. Chapter XXI consists entirely of journal entries, albeit in cut-up order. The death of Lude, Johnny's best friend, from a motorcycle accident provides the structural foundation for the chapter. It starts with several entries written shortly after Lude's death in late October 1998, all of which attest to Johnny's precarious psychological condition. At some point, he is surprised to find that his notes go back to May of the same year, and he confesses to be unsure whether or not he himself wrote them. Obviously, his agency once again dissolves into the reading process connected to the book.

In Virginia, he roams the streets of Richmond and Charlottesville and drives around the countryside to take Polaroids of random houses. Several images reprinted in Appendix II and on the spine of the book represent his fictional photographs. On a whim, he decides to abandon his mission and instead drives up to Ohio to spend a night in the forlorn Whalestoe Institute, where his mother was hospitalized until her death. Afterward, he searches for his childhood home, only to find it ripped down and replaced by a sawmill. The place still brings up traumatic memories, which make him abort his trip and return to LA. Once there, he retrieves his book and checks into a hotel, where he writes the introduction to the book and hears of Lude's death. Three entries from November 1998 and August 1999 follow, in which the reader encounters a final twist to the metamedial mechanics of the book.

As we have seen before, the title page of the book designates the first Pantheon edition as the "2nd edition." This information has no bearing on the plot until the first edition of House of Leaves unexpectedly appears in the text. In the final entry of the journal's chronology—and that of the entire plot—Johnny once again drifts through the country, homeless and worn out. In a bar in Flagstaff, Arizona, he listens to a rock band whose songs contain uncanny references to Zampanò's unpublished manuscript. When he asks the lead singer of the band "Liberty Bell" about the source of his inspiration, the young artist hands him "a big brick of tattered paper," whose cover page reveals it as the first edition of House of Leaves, published by the press "Circle Round a Stone" (513). As Johnny discovers, his book has had a life of its own:

As it turned out, not only had all three of them read it but every now and then in some new city someone in the audience would hear the song about the hallway and come up to talk to them after the show. Already, they had spent many hours with complete strangers shooting the shit about Zampanò's work. They had discussed the footnotes, the names and even the encoded appearance of Thamyris on page 387, something I'd transcribed without ever detecting.

Apparently they wondered alot [sic] about Johnny Truant. Had he made it to Virginia? Had he found the house? Did he ever get a good night's sleep? And most of all was he seeing anyone? Did he at long last find the woman who would love his ironies? Which shocked the hell out of me. I mean it takes some pretty impressive back-on-page-117 close-reading to catch that one. (513–14)

By locating the first edition within the diegesis, the passage metaleptically destabilizes the ontological status of the fictional world. However, the presence of the "big brick of tattered paper" has a more profound effect than narrative metalepsis. Like Navidson's copy of the book, which I discussed in the Introduction, the fictional first edition mirrors the pagination of the Pantheon edition of *House of Leaves*, as the band's members point Johnny to specific points of the plot on pages 387 and 117. Readers can double check the passages indicated by the band on the respective pages of the Pantheon book.

Again, the overall effect of this metalepsis is material: *House of Leaves* invites the reader to rethink the text as a book. What is more, readers can navigate the printed maze of the book and may finally realize the extent to which the printed product is calibrated and controlled. Against its fictional story of textual corruption and recovery, Danielewski's novel insists on its thick poetic and visual design, which carries a palimpsestic overload of signification on every page. As such, Danielewski transports the paratexts from the margins into the center of his aesthetics, where they oscillate between the instability of signification and the stability of the printed medium. Martin Brick describes this oscillation as a dialectical process in which an "unstable text . . . must be presented through a stable medium in order to make its instability apparent." In this unlikely convergence of stability and variability lies the supremely productive contribution of *House of Leaves* to the autopoiesis of literary communication.

Chronologically, Johnny's visit to Flagstaff is the final part of the narrative; yet, some entries still follow from the day in October 1998 when he supposedly wrote the introduction to the book. These entries call into question the veracity of his experiences in Flagstaff: "No idea what to make of those last few entries either. What's the difference, especially in differance, what's read what's left in what's left out what's invented what's remembered what's forgotten what's written what's found what's lost what's done?" (515). With a clear nod to Derrida, Johnny Truant here destabilizes his reliability as a narrator. After gathering up "the finished book" and climbing out the window of his apartment, he appears to walk to the beach reminiscing about his childhood and his parents. Then we read the following:

> The book is burning. At last. A strange light scans each page, memorizing all of it even as each character twists into ash. At least the fire is warm, warming my hands, warming my face, parting the darkest waters of the deepest eye, even if at the same time it casts long shadows on the world, the cost of any pyre, finally heated beyond recovery, shattered into specters of dust, stolen by the sky, flung to sea and sand.
>
> Had I meant to say memorializing? (518)

Danielewski returns the reader to the symbolically laden scene of a book burning. The pun on "character" creates a telling interplay between diegesis and external form. On the one hand, the characters on the page reference the typographic letters, which literally roll up into little scraps of burned paper. On the other hand, Johnny also comments on his own fate as a character within this book, whose very existence is tied to these inked markings on paper. As a fictional editor, he seems to recognize that he is merely an emergent cognitive phenomenon in the reader's mind. Johnny's existence relies on—yet is not fully determined by—the presence of a material text and the decoding apparatus of a human brain. In the character of Johnny Truant, Danielewski demonstrates how an encapsulated medial form enables text to transgress its mediality into infinity.

## ¶ An Uneasy Hybrid

*House of Leaves* has been Mark Z. Danielewski's most influential and lasting contribution to American literature, staging itself not merely as a book *of* fiction, but as an elaborate and minutely calculated book fiction. It has become the prototype of a form of writing that authors have since appropriated for novels in various genres. At the close of this chapter, I wish to append several observations on Danielewski's follow-up book, *Only Revolutions*. In its content, the book is so outrageously complex that fans, reviewers, and scholars alike have largely capitulated before the task to explicate it hermeneutically. Since excellent essays by Hansen and Hayles already present suggestive readings of *Only Revolutions*, I will solely focus on the way in which the book employs metamedial devices with a decidedly different—maybe even detrimental—effect as compared to *House of Leaves*.[12] The publication of this epic prose poem roughly coincided with the "Remastered Full-Color Edition" of *House of Leaves* in 2006. As if to prefigure their adjacent placing on a collector's bookshelf, the endpapers of both editions are elaborately intertwined. In the iconology of *Only Revolutions*, a circle with two parallel lines possesses central significance, symbolizing both the emotional bond of the two protagonists, Hailey and Sam, and the overarching structure of circularity that informs the whole book. In *Only Revolutions*, these symbols show up on the first pages, before the actual title page. In the remastered *House of Leaves*, both symbols are depicted on the inside parts of the paper cover at the front and back of the book.

The widely distributed hardcover edition of *Only Revolutions* contains elaborate endpapers with hundreds of words in small print, arranged in round, geometric shapes and printed in mirror-inverted form. The endpapers carry gold shading for Hailey's section, while in Sam's section they are green. In both cases, a headline reads "The Now Here Found Concordance." The first four words of this phrase are printed in red and are struck through. On these endpapers, Danielewski lays out compositional constraints akin to those used by Oulipo writers: None of the hundreds of words on these pages is to be used in the entire text of the book. As such, the concept of the concordance becomes inverted, which is underscored by the mirror printing, into a type of "anticoncordance" of forbidden terms (Hayles, *How We Think* 233). Two of the most remarkable semantic fields in the concordance directly engage with Danielewski's previous novel. One group contains terms and synonyms related to houses. The key terms of *House of Leaves*—such as "house," "hallway," "corridor," "room"—are ruled out for Sam's and Hailey's stories. On the endpapers, all instances of "house" are printed in blue and all struck passages are red. The concordance now strictly prohibits conventions familiar to Danielewski's readership for this new book. Instead, *Only Revolutions* erects its own, more fine-tuned visual vocabulary, consisting of new colors, new fonts, and new spatial arrangements. This decision quite naturally reflects the genre of the two texts. While *House of Leaves* tells a gothic horror plot about expeditions into the closed-off structures of a private home, *Only Revolutions* follows the conventions of a road novel. As such, its language takes the reader into the outdoors, with two of the most influential word fields consisting of plants and animals.

More consequential for the medial effect of *Only Revolutions* is a second forbidden category of words that encompasses those media of inscription, storage, and display that took center stage in the textual labyrinth surrounding the Navidson home. In a comprehensive list that starts with "8-Track" and ends with "Zincography," Danielewski scrupulously lists all kinds of material media and technologies, including several bibliographic ones, such as "book," "ink," "paper," and "printing press." Ostensibly, the author follows a poetic agenda that seeks to elide all the metamedial strategies of his debut novel. Where the earlier book embraced academic style and diction—partly for ironic effect, partly for philosophical depth—Sam and Hailey's love story completely ignores learned book culture. The largest word field on the endpapers, sprawling among and around several others, consists of academic catch phrases, buzzwords, and jargon. The rules of this anti-concordance purge the text of "philology" and "interpretation," "difference" and "differance," "text" and "subtext." Danielewski willfully surrenders the semantic tools for self-description, declaring the words "novel," "poem," "author," and even "literature" off-limits.

In its linguistic style, *Only Revolutions* therefore figures on a wholly different terrain than the earlier best seller. Its bibliographic form, however, outshines that of its predecessor. The result is an uneasy hybrid between an artist's book and a convoluted prose poem. As an artist's book, *Only Revolutions* proves to be a carefully crafted work of art that enmeshes the guiding metaphor of circularity in a mathematically calculated 360-page codex. Without its dust jacket, the book literally has no front and back. Both sections of the book are designed to reflect their narrative voices: the spine of the book is readable in both orientations; both sections have title pages that present Hailey and Sam as authors; the full copyright page is reprinted twice; two ribbons help the reader navigate the text from each side of the book.

In 2007, Danielewski published a foldout poster entitled "A Spoiler" in the French literary review *Inculte*. This poster reveals the full spectrum of mathematical calculation that underlies the book. To mirror the circular number 360 in as many facets as possible, the textual form of the book has to yield before its hyper-calculated structure. As such, the book has five large sections, consisting of 72 pages. These are further subdivided into three parts, with three subsections of eight pages each. Each page contains exactly 180 words and 36 lines of narrative, consisting of a section that is right side up and one that is upside down. Aside from the two epic poems relating Sam's and Hailey's versions of the same story, every page also contains so-called "chronomosaics" running alongside each section of text. These lists of historical snippets, containing everything from casualty counts to famous quotations and football results, span a time frame of 200 years—100 in each direction from the date of the Kennedy assassination on November 22, 1963. Hayles describes the computer-assisted composition process of these chronomosaics as a distribution of the Foucauldian author function. She holds, "Cooperating in the authorial project are the software programs, network functionalities, and hardware that provide sophisticated cognitive capabilities, including access to databases and search algorithms" (*How We Think* 236). With recourse to Actor-Network-Theory, she adds that machines come to "actively participate in the composition process, defining a range of possibilities as well as locating specific terms that appear in the text" (236). I concur with Hayles that the "writing-down system" figures prominently in the composition and production process of the text. However, as I have maintained throughout the chapter, this domain needs to be distinguished from the "textual condition" in which the work is released to the readers.

In the realm of typography, Danielewski lists eight fonts used in the book on the copyright page: Life, Dante MT, Lucida, Perpetua, Tempo, Myriad Pro, Spectrum MT, and Univers 57. With persistent use of Dante for his own name and the book's title, Danielewski manages to fashion an increasingly recognizable visual identity. The text proper renders the narrative in the Old Style font Spectrum MT, which provides a refined, bookish aura. The running historical sidebars are set in Myriad Pro, a sans-serif typeface. This font has an air of casual neutrality and seems less suited to a book of fiction than to an online database.[13] The letters and words are illuminated throughout, with gold and green used for all instances of the letter "o" and the numeral "0," thereby emphasizing the reigning metaphor of circularity. The circular form reaches its effective climax in the center of the book. Conventional books only have an ambiguous midpoint, as page counts never really match the number of printed sheets. The plot of an average novel will hardly align itself with such accidental factors. *Only Revolutions*, though, has an exact visual, material, and narrative center. As Sam's and Hailey's narratives start out on opposite sides of the book, they convene on pages 180 and 181, which visually present a perfect symmetry. The textual segments are equally large, half of each page devoted to either character. At this midpoint of their narrative, Sam and Hailey have temporarily halted their freewheeling road trip across the United States. Living and working in St. Louis, they experience the fleeting possibility of becoming one. For a few pages, green and gold letters occur in both of their sections. Also, page 180 has both narrators speak the exact same words. This romantic hope of spiritual union soon gives way to the mandates of passing time and the road trip continues toward death and rebirth.

As an artist's book, *Only Revolutions* ranks with the many works in this tradition that Johanna Drucker discusses in her pioneering *The Century of Artists' Books*. Danielewski's enhanced poem certainly fulfills the central criterion outlined by Karen Junod, who claims that artists' books are "typically envisioned and created by the artist who explores the structural, typographical, and conceptual possibilities of the book from its very inception" (484). From the work of Mark Z. Danielewski, I see two consequences for theories of the artist's book. First, the helpful differentiation between visual artists as creators of artist's books and writers as authors of "regular" books that underlies Drucker's work fails to account for a writer like Danielewski, whose aesthetics include both text and book to an equal degree. Second, to differentiate between an artist's book and a medially enhanced literary work, we need to engage with the overall narrative effect. Even if both text and experimental bibliographic style are present in a specific work, it remains likely that one of these levels will dominate the other.

The pleasure of reading *Only Revolutions* owes much to the presence effects that the book generates. Tracing perfect circularity and symmetry into every little sequence of the book can be a rewarding exercise. Each page is in itself a carefully crafted image-text, which feeds into the overall effect of this sculptured book. To illustrate (and to perform) his total control over the production process, Mark Z. Danielewski submitted seven versions of the first page of Sam's narrative to the biannual journal *Gulf Coast*.[14] The seven images chronicle a painstaking editing process ranging from a handwritten draft in 2002 to the final print form in 2006. In the process, the whole narrative changes completely, while only the overall tone and the method of enmeshing historical allusions with the narrative remain. Even the free-verse form of the final text is not yet apparent in the first versions. Accompanying the images are curatorial annotations that provide technical details on the design. To take one example, the entry for a mid-2004 version reads, "77 words (Chronomosaic + Date) + 90 words (Sam). Fonts: Spectrum MT (Sam); Spectrum MT (Chronomosaic); Times (Date); Times (Folio). Green: Pantone 348 C. Gold: Pantone 116 C. Violet: Pantone 259 C. Trim size: 5.4375 × 8.4375. Software: InDesign" (Danielewski, "Only

Evolutions" 184). Aside from the specifics on typography, word count, and page size, the entry lists the exact industry denomination for the individual colors used and the name of the Adobe software with which the author worked. Like Dave Eggers, Mark Z. Danielewski designs his books by himself during the writing process. The radical alterations to the textual content that we can see in the *Gulf Coast* excerpts indicate a shift in the aesthetics of the book from a medially enhanced narrative to a full-fledged artist's book.

Thus, the groundbreaking potential of Danielewski's second larger work lies firmly in the arena of book materiality. As a literary work, however, its merits are more ambiguous. For one, the relationship between the historical database and the stories of Sam and Hailey remains unbalanced. To actually read all chronomosaics and attempt to parse the interrelations with the main text would be a heroic, time-consuming task, without a clear narrative payoff in sight. Throughout, the voices of Sam and Hailey incorporate idiomatic words and phrases that etymologically date from the timeframe of the respective chronomosaic. This linguistic pattern points to a general feature of the narration, i.e. the paradigmatic selectivity among sets of data. Thus, there are several syntagmatic slots throughout the text (the cars Sam and Hailey travel in, the plants and animals they see, the people they meet) that are then filled from a virtually infinite set of names and synonyms. Frequently, the narrative devolves into a rage of free-associative naming that drowns metaphoric potentials in its explosive thrust toward an elusive gesture of freedom. Even the two protagonists never take on a specific form, as we can read in Sam's section: "We are without / edge, continually unwinding, uniting. / Every around retreating before / our freedom" (S 221–22). The success formula of *House of Leaves* most likely resulted from the combination of extravagant design experiments with the narrative of a compelling horror plot. In *Only Revolutions* there lurks a wide gap between the techno-compositional framework and the diegetic fiction—which is, after all, a love story. As the book willingly gives up all tools for self-description, readers are left to wonder why a shape-shifting, road-tripping couple ranting and raving in computerized vernacular has been incarcerated in the green-and-golden cage of a spectacular artist's book.

Mark Z. Danielewski holds a pivotal position in the evolution of meta-medial communication in the American literary system. His commercial and critical success flung wide open the door through which Dave Eggers and McSweeney's had only cautiously glimpsed. Inaugurated in the testing ground of the McSweeney's niche audience, metamedial aesthetics reached a mass readership with *House of Leaves*. Equally important for Danielewski's cultural impact are the American academic observers whose comments and theoretical framings recursively interact with the avid fan base and possibly even with the author; just as Hayles read Danielewski, Danielewski read Hayles. To be sure, there were prior examples of carefully designed book fictions in American literature.[15] As a veritable cult book, *House of Leaves* nevertheless figures as anchor and center of reference for the literary successors of the ensuing decade.

## 4. Convergences of a Different Order: Immersive Book Fictions and Literary Bibliographers

WITHIN THE FIELD OF MEDIA STUDIES, as well as within the industry, the concept of transmedia has recently become a buzzword. Transmedia aesthetics and practices permeate entertainment phenomena such as *The Matrix* movie series or the innovative marketing behind the mockumentary *The Blair Witch Project*, as media scholar Henry Jenkins points out in his seminal book, *Convergence Culture*. In its theoretical thrust, transmedia studies stresses interconnectivity and fluid transmission of media content from one platform to another. This setup rests on the underlying idea of media convergence, which holds that the availability of text, sound, and motion pictures as digital files separates content from its medial container and enables distribution across a multitude of channels. Jenkins sees convergence as referring to "a situation in which multiple media systems coexist and where media content flows fluidly across them" (282). As a historical process, Priscilla Coit Murphy explains, convergence entails that "the traits and functions of the older medium will be combined within the newer one—not disappearing but reborn in new and better form—for example book text on screen" (90). In the work of Jenkins and others, such normative assessments become entangled with a rhetoric of user empowerment inherited from British cultural studies, roughly associating "old media" with stasis and suppression, while identifying "new media" with active audiences and participatory culture.

This scenario of empowerment seemingly translates well to the literary sphere, where self-publishing and collaborative authorship have emerged as paradigmatic practices of digital culture. Nevertheless, the narrative of empowerment often presupposes the individual as consumer, so that new ways of participating increasingly equal new ways of harnessing revenue. Ted Striphas provides an important corrective for this scenario, showing how shifting industry practices around digital textuality increasingly wrest the control over commodities away from the consumer and into the hands of media conglomerates. Through controlled consumption, the consumer is transformed "from subject to object of capitalist accumulation" (Striphas 183). Often, the concept of convergence is used unwittingly to perpetuate the self-descriptions of digital culture (fluidity, interconnectivity, democratization) instead of critically engaging with them. The multifaceted interactions between printed books and digital media as presented so far are hardly compatible with the theory of convergence.

This chapter nevertheless meditates on convergence, albeit in a different sense than its transmedia version. It is less interested in usage practices along horizontal media flows. Instead, I use the notion of convergence for the authorial practices of several writer-designers, whom one might call "literary bibliographers." Just as the established—and thoroughly romanticized—figure of the singer-songwriter stands for an ethos of complete authorial achievement in musical performance, the literary bibliographer expands the traditional sphere of the writer. As photographers—according to the Greek etymology of the term—

write with light, literary bibliographers not only write books, they write *with* books.[1] In the figure of the writer-as-bibliographer, contemporary literary print culture sees a distinct break with predigital conventions. To these, the frequently cited diagnosis of Roger Stoddard applied: "Whatever they may do, authors do not write books. Books are not written at all. They are manufactured by scribes and other artisans, by mechanics and other engineers, and by printing presses and other machines" (qtd. in Chartier, "Laborers" 90). In the printed communication circuit of the present, however, the digitization of writing and designing has radically expanded the potential reach of an author's artistic influence. Danielewski and Eggers do more than simply invest extraordinary care into the look and feel of the book, as we have seen earlier. In their texts, the components of form, content, and medium converge into a tightly knit signifying structure whose parts cannot be interchanged without altering the overall effect.

The authorial construction of the literary bibliographer also brings to the fore the dimension of gender. By focusing on some of the most explicit examples of metamediality in recent American literature, this book presents a very male-dominated picture. In a peculiar way, it thus echoes other recent considerations of medially innovative American literature. N. Katherine Hayles's extensive writings on the subject concentrate on a group of authors consisting of Philip K. Dick, Neal Stephenson, Talan Memmott, Tom Phillips, Mark Z. Danielewski, Steve Tomasula, Steven Hall, and several others. Jessica Pressman's *Digital Modernism* and Mary K. Holland's *Succeeding Postmodernism* reflect the same tendency. How are we to explain this obvious gender imbalance? This is a pressing question, but it is one that is all but impossible to answer within the methodological framework used here. Still, I wish to point to some starting points for investigations in this direction. Amy Hungerford has done pioneering research on the gender dynamics within the McSweeney's network of writers, based on which she terms its field imaginary a "boy's world" (662). Hungerford's argument refers back to the male-inflected outlook on high art that often underlay modernist conceptions of poetics and literary craft. Furthermore, as

Kathleen Fitzpatrick has convincingly argued, even within the shift from modernism to postmodernism in American literature, the older alignments of the high/low divide with gender categories proved to be strangely resilient (201–33).

Some of the writerly ethos of strong authorship is also at work in the realm of design. Merely sampling scholarly and artistic discourses, we may provisionally diagnose that women writers have not generated a critical mass of accounts that expose authorial involvement with book design and embodied fiction. Conversely, the male archive in this arena presents a long lineage as Jerome McGann has shown with regard to Blake, Byron, Joyce, Pound, and Yeats (Textual). This archive also includes such writer-publisher figures as William Morris, Samuel Richardson, and Octave Uzanne. For today's writers, this heritage may facilitate the construction of a confident self-image of male artistry, craft, and control. Still, there are several women writers such as Geraldine Brooks, Jennifer Egan, and Nicole Krauss who have occasionally drawn on metamedial devices in recent novels. If we add to this the names of those writers, designers, and publishers who do make an appearance here—Anne Burdick, Johanna Drucker, Anna Gerber, Britt Iversen, Shelley Jackson, A.L. Kennedy, and Judith Schalansky—there is little reason to believe that metamedial writing is intrinsically gender biased. Even though the plots of the novels discussed in this chapter stray far from the confines of white, male, straight, middle-class subjects, we have to take note of the fact that today's writer-designers stand on the shoulders of those assertive craftsmen who dominated the Western publishing and printing trades in the past.

While the public persona of authors has often influenced the reception of their writings, the cultural work of literature relies more firmly on the agency of its artifacts; thus the character of the literary bibliographer is contingent on the reading process. In the communication system of literature, books authorize themselves, with the empirical author becoming a mere functional role, as envisioned in Michel Foucault's concept of the author function, as developed in his seminal essay "What Is an Author?" On the pages of House of Leaves, a dense effort of authorization occurs that draws book design into the signifying territory of the work. The aesthetic convergence of writing and design comes on the heels of a professional one that gradually renders permeable the boundaries between designers and writers. While early scholarship has adopted the authors of *A Heartbreaking Work* and *House of Leaves* as literary writers, one might also approach them as designers. Writing before the advent of desktop publishing, Gérard Genette understandably decided to associate book design almost exclusively with the publishing company. Genette's model corresponded to the division of labor in the publishing industry at the time. Once authors submitted their text to the publishing houses, they underwent a standardized process conducted by professional typesetters and freelance design artists. Design began when writing ended. As a result, these groups assembled the book in streamlined processes, with authors often as extraneous to the material product as the average reader. In addition to this standard division of labor, we currently witness an emergent paradigm of collaboration that penetrates the composition of literary texts.

This chapter traces the work of Chip Kidd, Salvador Plascencia, and Reif Larsen—three literary bibliographers who embody the convergence of writing and design while advancing the divergence of screen and paper. Proceeding from the playful McSweeney's style and the experimental work of Mark Z. Danielewski, these authors represent the adaptability and increasing normalization of metamedial forms within the realist novel. In his influential analysis of postmodernist "concrete prose," Brian McHale argues that experimental visual typography and layout in the works of Barthelme, Federman, Sukenick, and others foregrounded "the printed book's most basic physical components, namely paper and print" (*Postmodernist* 182). The overall effect results, according to McHale, in anti-mimetic defamiliarization, as readers focus more on the medial presentation of the text than on the fictional world (190–93). Opposing this reading in his pioneering study on British literature and (typo)graphic design, Glyn White claims that "defamiliarisation is not enough" (17). Typographic experiments, he holds, "may be the result of efforts to make the text function in a *more* mimetic manner" (21). We can synthesize these two positions with recourse to the evolution of postmodernist literature. Where early readers of experimental fiction were most likely taken aback by typographic trickery, contemporary audiences have increasingly become habituated to such devices. Whether or not metamedial uses of typography and pictorial matter in literature function to heighten immersion or serve to carry out anti-mimetic strategies rests on the individual artifact in question.[2] As my readings in this chapter show, immersive book fictions enable readers to become absorbed not merely in narrative, but in the entire designed artifact.

### ¶ Between the Covers: Chip Kidd

Chip Kidd, currently art director at Alfred A. Knopf in New York, claims that literary writing is merely "designing with words" (Book 354). As designer, Kidd represents all those actors in the American book industry who contribute to the literary system of communication without being authors themselves. He joined the small design team at Knopf in 1986 during a momentous period in the publisher's history. In the same year, the long-time editor-in-chief Robert Gottlieb left Knopf to take the reins of the New Yorker magazine. As his replacement, the firm hired Ajai Singh Mehta, formerly editor at Picador in Britain (Vienne 8). Under Mehta, Knopf assembled a steady team of designers, including Barbara deWilde, Archie Ferguson, and art director Carol Devine Carson. Kidd thrived in this creative environment and has since produced well over 1,000 book designs, mostly dust jackets, many of them adorning best sellers.[3] Several of his designs have become iconic in their own right, the most pertinent example being his abstract, monochrome dinosaur skeleton for the cover of Michael Crichton's Jurassic Park (1990). The image became the trademark for the ensuing movie franchise and was eventually printed on millions of movie posters and merchandise articles. Kidd also designed several books for authors such as Bret Easton Ellis, Cormac McCarthy, and John Updike.

Through his work as book-jacket designer, he has given shape and form to a significant portion of American literature since the late 1980s. For many of his covers, Kidd uses the outside layer of the book not merely as a neutral surface, but as a space with intrinsic medial potential. As such, he visually infuses books with an air of tactility that forms a material correlative to specific aspects of the text. David Rakoff's essay collection Fraud (2001) and Augusten Burroughs's memoir Dry (2004) are two examples of this style. The Doubleday edition of Rakoff's collection of humorous, often self-loathing nonfiction pieces bears Rakoff's name in elegant typography on the cover, surrounded by much white space (Kidd, Book 125). On the front, back, and spine of the hardcover appears the word "Fraud" as if handwritten in capital letters with a red marker. After having toyed around with different cover drafts, Kidd explains, he finally imagined a scenario in which a dissatisfied reader takes out "a big red magic marker" after reading the book and scribbles all over the dust jacket (124). By simulating this story on the cover, Kidd creates a miniature diegesis that covers the actual text like a thin, decorative varnish. The design takes its medial positioning for granted and enacts a possible world in which an angry reader has defaced the surface of the document.

Such a miniature fiction also envelops the Picador paperback edition of Augusten Burroughs's Dry. Here, Kidd employs a purely typographic cover in an elegant serif font (Kidd, Book 284). In stark visual contrast, however, the letters are made to appear as if they have been smudged by water. The ink spills downwards from each individual letter across the white paper. Once more, the design evokes a publishing fiction, in which the copy of the material book was mishandled and became wet. The whole setup thereby feeds into a tangential story, which metaphorically resonates with the autobiographical account of an alcoholic who attempts to "become dry." Chip Kidd likes to relate an anecdote during public appearances, in which Burroughs himself witnesses a customer complaining about the supposedly spoiled book to a bookstore clerk (284). The success of this ruse owes to the refined printing techniques of the present, which can generate such visual-material trompe l'oeil effects with relative ease. As these examples show, Chip Kidd's influential aesthetics introduce medial self-awareness to the outer layer of mass-marketed books.

In the early 2000s, Kidd wrote and designed two novels that portray the formative years of a young design student. With his debut *The Cheese Monkeys* (2001), Chip Kidd encroached on the territory of literary authorship while retaining his design ethos. *The Cheese Monkeys* narrates a semiautobiographical coming-of-age story, set in the 1950s at an unnamed state college. The Scribner hardcover edition presents the book as unfinished and clumsily composed. The design emulates raw, brown draft paper, worn by stretches and tears. A broad sleeve conceals the front cover, bearing the title of the book in hand-drawn typography by Chris Ware. Peculiarly, the final version still shows what seems to be an early draft of the hand-lettering. Pencil-drawn guiding lines lay bare the geometric grid for each of the black letters. The cursive script of the word "*The*" stands in contrast to the thick, sans-serif capitals of "*Cheese Monkeys.*" Once readers remove the slipped-on wrapper, they face a second cover illustration that repeats the unfinished, drawing-board style of the first. Instead of using words, this cover expresses the obscure title of the book in a rebus of two drawings, depicting a piece of cheese and a group of three monkeys. The spine and edges of the book are decorated with a blue pattern, suggesting the surface of a cloth-covered board, as used to display drawings and drafts.

While the cover design reflects the novel's art-school setting, the narrative itself also engages with the shape and design of the book. Fostering the medial diegesis, Kidd inserts a replica of his book as a final assignment for a class by design professor Winter Sorbeck. The narrator nicknamed Happy makes arrangements for his project at the end of the book. Using discarded letterpress equipment in the basement of the design workshop, he plans to "make a series of six broadsides based on notes I had taken all semester," all of which he wants to gather in a "cloth-bound portfolio case" with the label "THE CHEESE MONKEYS" (252–53). Kidd here positions the bibliographic ekphrasis of a cloth-covered book object within the text, only to materially recreate this same object in the hands of the reader. The complex interweaving of medium and text does not stop here, though. After the end of the actual narrative on page 273, a final snippet of text appears printed on the endpapers, which continue the novel's pagination, suggesting that they, too, belong to the diegetic world of the novel. Rendered in italics, an anonymous, possibly authorial voice similar to that of the draconian professor Winter Sorbeck, gives a class assignment: "I want you to design a moment in time . . . At some point this semester (pick a point, any point), you will take something you have made and use it to claim a moment for yourself—yours and only yours—in front of the class. It could be a word, a picture, a poster, a combination of these, hell . . . maybe even a book—you get the idea" (274; last ellipsis in original). Finishing the novel, the reader thus recognizes the significance of the material book for the narrative illusion: it represents Happy's—and Kidd's—class project, propped up in front of the eyes of the public, awaiting the inevitable critique. As the chapters in the second half of the novel follow the organization of Happy's design course—"The First Critique," "The Second Critique," etc.—*The Cheese Monkeys* extends the plot into the empirical publishing world by presenting itself as a handcrafted exercise in graphic design.[4]

To get through the opening paratexts, readers need to skip across eleven pages on which Kidd spreads the content of a regular copyright page in a single line of text. Aside from the standard copyright data, this section also contains the following statement: "Book design by Chip Kidd, who wrote it in Quark 3.2. Text is set in Apollo and then, at a certain point, Bodoni." Highlighting specific design choices and lavishly expanding the paratextual space, this front matter attunes readers to the typographic form of his novel. The first-person narrative follows Happy's freshman year in the design department of his home state college. Through the autobiographical avatar of his protagonist, Kidd reenacts his college career at Penn State as it might have occurred had he entered college thirty years earlier than he actually did. The first section of this "Novel in Two Semesters" covers the fall term of 1957, during which Happy attends "Art 101" and tries his hand at several art and design techniques. In equal measures, the narrator recounts his first contact with academic theories of art. For the latter, Happy's fellow student Himillsy Dodd becomes his tutor. This blasé young woman deconstructs both the paradigms of art history and the ruling stylistic tenets of high modernism, hereby presumably acting as a mouthpiece for Kidd's postmodern visions. Himillsy also figures as one vertice in an odd triangle of romance, inspiration, and hate. The third character in this triangle is the enigmatic Winter Sorbeck, whose course "Commercial Design" serves as setting for the bulk of the plot.[5]

Within the small 5 × 8.5 inch format of *The Cheese Monkeys*, Kidd sets his text in blocks that cover only about half of each page. Through the extensive use of white space, the text takes on a more opaque quality vis-à-vis a conventionally proportioned page. Through these wide margins, the text appears like a curated piece of typographic design. While somewhat forestalling immersion in the plotline, this design immerses readers into the typographic signification process. As such, alert readers will notice that the pivotal instance in which the Bodoni typeface supersedes Apollo occurs right at the beginning of Sorbeck's graphic design course (see fig. 5). At this transformative moment in *The Cheese Monkeys*, Happy and Himillsy are about to enter the classroom: "At twenty-five after, we made our listless way into 207 and found seats. A minute or two of silence. Then, from behind us: 'That was *lousy*. Do it again.'" (98). Right before the final quote, the narrative changes its font. Winter Sorbeck's disapproving pronouncement—the first of many—begins the part of the book set in Bodoni. Here, the professor starts his stylistic

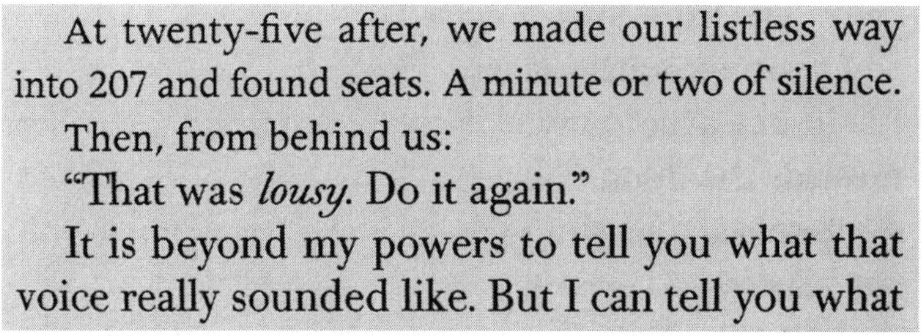

At twenty-five after, we made our listless way into 207 and found seats. A minute or two of silence. Then, from behind us:
"That was *lousy*. Do it again."
It is beyond my powers to tell you what that voice really sounded like. But I can tell you what

Fig. 5. Detail from Chip Kidd, *The Cheese Monkeys: A Novel in Two Semesters* (New York: Scribner, 2001), p. 98. Copyright © by Chip Kidd. Courtesy of the author and Scribner Publishing Group, a division of Simon and Schuster, Inc. Photograph by Alexander Starre.

criticism by ridiculing the clumsy way in which the students walked into class. The piercing critiques of the design professor are an inspiration to several students through the remainder of the book, while they drive others into despair. The change in typeface reflects the evolving design sense of the narrator. As soon as Sorbeck lays his piercing eyes on Happy, the narrator can no longer pretend that typography is merely a neutral, invisible container for language. The anachronistic Apollo font—designed by Adrian Frutiger in the early 1960s—gives way to a classical book font available during the historical setting of the book.

Sorbeck begins his class by delivering an impromptu lecture on his approach to graphic design. Rejecting the label "commercial art" that describes his class in the course catalog, he elaborates: "Uncle Sam . . . is Commercial Art. The American Flag is Graphic Design. Commercial Art tries to make you *buy* things. Graphic Design *gives* you ideas." (106–07; ellipsis in original). Graphic design, Sorbeck continues, holds a precarious middle position between commercial effectiveness and autonomous art. There is no graphic design "for its own sake," he insists: "Design must always be in service to solving a problem, or it's not Design" (108–09). This aesthetic philosophy sends Sorbeck into numerous tirades, covering everything from gum wrappers to high art.

In the progression of this bildungsroman, learning to see is the key rite of passage. Winter Sorbeck, both nemesis and tutor to the two protagonists, sets an impressive benchmark during a class session in which Himillsy tries to conceal her lackluster work by relating a fabricated personal story of the Ukrainian town "Kimprobdag." Sorbeck sees through her ad-libbing on the land of Brobdingnag as described in *Gulliver's Travels*, putting her on the spot: "As in the book by Dean Swift, which is peeking out of your handbag—Penguin Classic, with the orange bands at the top and bottom; and the Gill Sans thirty-six-point title, all caps, centered and medium weight, in black on the white band in the middle" (Kidd, *Cheese Monkeys* 127). Referencing Jan Tschichold's famous design of the Penguin paperbacks, Kidd's character Sorbeck presents himself as a scrupulous, pedantic observer of everyday objects. While his impromptu lectures often undercut the realism of the book, they represent fragments of Kidd's implied authorial aesthetics. Later in the narrative, Happy notices how Sorbeck's designer's gaze rubs off on him. Returning to his parents' home for Easter, he loathes the incoherent use of typography and logos on the local buses. Also, he scrutinizes the schedule pamphlets, noting that the "flimsy paper stock" hardly corresponds to their intended long-term use (167). Happy concedes, "And that's when I realized things like this had been occurring to me a lot lately. All signage—indeed, any typesetting, color schemes, and printed materials my eyes pounced on were automatically dissected and held to Draconian standards of graphic worthiness" (167). In a very direct form, reflexivity in The Cheese Monkeys wants to educate the readership. The book attempts to replicate its discovery plot in the empirical reading situation by providing didactic material for every reader to emulate Sorbeck's design gaze with the codex in hand.

Kidd's novel therefore proliferates what Niklas Luhmann calls "specific forms for an observation of observations" (Art 69). Reading literary texts, we become second-order observers: we witness other, fictional persons observing the world, thus confronting how we ourselves perceive our environment. This preoccupation with ways of seeing was a prominent aspect of the late-nineteenth-century realist movement. As Martin Klepper points out, authors such as Henry James and William Dean Howells attempted to shape an autonomous American literature through their insistence on "the power of art to appreciate, to represent and to juxtapose impressions, observations or, to use a technical term, perspectives" (48). The ensemble of authors introduced here performs similar cultural work in the literary sphere of the present. Pointing to the book's exceptional function in the system of art, they claim it as a site of artistic signification and self-description. While other domains like science, law, and education use the book chiefly as a channel of communication, literature can turn it into an object of second-order observations. In a way, Kidd's design approach refocuses the impulse of James and Howells, who "strongly believed" in the power of art "to civilize and cultivate the observer," to the designed artifacts that give shape to literary imaginaries (Klepper 48).

After graduating from college about three years later, Happy starts to work as a design assistant at the advertising agency Spear, Rakoff & Ware in New Haven—the firm where Winter Sorbeck began his career. In the beginning of *The Learners*, Kidd's second novel, Happy starts his apprenticeship there. *The Learners* is a negative companion volume to *The Cheese Monkeys*, as it examines the potential of graphic design to deceive and destroy. Happy briefly reunites with his estranged friend Himillsy, who has aimlessly drifted after dropping out of college. Shortly afterward, she kills herself with the exhaust fumes of her parents' car. Although Happy grieves and suffers much throughout the novel, he is very fond of his design projects at work. His first proper assignment, however, proves to be fateful. He receives the text for a help-wanted ad to be placed in the local paper. The item advertises the infamous experiments conducted by psychologist Stanley Milgram in 1961, during which volunteers acted as "teachers" who punish fake "learners" with electric shocks. Kidd reprints the original public notice and has Happy philosophize about the "invisible art" of typography during the design process in the adjoining commentary. In this side note, the narrator's voice overlaps with the implied authorial perspective: "What most people don't understand is that typography is the use of language that in itself is its own language—one that can take a lifetime to learn and perfect, and that few ever do" (58–59). In a more direct manner than in *The Cheese Monkeys*, Kidd establishes a channel of communication that appears to hover above the fictional world. Here, he addresses readers with an educational, almost conspiratorial tone, introducing them to a frame of perception that reveals presumably concealed information. Unlike in a typical conspiracy plot, however, the truth is not hidden below the surface; it is plainly evident on the surface. The true deception of graphic design, Kidd implies, is to make us believe that there is no surface.

In the central chapter of the book, Happy participates in the experiment and tortures a "learner" to his simulated death. After the experiment, Stanley Milgram introduces himself to the narrator and reveals that the whole setup was a sham and that the experiment was not about memory and learning, but about "people's responses to authority" (146). Still dazed from this revelation, Happy berates the confused Milgram: "The *form*, of your experiment—the memory study. It completely camouflages the *content*. God, it's amazing" (146). Having just embarked on a career in graphic design, Happy recognizes that his refined way of seeing and perceiving has failed to alert him to the ethical perils of this laboratory experiment. Since the erudite and cynical Himillsy has fallen into the trap as well—and likely killed herself in response to the traumatic experience—he conjectures that form-based finesse might actually nurture blindness toward the real meaning of the experiment.

Where *The Cheese Monkeys* largely celebrated the possibilities of typography and graphic design, *The Learners* stresses their limitations. In the last one of several interludes, the narrative voice asserts that language—even in mediated, written form—can still be used to genuine effect. The speaker in this interlude is "Content as Sincerity," who holds: "I can be a bore. I am your driver's license. I am a price tag, a phonebook, a lease, a road map, a will. But . . . I'm also a construction paper birthday card, scrawled in crayon with hysterical devotion by a child who actually loves you . . . I am the Constitution of the United States" (254, first ellipsis in original). In the beginning of this quotation, Kidd aligns himself with the modernist aim to rescue poetic language from the diversions of pathos and cliché. Like Hemingway's shell-shocked Lieutenant Frederic Henry, who preferred the names of roads and villages to abstract concepts such as love and glory, Kidd's authorial persona retreats from irony and well-designed deception to the utilitarian, deictic functions of maps and price tags. Beyond this, he extends the notion of "content as sincerity" to the founding document of the American nation. Overall, then, it is not the empirical or experiential proximity between text and context that creates sincerity. Instead, the key to sincerity lies outside the text: "What it all boils down to, what only ever really matters the most when it comes to Content, is Intent" (254).

As a metamedial novel, *The Learners* transcends the plot level and repeatedly foregrounds the fusion of bibliographic and linguistic codes. Besides the typographic manipulations discussed above, the book uses the perceptual unit of the page to structure the reading experience. Within Happy's narrative, the textual layout often uses page breaks as a way to create moments of suspense. In numerous instances throughout, the last line on the lower-right-hand side of the recto page announces or foreshadows some fact or event that will be revealed on the flipside.[6] Kidd's most intricate use of this implicit metamedial device occurs during Himillsy's burial service. Upon entering the church, Happy sees that his friend is laid out in an open casket. He is overcome with dread, having never seen a dead body before. Suspense builds as he moves up the line of mourners: "Endless, terrible minutes, drawing forward until I couldn't avoid it anymore. The time had come. I was too close, there were people watching, I had to do the right thing, what was expected, I had to turn and look, look at—" (85). At this point, the page break interrupts the reading process. In the vast majority of instances, the end of a page in a printed book is merely a medial constriction. Established cultural protocols prompt the reader to ignore the physical interruption and reconstruct the cut-up text as a seamless continuum.

In this case, however, the page break enhances the narrative. For one, the closing dash and the pause needed to turn the page briefly heighten the suspense, as readers wonder, "What is he looking at?" Furthermore, Kidd entwines the diegetic world with the material medium. The front and back of pages 85 and 86 metonymically stand in for the body of the narrator. Happy has to "turn" his body and "look" just as the reader has to turn the page and read on. At this juncture, narrative, medium, and reader are engaged in complex interactions involving cognition, bodily motion, and eye movement—all of which replicate the fictional character's actions. Happy quickly relaxes as the dead body appears to him completely remote from the person he used to know and admire: "And a burst of something like relief popped in my heart because, it . . . wasn't her" (86; ellipsis in original). Both text and paratexts have schooled the reader at this point that such presence effects are not arbitrary. As with any textual feature, we can never be completely sure that the writer intended it to function in a specific way. Authorized by the paratexts and foregrounded by the narrative mechanics, however, these devices feed hermeneutic proficiency that extends beyond words to the multimodal and material ensemble of bibliographic codes.

Chip Kidd and his employer Alfred A. Knopf complicate orthodox methods of literary historiography. Even though it has so far failed to generate scholarly interest, Kidd's work both in fiction and in book design actively constructs a network that challenges several models and practices. In literary studies, authors and genres represent two of the most conventional organizing principles for making sense of large amounts of information. Even though authors exist as persons, the notion of the "author" primarily has discursive value. As Luhmann holds, it serves a "structuring function within the autopoiesis of art" by making successful communication more likely (Art 49). The name of an author can order everyday conversations as well as fields of research. Instead of perceiving literary works as aligned by their authors, however, one could also systematize them according to their publishers.[7] In this regard, there are significant parallels between the small-scale influence of the McSweeney's style, and the more implicit, mass-marketed book aesthetics at Knopf. Just as the McSweeney's Universe arranges many of the individual texts discussed here into an interrelated network, Alfred A. Knopf, Inc.—including Pantheon and the Vintage paperback imprint—also establishes a suggestive grid within American literature. Chip Kidd can be seen as an emblematic marginal figure whose influence on American literature in the twenty-first century has remained obscure precisely because it is so extremely obvious.

## ¶ The Bibliography of Separating: Salvador Plascencia

As an insider in the publishing business, Chip Kidd will likely have met with little resistance when he pitched the extravagant design of his novels to the editors at Scribner. Writer-designers with less renown face higher obstacles at major trade presses. Having graduated from Syracuse University's MFA program in creative writing in 2002, Salvador Plascencia began to receive rejection letters. Several mainstream publishing houses, among them Grove, Random House, and Picador, turned down the manuscript of his debut novel *The People of Paper*, deeming its formal features too complicated to render for a general audience (Kun 82). Eventually, McSweeney's picked up the book through the initiative of editor Eli Horowitz, who closely cooperated with Plascencia during the layout and production process. Published in 2005, the book became one of the firm's most successful titles; Harcourt soon bought the paperback rights and brought out the trade paperback in 2006. The book has since been translated into several languages. As an artifact, the novel is quite noticeably a McSweeney's book. The elaborate printed cover boards, the Garamond font, and the experimental page design all align with Dave Eggers's house style. While I discuss the book as a stand-alone novel in this chapter, *The People of Paper* grows out of and recursively inscribes itself back into the McSweeney's Universe as portrayed in Chapter 2. It is as much a serial episode in the development of Eggers's publishing house as an autonomous literary work.

Succeeding Danielewski's horror novel and Kidd's typographic bildungsroman, the bibliographer Plascencia brings a postmodern romance into close contact with its medial surfaces. According to Hayles, *The People of Paper* functions as an emblem of computation and digitization in literary writing (*Electronic* 171–75). Against this technological reading, Ramón Saldívar holds that the novel incorporates an "aesthetic idiom . . . committed to social justice" (584). Neither Hayles nor Saldívar discusses the publishing context of the book, disregarding the McSweeney's network. While the two critics capture important facets of the text, I contend that Plascencia's prime concern lies with the relationship of human emotions and medial materiality. In his novel, he redefines the novelist's occupation as a specific form of artistic bibliography. The title of the novel already indicates that Plascencia uses paper as more than a neutral inscription surface. Refracted through several chronological and ontological layers, *The People of Paper* relates a fairly straightforward love story in a highly complex fashion. As such, the novel extends the metamedial mode of American literature into yet another genre.

What is more, this romance is interwoven with the author's biography: After Plascencia's family had immigrated to the United States from the Mexican city of Guadalajara, the author grew up in El Monte, a suburb of Los Angeles with a large Latino population. Most of the plot takes place in a fictionalized version of this town. *The People of Paper* contains hosts of anecdotal divergences from the central plot. Plascencia splits the text into columns, with each chunk focusing on the character named in its headline. Throughout the book, dozens of characters receive a designated column in which they narrate in the first person. In one recurring column, an authorial narrator attempts to chronicle life in El Monte, while the characters constantly challenge his power to control the fictional world. Readers soon learn that Plascencia's authorial avatar with the telling name Saturn attempts to mirror his own love life in the relationship between the character Federico de la Fe and his ex-wife Merced. Saturn/Plascencia and a woman named Liz separated because the author had devoted all of his time and attention to his novel. The authorial voice attempts to suppress the cause of their breakup and instead calls upon a broad array of external reasons, which show Saturn in a more favorable light. Still, this fictionalized author-narrator cannot help but subvert his own narrative, exposing his unreliability and revealing the whole narrative as a manic exercise in heartbroken fabulation.

Plascencia dedicates the novel to his family and to his ex-lover Liz who taught him, as the dedication reads, "that we are all of paper" (7). Embodiment thus becomes the guiding metaphor of the novel. In the character Merced de Papel, Plascencia carries this metaphor to extremes, as he envisions the daily life of a person physically made of paper. This paper-woman is a thoroughly secular Eve, brought into existence in a mystical factory "not from the ribs of man," as the book's Prologue relates, "but from paper scraps" (15). Her shoes continually grind at her frail feet, while every interaction with tools and objects threatens to destroy parts of her outer layer. She needs to repair herself after every physical encounter, preferably with "fresh, tight wraps of newsprint" (162). Like several other characters, Merced de Papel also migrates from Latin America to southern California. In her case, though, this migration is pragmatically motivated, as she needs an arid environment to survive. In Los Angeles, scores of men fall for the paper woman. Making love to Merced de Papel, preferably through oral intercourse, proves to be a painful and bloody exercise. Her lovers incur deep paper cuts and stain the outer layer of her thighs with blood. While humans made of flesh and blood retain their scarred mementos for life, Merced de Papel discards all their markings as soon as possible. For her species—the people of paper—the notion of romantic love and "the contrived melancholy" (168) of forlorn lovers seem absurd.

Within the novel's fictional diegesis, readers become deeply involved with Merced de Papel as well. The idiosyncratic character Baby Nostradamus—a "slobbering" and "brain dead" baby (23)—has prophetic visions that extend to the reader's interactions with the artifact:

He knew the different grips of the readers, how some cradled the open covers while others set the book on a table, licking their fingers before turning each page, saliva soaking into the margins.

And there were those readers who, when alone, opened the book and licked the edge of the pages, imagining that they too were going down on Merced de Papel, their blood gathering and channeling in the furrows of the spine. And they, these readers who were intimate with paper, went out into the world licking their lips, showcasing their scars and sore tongues, adding to the loves of Merced de Papel. (166)

The Baby Nostradamus creates in his mind the reading site of the book, the empirical location in which each reader encounters the text. At first, his visions only show everyday interactions with the book, as some readers hold up the book while others lay it down on a surface. In the second paragraph, however, the reader's interaction with the book turns into a surrogate for sexual intercourse. *The People of Paper* hereby describes itself as the ultimate fetish for bibliophiles. While the idea of making love to a book may seem absurd, the combination of arousing stories and book materiality undeniably encourages what has been called "one-handed reading."[8]

Such eroticized portrayals of the reading process also permeate theoretical writings, for example in Roland Barthes's *The Pleasure of the Text*. Barthes's collection of short musings, fragments, and aphorisms develops a bodily semantics of reading, steeped deeply in sexual terminology. His central concept of jouissance—translated as "bliss"—correlates the romantic notion of artistic sublimity with the experience of an orgasm. Anticipating Gumbrecht's "Farewell to Interpretation," Barthes perceives the pleasure of reading as an irreducibly embodied phenomenon. He holds, "The pleasure of the text is that moment when my body pursues its own ideas—for my body does not have the same ideas I do" (17). Hermeneutics, Barthes elaborates, can only ever expect to rationalize pleasure or plaisir. Since sensual, erotic jouissance is singular and presentist, it effectively eludes critical explanation (21–22). While Barthes argues for an embodied understanding of the reader, he seems to be oblivious to the embodied nature of the text. Even when he calls the text a "fetish object" (27), he ultimately does not see it as a material entity. This discursive notion of textuality fits well into Barthes's larger semiotic framework. His disembodied notion of text exemplifies the dominant self-description of literary art during the extended era in which the printed book was the unquestioned, naturalized, and thus invisible delivery vehicle for literary texts. A text, the semiotician Barthes asserts, "consists of language" (30). Writers of Plascencia's generation now appear to append textuality with the semantics of embodiment. Through the visions of Baby Nostradamus, Plascencia portrays sexual intercourse as a valid type of world appropriation—an embodied method of knowing. In this scenario, Merced de Papel becomes the emblem of neo-Barthesian textual pleasure. Reading about her papery body, picturing her face, and reliving her erotic encounters are merely the traditional methods of aesthetically experiencing her sections of the story. We may receive a similarly accurate and more visceral impression of Merced de Papel, the narrator suggests, by licking the sharp edges of a page in the McSweeney's book.

The People of Paper transposes the classic postmodernist motif of an author's struggle with his characters onto the medial plane. The novel incessantly recalls Latour's dictum that "objects too have agency" (Latour 63). In Plascencia's bibliographic aesthetics, the agency of fictional characters such as Saturn, Liz, or Federico de la Fe becomes equal, maybe even secondary to that of the bibliographic artifacts that populate the text. While the novel depicts dozens of books and documents, two items crucially influence the plot. For one, Merced de Papel records her life in an autobiographical book of her own. Also, the existence of a mysterious *Book of Incandescent Light* hovers above the entire fictional world.

For Merced de Papel, bibliographic fixity is a question of asserting her agency. As the object of male love, dispersed memories of her exist in the gray matter and the scarred tongues of her lovers. Distrusting the melancholy of her ex-lovers, she fears that their heartbroken chronicles will misrepresent her. To become a subject, and to remain one beyond her death, she has to write herself into the archive: "Merced de Papel was cautious of a legacy left in scar tissue, and for this reason she kept her own account, written on the scraps that she shed. She compiled her own book, which she titled in her native Spanish: *Los Dolores y Amores de la Gente de Papel*" (198). From the ephemeral scraps that fall from her body, Merced de Papel assembles a more durable artifact. In this book, she attests to having had an affair with Saturn/Plascencia who, like other men before him, had attempted to permanently mark her body. Where others had jotted down notes or reminders on her paper skin, Saturn "had written the name Liz a thousand times over in blue ink" (165). Just like the newspaper she's made of, however, Merced de Papel is ephemeral. Saturn cannot use her to record his feelings of loss, even though he scrawls Liz's name all over the paper woman. The novel here inquires into the storage capacities of paper as a medium for human memory. As the very stuff of life for the emergent consciousness of Merced de Papel, paper is as unreliable and fleeting as the cells that make up the human body. Flung about carelessly, paper disintegrates, burns to ash, or degrades into wet pulp. Only through careful inscription and arrangement, through proper storage and binding can paper become a relatively permanent mnemonic medium.

In its self-reflexive Spanish title, Merced de Papel's personal record book suggests that she—like many other characters of the novel—is not to be understood as a character separate from the author who envisioned her. Her fictional book functions both as context and counter- text to Plascencia's novel. It presents the female counter-narrative to Saturn's narcissistic, self-indulgent "melodrama of beset manhood," to use a phrase by Nina Baym (130). Merced de Papel's personal book is crucial for her own sense of subjectivity, as well as for the archival record of her species: "Merced de Papel was the only known survivor of her people, and as is always the case with those nearing extinction, she chronicled everything" (Plascencia, *People* 162). As a hybrid text of observations, instructions, daily routines, and extraordinary events, her manuscript shares many of the traits of everyday writing forms such as the biji or the consuetudinary, as presented in *McSweeney's* 31. The book *Los Dolores y Amores de la Gente de Papel* remains Merced de Papel's only trace after her death in a car crash. With this paper creature, Salvador Plascencia connects the realm of the dead, as manifested in durable storage media, with the stuff of human life. Rethinking human cell tissue as an ephemeral archive, he suggests that bibliographic artifacts do not radically transcode human experience. As anthropomorphic objects, they simply extend the lifespan of individual identities.

Whereas Merced de Papel's records have little relevance within the overall plot structure, another artifact interacts centrally with Plascencia's text. The origin of this second book can be traced back to the creation myth from the prologue of the novel. A Franciscan order of monks, who used to create humans from ribs and mud, vowed to march the earth in single file for as long as it takes for each member to forget the location of their factory. During their procession across continents, the monks lose one member who remains unaccounted for. The El Monte town healer Apolonio, however, meets this very monk and learns about his life of penance following his fateful decision to abandon the orderly march:

> In his quest for forgiveness he had written *The Book of Incandescent Light*, a manuscript that took three decades of research and twenty-six months of fevered writing to complete. It was published posthumously but lauded as the greatest apology since the blood letters of the expelled seraphim angel Juan Vincente, who wrote with his index finger and the ink of his own veins, standing on his head and shaking his wrist when the ink began to fade. (102)

The monk's *Book of Incandescent Light* serves a different function than Merced de Papel's autobiographical chronicle. As a form of public contrition, the strenuous work on this manuscript over thirty years is supposed to cleanse the soul of its author. Later published by the Vatican, this "treatise on sadness and love" (219) becomes a religious best seller.

While the characters frequently talk about this book, Plascencia mentions its physical presence on the intradiegetic level only once during the opening section in which Antonio creates Merced de Papel out of its leaves of paper. Neither Apolonio, nor the other residents of El Monte ever claim that they possess a copy. Conversely, the book figures strongly on the extradiegetic level. As such, chapter 19 presents "The Ballad of Perfidy," a "silent hymn" excerpted from *The Book of Incandescent Light* (179). Three hand-drawn, but otherwise empty lines of musical notation depict this farcical song of silence. Since Salvador Plascencia and his authorial persona Saturn control the chapter structure, readers are led to assume that the author possesses a copy of the book from which he lifts this piece. Several other indicators throughout the book all point to the same conclusion: *The Book of Incandescent Light* originates with Saturn, not with the fictional monk. The "treatise on sadness and love" is an alternate version of the novel *The People of Paper*. The author himself actually performed the "three decades of research and twenty-six months of fevered writing." For Plascencia, his entire life—he was born in 1976—was research for the publication of this book in 2005. Overall, however, the published version of the monk's apology remains merely an unrealized alternative for the final form of Plascencia's novel. The gesture performed in the writing of this treatise—an act of contrition to make amends with the community—will not be repeated.

Building on these intradiegetic versions of his novel, Plascencia creates a signifying material structure around the fictional world through ingenious manipulations of the bibliographic form. Saturn watches the town of El Monte and its residents from above, orbiting their fictional world like the eponymous planet.[9] Aside from this fictional scenario, however, his textual presence physically hovers above the residents in the material book. Across the numerous chapters that represent Saturn's narration alongside other characters in separate columns, the authorial persona is exclusively present on the verso pages (see fig. 6). As readers progress through the book from front to back, they enact this spatial arrangement on each page: while turning the page from right to left, Saturn's column briefly floats over those of the characters on the recto page. Remarkably, the author presents himself as a privileged observer, not an omniscient narrator. Plascencia hereby creates a material version of the "third person limited" perspective. This perspective generally assumes its "impersonal separateness" through narrative techniques that are "built into its grammatical structure" (McGurl 142). *The People of Paper* attempts to create this separateness in the bibliographic structure of the printed sheet itself: Saturn can only observe what happens on the adjacent page.

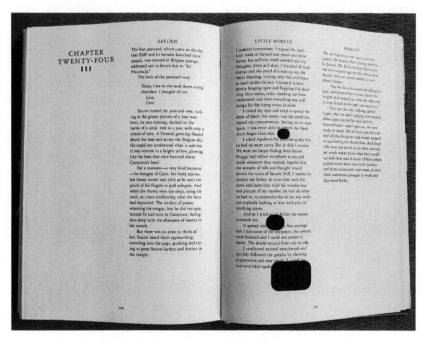

Fig. 6. Salvador Plascencia, *The People of Paper* (San Francisco: McSweeney's, 2005), p. 208–209. Courtesy of McSweeney's Publishing. Photograph by Alexander Starre.

Even though Saturn's senses are supernaturally enhanced, he cannot fully control his fictional world. His characters devise strategies to shield their privacy from the author. Early on, Federico de la Fe discovers that he can hold Saturn's oppressive gaze in check by using lead. In his curious arms race in preparation for the war against Saturn, Federico buys up the shells of mechanical tortoises, obscure creatures that resurface throughout the plot and speak in digital code (97). Federico frequently hides within these shells: "Saturn was aligned directly over Federico de la Fe, following him wherever he went, budging a half a space centimeter for every five hundred land miles de la Fe and Little Merced traveled. But once Federico de la Fe retreated into the lead shell . . . Saturn withdrew into his orbit" (30). The passage exhibits Plascencia's sophisticated spatial vision of authorial perspective. Several interpretations for the choice of lead as shielding material are possible. The most obvious reading would associate Saturn's gaze with X-rays, which can be deflected through lead shielding. Aside from this evident metaphorical link, the choice of lead also resonates with the history of the book. Traditionally, lead has been the main component in the metal alloys used for manufacturing movable type. Even though the McSweeney's book certainly sprang from offset printers, Plascencia calls up the conventional association of printing with lead. Hereby, he portrays the ontological separation between author and fictional world as an impenetrable wall of lead. The author's influence thus stops where the lead type of the printing house intervenes in the communication process.

The most striking episode of medial self-inspection fleshes out the device of ontological metalepsis. Plascencia's version of metalepsis couples the puzzling dynamic of entwined ontologies with thoroughly realistic descriptions of penetrable borders. Smiley, a very shrewd resident of El Monte, comprehends the ontological status of Saturn and goes on a quest to find the author of the book. Ascending the Southern Californian San Gabriel Mountains to their highest peaks, he finally hits upon the ontological boundary. The sky above his head turns out to be a visual illusion painted on papier-mâché. Using his carnation knife, Smiley opens a hole in the sky, through which he pulls himself up into the higher ontology of Saturn (103). Once in the author's presence, however, Smiley is severely disappointed. Instead of having a "dignified meeting" with his creator, Smiley finds Saturn asleep on his bed, bereft of all omniscience and authorial control. Saturn's bedroom is a mess; also serving as his writing space, the room represents the heartbroken disarray of its owner. Smiley sees "books stacked in badly planned towers that disregarded alphabet and size, falling and collapsing into rubble. And paper, unbound and scattered everywhere" (103–04). Soon, Saturn wakes up without paying any attention to Smiley and calls his ex-girlfriend Liz, who refuses to talk to him.

Smiley remembers the tactical instructions drafted by the war committee in El Monte. These instructions dictate that Saturn's throat needs to be cut, but not just in order to kill him. As Smiley describes the ritual, ink, not blood, will seep from the author's wounds. The liquid will then leave permanent traces in the author's home in the form of "dense warm prose that stains the floors and always reappears six coats of paint later. Something that will remain longer than any novel will" (105). Smiley also recalls the rules of engagement regarding the author's current writing project: "At the very least, if rushed, steal the plot lines and the hundred and five pages that have been written. Leave nothing behind but the title page and table of contents, on which you write, 'You are not so powerful'" (105). Metamedial devices familiar from Danielewski reemerge here, as Plascencia reflexively calls up the page numbering and places a mise-en-abymic copy of the book within the diegesis. Since the passage is located exactly on page 105, Smiley would steal the entire work in progress.

Conversely, readers now discover that they not only witness the events unfolding in El Monte. Alongside the main narrative, Plascencia reenacts the writing process, during which Liz split up with Saturn. Increasingly frustrated with Saturn's desperate phone calls, Liz addresses the novel and its intolerable invasion of her privacy. She accuses Saturn of capitalizing on his pain: "In a neat pile of paper you have offered up not only your hometown . . . but also me, your grandparents and generations beyond them . . . You have delivered all this into their hands, and for what? For twenty dollars and the vanity of your name on the book cover" (138). Fearing that her children or other people she cares for will one day discover the text, she pleads with Saturn to edit her out: "Start this book over, without me" (138). And so he does. On page 141, the novel begins again, complete with a new title page—but without the dedication addressed to Liz.

Like many of the other works discussed in this book, *The People of Paper* experiments with the form of fiction not merely by diverting closure and signification indefinitely. Ramón Saldívar reads the novel as a parable on the fragility of social bonds, especially for diasporic cultures within the larger framework of the United States. Therefore, he argues, the novel "remains an open form, permanently unfinished, precisely because the process of ethnic and racial identity construction, within the general, brutal structure of commodity fetishism and the reification of labor, is, historically speaking, itself awesomely incomplete" (583). While I acknowledge the political import of Saldívar's reading—he contends that Plascencia envisions "social justice" (593) and the "transformation of society as a whole" (596)—I would challenge his formal description of the novel as an "open form." The narrative and typographic experiments coupled with the extremely meticulous attention to bibliographic form instead achieve what Niklas Luhmann has called the "stabilization of a relationship of redundancy and variety" (*Reality* 50). In its deictic anchoring on the pages of a book, *The People of Paper* is an extraordinarily closed and finite artifact. It enforces what Eisenstein calls "typographic fixity" through aesthetic binding operations. We can observe this stability in the succeeding paperback printings by Harcourt, which keep intact the entire textual layout, including page numberings, typeface, and paper size. Above all else, Plascencia's novel is a tightly closed form.

This bibliographic closure is necessary for the whole experimental ensemble to be kept intelligible to the reader. For reprints and intermedial transpositions, Plascencia's design implies additional work. American readers have encountered the book either in the McSweeney's or in the Harcourt edition. The original edition establishes the textual condition of the novel; further printings threaten to corrupt the text. To give a couple of examples: During one of the skirmishes between Saturn and the so-called "El Monte Flores" gang, Federico de la Fe instructs a man named Pelon to stop thinking about anything incriminating. If need be, Pelon should think of rooster fights. His column of text then runs down the length of the page, while he calls up random images. At the very end of the page, extending below the page number, his interior monologue reads: "the red crest of the roosters, the red blood on the razor blade that cuts the fighting cock's crest, the sharp beaks of the hens that pick at the severed" (91). After the last word, "severed," the column terminates at the bottom edge of the page, suggesting that Pelon's text would run on if the page had not been cut. Nowhere else in the book does the text descend into the bottom margin in this fashion. The cut of the razor blade materializes in the edge of the page, which has itself been trimmed into shape by a sharp blade at the printing house. In the paperback edition, however, this metamedial effect does not work as well, as the printing machines were not properly configured to produce a page with no margin. Additional white space looms below the last line on page 91 in the Harcourt edition, so that Pelon's column appears to end before it is cut off.

The transcript of a phone call between Saturn and Liz exhibits a second instance of medial closure. After Liz listens to Saturn's jealous rant for a while, she defends her new partner by saying, "You went away to fight de la Fe and [ ] was here" (117). Saturn retorts, "Don't say his name. I don't want him in here. I will cut him out" (117). In the McSweeney's edition, the empty space denoted by the brackets consists of a die-cut hole in the material page (see fig. 7). Two pages later, Saturn repeats this maneuver when Liz says "I love [ ]" (119). Enhancing a mass-produced book with die-cuts adds a considerable amount to the overall printing cost. As described above, however, such material manipulations are defining components of the McSweeney's publishing program. With a mainstream publisher like Harcourt, authors will surely have a harder time in negotiating such extravagant features. Without die-cuts, the text still demands visible imprints that represent Saturn's interventions. To solve this problem, the Harcourt edition slightly modifies

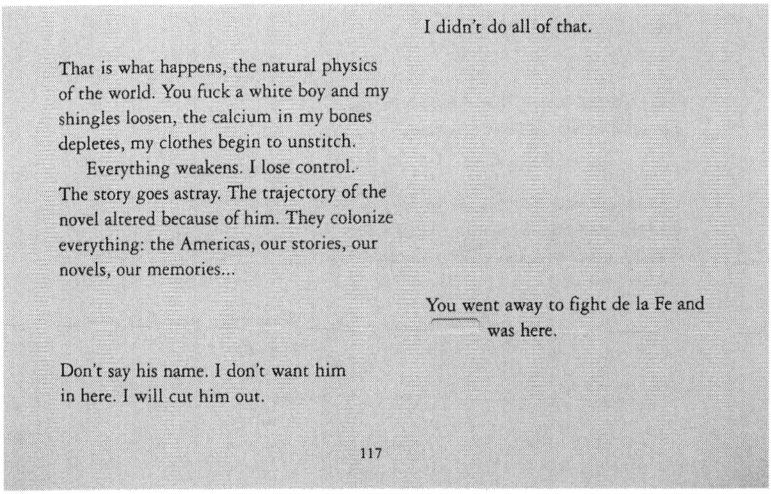

I didn't do all of that.

That is what happens, the natural physics of the world. You fuck a white boy and my shingles loosen, the calcium in my bones depletes, my clothes begin to unstitch.
  Everything weakens. I lose control. The story goes astray. The trajectory of the novel altered because of him. They colonize everything: the Americas, our stories, our novels, our memories...

You went away to fight de la Fe and ~~——~~ was here.

Don't say his name. I don't want him in here. I will cut him out.

117

Fig. 7. Detail from Salvador Plascencia, *The People of Paper* (San Francisco: McSweeney's, 2005), p. 117. Courtesy of McSweeney's Publishing. Photograph by Alexander Starre.

the text. Saturn now says, "I don't want him in here. I will scratch him out." Accordingly, thick, black scribbling conceals the man's name, as if drawn with a black marker. Alterations in the medial form of *The People of Paper* necessitate changes in the discursive content of the book. Plascencia's novel hereby urges literary scholars to approach material variants with the same amount of care routinely devoted to semantic variants in critical editions.

In the realm of literary communication, the narrative of El Monte continues the autopoietic coevolution of art and technology. Plascencia self-reflexively portrays the mechanisms of love in a culture of symbolic communications carried out via books, letters, and maps. In the process, the novel reflects on the capacity of literary artifacts to transcend space and time, but also on their tendency to distort reality in such convincing ways that future generations will decode fiction as fact. Saldívar holds that the book confronts readers with "the overlay of literature and politics in the Americas, which Plascencia calls the commodification of sadness" (595). Against this, the metamedial form of the novel suggests that "commodification of sadness" refers to something else beside the immigrant experience of diasporic Latino communities. As Saldívar also points out, Plascencia aims to emancipate his writing from the realist tradition of politically engaged Chicano literature. The sadness permeating the whole book may be read as fully reliant on the author, which is reinforced by the symbolism of Saturn, the planet of melancholia. It becomes refracted through scores of personal histories, all of them either fictive or originating with other heartbroken authors. It may touch upon "the local histories of sadness on the US-Mexico border" (Saldívar 581); yet the majority of this plight consists of projected sadness—melancholia originating with the author.

The commodification against which Federico de la Fe wages war references the basal, medial foundation of the emergent communicative system of modern literature. Without mass produced commodities—books—this system would cease to exist. The "war on omniscient narration (a.k.a. the war against the commodification of sadness)" is therefore always already lost (Plascencia, *Paper* 218). Smiley correctly conjectures, "I knew that the defeat of Saturn would bring our own end, that everything would conclude with its crash" (101). The representational flexibility of the novel form may allow its characters to revolt against authorial control. Ultimately, however, the overthrow of the author would not free but annihilate them. The autopoiesis of literature hardly relies on its overlay with politics; it rests with its capacity to fulfill unique functionalities in the communicational realm that is U.S. society. As the product of literary bibliography, *The People of Paper* engages directly with the accepted tenets and conventions of novelistic communication. Plascencia explodes the post-humanist idea that "we are all of paper" to erect a narrative universe in which humans enter into strange alliances with papery artifacts. The transference of mind into medium comes at a cost, though, as these artifacts take on lives of their own—a process personified by Merced de Papel. Salvador Plascencia's book is anything but a neutral communication medium. In the hands of its readers, it becomes a thing capable of coevolving with its observers. As such, the novel engages with the figural and literal scabs and bruises that humans incur when they chafe against people and things in their environment. Whether these come in the form of broken hearts or paper cuts ultimately matters little.

### ¶ Unpublished Histories of Frustrated Ambitions: Reif Larsen

Like Salvador Plascencia, Reif Larsen underwent professional instruction in creative writing—in his case at Brown and Columbia. During this formative period, Larsen directly witnessed the hypertext fiction hype surrounding Robert Coover's workshops at Brown. In a recent article in the McSweeney's *Believer* magazine, Larsen reminisces about his introduction to the world of hypertext:

> [A]s I walked into my first hypertext "show" at Brown in which students were demonstrating their hyperspace stories (several of which were just borderline cybersex *Choose Your Own Adventure* pieces repackaged as groundbreaking postmodern electronic literature), as a "reader" of these stories, I came up against the obstacles that have, at best, prevented hypertext fiction from blossoming beyond the geekworld, and, at worst, sunk the ship before it ever set sail. That is, hypertext fiction, with very few exceptions, was mostly bells and whistles, fireworks and birdcalls, virtual heavy petting and mouse clicks. ("Crying" 8)

Larsen still admits that his debut novel, which he drafted while attending Columbia, ended up being "essentially an exploded hypertext" (8). *The Selected Works of T.S. Spivet* (2009) indeed uses an ergodic, multidirectional structure with visualized hyperlinks to tell the story of a young boy with uncanny skills in cartography.

The format and size of the American Penguin edition, specifically the paperback version, closely resembles Danielewski's *House of Leaves*. Expanding the horizontal space in its 7 × 9 inch format, the novel appears even more square shaped than Danielewski's book. In its dimensions, the novel strays from the upright orientation of a standard book. Larsen also constructs a medial diegesis for his novel by attributing authorship to his narrator, T.S. Spivet—whose first-name initials fittingly recall the abbreviation for the bibliographical term "typescript."[10] The child prodigy Tecumseh Sparrow Spivet devotes himself to the "lifelong task of mapping the real world in its entirety" (338). In his youthful scientific exuberance, T.S. aims to create a map akin to the one Jorge Luis Borges described in his brief story "On Exactitude in Science." Borges envisioned a map of an unnamed empire "whose size was that of the Empire, and which coincided point for point with it" (325). Having started mapmaking at age six, T.S. already had to turn his bedroom into a small research library so as to house his large cartographic oeuvre. In his rural Montana home, he spends his days filling notebooks with hand-drawn maps of anything from geology to insect anatomy. T.S.'s interest in insects owes to his mother Clair Linneaker Spivet, a specialist in coleopterology, the study of beetles. While the thrust of Larsen's narrative derives from the boy's adventurous cross-country voyage, the novel also chronicles the history of the Spivet family.

T.S. is the fifth-generation descendant of an immigrant family from Finland. As his self-made family tree shows, T.S.'s male ancestors all worked in menial jobs as miners or ranchers (143). The female line, however, features two artists—a painter and a poet—and two scientists. Beyond T.S.'s mother, the scientific strain of the family hearkens back to the "first female geologist in the entire country," a woman named Emma Osterville (143). Shortly before the onset of the plot, the tragic death of T.S.'s brother Layton from an accidental gunshot unsettled the peaceful family life. In the aftermath, the parents begin to shroud this traumatic event in silence. In this stifling atmosphere, T.S. receives notice that he will be awarded the Smithsonian Institute's Spencer F. Baird Award for the popular advancement of science. A friend of his mother had supposedly submitted a portfolio of the boy's maps to the Smithsonian, omitting the boy's age.

While reviews and scholarly readings of the text focus largely on T.S.'s transcontinental voyage to Washington D.C. and the multimodal potentials of cartographic narrative, my aim is to show the crucial function of the interpolated story of Emma Osterville, as written down by T.S.'s mother Clair.[11] Before secretly departing for Washington, D.C., the young boy visits his mother's study for a last time. In a hurry to leave,

T.S. grabs the burgundy, bound notebook marked "EOE" that lies on her desk. His mother's room contains a full shelf of these notebooks, leading the narrator to presume that she uses them for notations in a long-running entomological project. To T.S.'s surprise, the notebook contains anything but scientific data sets. As he reads through the whole manuscript in several bursts during his train ride east, he discovers that Dr. Clair has written a biography of his great-great-grandmother. The three letters stand for Emma Osterville Englethorpe, the latter name deriving from the second husband of Emma's mother.

The mise-en-abymic artifact of the EOE notebook is the metafictional and metamedial key to Larsen's novel. It leads T.S. to consider the constructive relationship between the materiality of primary documents and their creators or owners—a relationship that readers of such a primary source may retrace. In a reversed initiation plot, T.S. slowly loses faith in the objective representational capabilities of maps and hard science, while discovering the world-making values of fiction and the imagination. In itself, the fictionalized biography of Emma Osterville relates a history of female emancipation and retroactive Americanization. Freely combining unpublished personal memoirs with published national history, Dr. Clair constructs an adequate narrative to vindicate her own biography of unfulfilled ambitions. Overall, Larsen's novel depicts the agency of primary documents within the unlikely genealogy of a family whose heritage becomes bound to the collective memory of the period in literary history that F.O. Matthiessen called the American Renaissance.

At the beginning of Clair's notebook, Larsen refutes the Kittlerian thesis that electric recording media have put an end to the imagined sensuality of printed words. Kittler argues that "words quivered with sensuality and memory" only as long as the discourse network 1800 with its prime reliance on handwriting was in place (*Gramophone* 10). Through illustrations that depict Clair's notebook, Larsen attempts to transport this twice-mediated sensuality. Larsen suggests that T.S. Spivet drew all of these sketches by hand; their style matches that of his maps and drawings. The first sentence carries a dotted-line hyperlink, which points to a miniature reproduction of the notebook. With a common cartographic technique, T.S. magnifies this line, providing an enlarged sample of Clair's handwriting on graph paper above the small picture. Below the image, the narrator ponders the form of her manuscript: "As I began to read Dr. Clair's notebook, I realized how personal someone's handwriting actually is. I had never thought of Dr. Clair as separate from the way she wrote: those E's that looked like half 8's had always been a part of her . . . I now saw that my mother's writing was not a given, but the result of a life lived" (Larsen, *Selected* 144). In a Darwinian epiphany, T.S. recognizes that the unique appearance of handwriting is not a natural given. Script attains its sensuality because it is always the end result of an ongoing process of coevolution, as someone's environment triggers changes in mental structures and bodily automatisms. As such, Darwin's handwritten notebooks, visually reproduced in a different section of the book (57), not only speak of evolution in their content, but also in their outward form. Clair's manuscript fulfills T.S.'s wish to take along a piece of her. Throughout his long journey, he cradles the autographic representation of his mother's embodied self.

To the young cartographer, writing mostly figures as an informational tool. His true fascination lies with the pictorial representations of maps. Here, however, he witnesses a similar medial transfusion of the self onto the page. At the beginning of his train ride, T.S. remembers a lecture by the elderly cartographer Corlis Benefideo that he attended at Montana Tech. Benefideo presented a selection of his hand-drawn maps of North Dakota, which systematically represent the state from a variety of scientific perspectives. After the talk, T.S. recalls, a young audience member asked the old man: "But what about the *now*? Why is this field so rooted in the last century? What about mapping McDonald's or wireless hot spots or cell phone coverage? What about Google mash-ups? Democratizing GIS for the masses? Aren't you doing a disservice by ignoring these trends?" (137). This minor character of course stands in for the tech-savvy mainstream of contemporary Internet users by directly naming the latest digital tools and Web services. Larsen here voices the populist ideology of the inherently democratic nature of networked computers that dispense information to the masses at no cost.

On the scientific level, neither the old man nor the young boy can adequately counter this argument. Yet, in an effort to make sense—not just to retrieve data—hand-drawing maps has surplus value, as T.S. tries to articulate: "Like him, I made maps without the aid of computers or GPS devices. I was not quite sure why, but I felt much more like a creator this way. Computers made me feel like an *operator*" (138–39). At a loss for words, the narrator tries to account for the fact that he prefers individually penned maps, even though the end result of a computer-generated map will be scientifically superior. He is not ready to admit it yet, but he inches toward comprehending the importance of his maps: in manually tracing the external world, T.S. develops his internal capacities to become a more proficient observer. As he registers the difference in sensory experience between writing on paper and manipulating pixels through mouse clicks, he sees that his maps of Montana are finally not about Montana at all. Instead, they represent externalized traces of the subjective being T.S. Spivet and his evolving mind.[12]

Dr. Clair's handwritten notebook similarly mediates her subjectivity. While T.S. provides several snapshots of her handwriting, her text undergoes a second, typographic mediation as it is printed on the pages of the Penguin book. Aside from its visual and tactile features, the notebook also emanates the "formaldehyde and lemony scents of her study" (211), which trigger homesickness in the little boy: "I wanted to hold her hand and apologize for taking this book, for leaving without permission, for not saving Layton, for not being a better brother, or ranch hand, or scientist's assistant. For not being a better *son*" (211). Just as implied readers of The People of Paper supposedly mark the book with their spit, T.S. imprints his sadness on the paper in the form of tears that leave "two pear-shaped stains on the binding" (211). Evoking inscription technologies and personalized markings, the novel thus attempts to recreate a paradoxical effect of proximity through distance. Larsen does not stop here, though. He follows the nexus of writing and identity from the scene of inscription to the bibliographic storage medium of the book. As such, the cardinal points of Emma Osterville's life story revolve around material texts.

According to Clair's manuscript, Emma is the only child of Elizabeth Tamour and Gregor Osterville of Woods Hole, Massachusetts, where her father makes a living as a fisherman. Only months after Emma's birth, a violent storm sweeps away Gregor and his boat—his body is never found. Elizabeth clings to the desperate hope that her husband is still alive until someday, months later, a severely damaged copy of Gulliver's Travels washes up on the shore. Gregor had only owned two books, the King James Bible and Swift's novel. Elizabeth grasps the significance of the soaked edition right away: "The pages were discolored and bloated; only the front half of the book remained, the rest gone. She wept. It was proof enough" (150). Afterward, Elizabeth cherishes the torn book as the only memento of her husband. Clair's narrative then skips a decade and reencounters Emma and her mother in Boston, where the little girl will soon be introduced to scientific learning. After hearing that her father never bothered to study his Bible and instead kept rereading Swift, Emma begs her mother to read to her from Gulliver's Travels. Since Gregor's marred copy is illegible, they pick up "a brand-new copy of Gulliver's Travels at Mulligan's Fine Books on Park Street" (151). The narrative then fast-forwards another decade, to Emma's career pinnacle when she is offered a professorship at Vassar College. On her private bookshelf, Clair writes, Emma retains the tattered remains of Gregor's copy alongside the pristine Gulliver's Travels purchased in Boston.

This bibliographic coupling becomes the archetypal anchor through which Clair projects her sense of self back through several generations. It is Clair's voice that emanates from the imagined thoughts of Emma, as she realizes that "the initial, elusive push on her course to becoming a surveyor (born inside the wrong sex) could be traced back to her father's nighttime studies of Gulliver and his travels" (152–53). This poignant passage induces T.S. to illuminate Clair's manuscript with a visual rendition of the two books on the shelf. The boy then contemplates the relationship between the arrangement of books and a person's character: "I suddenly missed the curious shelving patterns of my room, those old planks from the barn groaning under the weight of the notebooks. Shelving is an intimate thing, like the fingerprint of a room" (153). Unlike digital text files, books do not pass out of physical existence once read. Thus, the presence of books in people's lives extends for as long as they are kept on display. While this is a subtle and elusive presence, the personalized bookshelf represents a rich material metaphor—a map, one might even say—of an individual's reading life. As such, personal collecting practices constitute a key element of the collective material culture within a given community.

Triggering what I have called T.S.'s reversed initiation plot, the notebook reenchants the prematurely skeptical narrator and forces him to acknowledge the personal and social function of fictional storytelling. The astute child prodigy presents himself as a serious scientist caught in the body of a twelve-year-old. Despite his tremendous learning, he cannot fathom the peculiar social behavior of adults. Like Huckleberry Finn, he fails to grasp the workings of romantic love; like Holden Caulfield, he despises the phoniness of public performances, as exemplified by the speeches given at the Smithsonian ceremony (305). However, as soon as he observes and catalogues the nonhuman world, his academic diction resembles that of a man four times his age. In his quest for complete cartography, T.S. does not want to waste precious time reading fictional stories. He bluntly asserts: "I am not a reading nerd" (199).

Not surprisingly, T.S. is shocked and infuriated when he discovers that his mother devotes most of her time to imaginative writing instead of rigorous science. After reading the first few pages, he anxiously wonders, "Was my mother not a scientist but a *writer*" (148). The italicized word "writer" reveals T.S.'s outrage at this trivial occupation. While reading the notebook, the young cartographer attempts to forestall cognitive immersion in the story. He simultaneously maps the eastward progress of his freight train into one of his own notebooks. This train route, including significant cities and sights, runs along the margins of Clair's text. After Emma's life story brings him to tears, however, T.S. grudgingly admits that the EOE notebook absorbs him to such a degree that he cannot keep up with his topographical sketches. Between pages 220 and 225, the vertical lines representing the train tracks slowly dissolve and ultimately disappear, signifying T.S.'s total immersion. A little later, he runs into a gap in his mother's prose. Disrupted by the white space—which is represented in the novel as well—T.S. is thrown back to his usual frame of observation, once more scolding his mother for her audacity to "speculate—no, *invent*—all of these emotions in our ancestors" (237). Nevertheless, he concedes that this free manner of narration causes him to turn page after page without looking up. He infers from this process that he might be witnessing himself growing up. In fact, however, his reading follows an opposite direction: it becomes more immersive and naïve with every page.

Concealed behind the lighthearted quest plot surrounding a young boy, *The Selected Works of T.S. Spivet* tells the story of the boy's mother, who has given up her academic career in favor of secluded, rural family life. Clair's passion for science has alienated her from her children. In fact, the entire Spivet family has fallen into repressive silence since Layton's death. For Clair, the creative retelling of Emma Osterville's story is a therapeutic exercise. She derives comfort from the act of interweaving her family's ancestral history, which is largely devoid of traces in the printed record, with publicized American scientific and literary history. The constructivist nature of her whole enterprise is obvious, as she is not even directly related to Emma Osterville. She nevertheless perceives a parallel life in the nineteenth-century geologist, using it as a shell to project her own dreams into a mythic past. In her private sanctuary close to the continental divide in Montana, Clair Linneaker Spivet crafts a sense of belonging to an imagined community of American intellectuals. At the outset of her notebook, Clair reveals the scarcity of historical sources for Emma's story. As an attachment, T.S. finds a photocopied excerpt from an old diary, written by William Henry Jackson, the actual photographer of the Wyoming Geological Survey in the 1870s.[13] Jackson mentions a "Miss Osterville" who allegedly accompanied the exploring party; he also praises her scientific skills. In an additional loose-leaf note, Clair discloses her insecurity: "I often wonder what I am doing lurking in this world, when the data sets are so weak. This is not science. I have Englethorpe's book, a few diaries, the Vassar archives, not much else—why am I compelled to speculate? Have I any right to do so? Would EOE approve?" (142). Apparently, Clair overcame these reservations and freely reconstructed Emma's life.

Having moved to Boston with her widowed mother, Emma makes the acquaintance of Orwin Englethorpe, a surveyor and biologist. Orwin grants her entry to the scientific elite in and around Harvard University. Through his studies, Orwin has turned into a fierce rival of Louis Agassiz, who first established the study of zoology and geology at Harvard. Whereas Agassiz devotes his life to refuting Darwin's theory of evolution and natural selection, Orwin wholeheartedly embraces the concept. Before long, Orwin and Elizabeth get married and the biologist becomes Emma's private tutor. Under several pretenses, Orwin keeps her away from the girls' school run by Agassiz's wife. Shortly before leaving Boston for Concord, the hub of New England transcendentalism, Emma personally meets Agassiz for the first and only time. After some trivial chatter, Agassiz excuses himself to return to his desk to resume "that infernal act of writing, an endeavor to which I have apparently signed away the rest of my days" (215). He explains that he is struggling to complete the projected ten volumes of his *Natural History of the United States*. With spontaneous ambition, Emma retorts, "I should like to write ten volumes someday" (215). Agassiz answers with reservations, hinting that he does not believe in the equality of the sexes within the domain of science. Emma brusquely tells him off by announcing, "You are just scared of evolution. Well, things evolve, sir" (216). Orwin and Emma settle at Concord in high hopes of spreading the theory of evolution and the feasibility of female science. Elizabeth befriends Louisa May Alcott, who in turn introduces Orwin to Ralph Waldo Emerson. On the eve of the Civil War, Emerson and Orwin take "long walks around Walden Pond," conversing on science and philosophy (218).

With the beginning of hostilities, however, fortunes seem to shift. Orwin's ambitious book project—"a New World companion volume to *On the Origin of Species*" (217)—is stalled at the draft stage, even after more than a year of work. His brilliance in collecting, itemizing, and classifying does not extend to his composition skills. Shortly after, he contracts a mysterious disease and dies before seeing his magnum opus in print. Vassar College has meanwhile admitted Emma, but she has second thoughts after Orwin's untimely death. Elizabeth implores her to take this unique chance: "To close yourself off to what is possible is to kill part of yourself, and that part will never grow again. You can marry and you can bear many beautiful children, but a part of you will be dead and you will feel that coldness every time you wake in the morning" (234). Finally entering Vassar, Emma excels academically. After her graduation, the university offers her a professorship in geology, which she gladly accepts. At the annual meeting of the National Academy of Sciences, she is to hold an address entitled "Women and Higher Learning." What she envisions as a triumphant performance turns out to be a sexist nightmare reminiscent of the "Battle Royal" chapter in Ralph Ellison's Invisible Man. Led off the stage in eerie silence and greeted with nothing but condescension by the "fat old men and their cigars," Emma immediately decides to leave the ivory tower and prove her resilience as field geologist with the Wyoming Survey (321). Throughout the trek west, Emma endures severe physical and psychological hardships. Instead of proudly returning to Boston as a seasoned frontierswoman, however, she meets the Finnish immigrant Tecumseh Tearho Spivet beside the railroad tracks in Wyoming's Red Desert. Clair's notebook breaks off here.

The EOE notebook reframes the ancestral lives of the Spivet clan as stories of failed ambitions. In the eyes of T.S.'s mother, the failures of Orwin, Emma, and even Elizabeth, are not related to their overall paths in life. Instead, the tragedy of the ancestral Spivets—especially the female lineage—solely lies in their failure to write down the results of their scientific studies and to publish them. For Orwin, the very idea of publishing a typographically fixed text runs counter to the evolutionary paradigm. Discussing the affinities of religion and science, he argues that in an ideal world both fields would embrace their adaptive nature, providing the world with a constant flow of new ideas that can then be tested for their usefulness. The holy book of the Bible, as an immovable artifact, stands in the way of this goal: "[H]ow can you have a single text and not keep editing it? A text is evolutionary by its very nature" (190). In essence, Orwin acts as the mouthpiece of post-bellum pragmatist intellectuals such as John Dewey, Oliver Wendell Holmes, William James, and Charles Sanders Peirce. As Louis Menand claims in The Metaphysical Club, these men had a common outlook on epistemology: "They believed that ideas do not develop according to some inner logic of their own, but are entirely dependent, like germs, on their human carriers and the environment. And they believed that since ideas are provisional responses to particular and unreproducible circumstances, their survival depends not on their immutability but on their adaptability" (xi–xii). From Orwin's perspective, publishing a text is a disservice to the nature of communicative evolution. He maintains that one cannot do greater justice to adaptive textuality "than to return to it and re-examine its contents," thus constantly rewriting it (190). As a result, he never finishes his book, and even though Clair claims that she possesses a copy of it, its existence seems dubious. Contrary to Orwin's celebration of free adaptive flow, Jaron Lanier has recently stressed the value of "encapsulation" for biological, scientific, and technological evolution (140–41). Rephrasing Lanier, we could say that Orwin miscalculates the value of temporary fixity for adaptive processes. Encapsulating a text and testing it in larger communicative systems will, according to Lanier's position, increase the chances of creative development. Alterations and corrections could then enter into subsequent editions, as the text's evolution takes place incrementally.

While Agassiz still has a place in the collective memory of the United States, the evolutionary biologist Orwin leaves no traces in the printed record. The hackneyed phrase "publish or perish" rings literally true here, as discursive death follows on the heels of Orwin's physical death. The Osterville women share his fate. Elizabeth has little interest in science, and her vague dream of settling out west also remains unful-filled. During her final years in Concord, however, she dabbles in belles lettres. Clair informs us that she "penned a couple of ordinary poems, which she timidly showed to Louisa May [Alcott], who proclaimed them 'emotive & telling'" (234). None of these poems survives, however. As

Agassiz relates to Orwin, so Alcott and Emerson relate to Elizabeth. These pairings represent the published and the unpublished histories of American literature.

Emma finally strays from her spontaneous ambition to write ten volumes. Her failed quest on the Wyoming Survey eradicates any chance for her to become a published scientist. As book historians have pointed out, political, social, ethnic, financial, and gender-related factors are all intricately bound up with the publishing circuit.[14] Steep barriers of access keep the female geologist relegated to the discursive margins. Emma's only substantial work, her childhood sketchbook, has been lost. In a side note, T.S. accordingly wonders: "What had happened to that sketchbook? What happened to all the historical detritus in the world?" (191). He then mourns the passing of embodied textual memories and the disappearance of the intimate stories contained in them. Clair's biggest problem with her fictionalized biography is that Emma has left no inscriptive trace at all. This is both a bane and a boon: the tabula rasa of Emma Osterville allows Clair to reinscribe her own biography onto this woman. In the process, she refines and Americanizes her family history.

Overall, the devastating development of the family plot proves to be a strong corrective to T.S.'s droll narrative. The text never confronts the trauma of Layton's death. Nor does T.S. reunite with his mother at the end. The novel closes with a heartfelt but still awkward interchange between T.S. and his father, as the parents' marriage appears to be in shambles. Against these loose threads, Larsen follows two important paths to narrative closure. One of them takes place within the text; the other occurs on the implied level of medial communication. As to the first: T.S. manages to retract his great-great-grandmother's course from the coastal cradle of science and learning into the Western intellectual wilderness. In Washington D.C., T.S. delivers a touching and warmly received acceptance speech to the distinguished audience at the Smithsonian. Afterward, his mentor, Dr. Yorn, reveals to him that it was actually his mother who prearranged his introduction to the scientific community and who suggested him for the Baird Award

(356). Clair therefore plotted not only the biography of her ancestral soul mate, Emma, but also nurtured T.S.'s cartographic skills behind the boy's back. In this regard, Clair's redemption arrives in the form of her children.

Aside from T.S.'s genius, the presence of Layton has a crucial function as well. At the bottom of the last, otherwise empty page of her EOE notebook, Clair writes out Layton's name. The discovery of his brother's name in this location upsets T.S., as he cannot understand its significance. On page 243, T.S. illustrates the enigmatic "Layton" signature with a sketch of the corresponding notebook section. He also lifts the minuscule detail of Clair's handwriting off of the page and enlarges it visually. Turning the page, readers discover Layton's name once more within the sidebar. It has grown to more than double its previous size. The visible remnants of Clair's graph paper now seem to blend with the page of the Penguin book. The chapter ends on this page, with T.S. declaring in a frustrated tone: "I stared at those six letters. The answers to my questions would never come" (244). Ironically, however, the answer is right in front of his eyes; he looks through it, instead of at it. The facing page reinforces this recognition in an even more obvious manner. The handwritten name "Layton" is blown up to such gigantic size that it covers more than half the page. At the end of this quadruple magnification process, each stroke of Clair's pen, each figment of ink becomes visible and creates an extraordinary presence effect. At about the position of the letter "o," the schematic train tracks that T.S. previously lost reemerge and lead the reader across the page break into the next chapter, where he arrives in Chicago. In this image, we can perceive the second path to narrative closure, as Layton's name enacts the main concern of the book on the metamedial level. The first step to effectively end the gloomy history of frustrated ambition, Layton's signature suggests, lies in the encounter of pen and paper. The final fulfillment, then, cannot be reached on the diegetic level.

The book itself becomes the destination of the Spivet family. Its final form relies on the collective act of authorship, as performed by T.S. and his mother. Even the idiosyncratic layout—two-thirds text, one-third illustrative margin—has its origin in the interplay of these two authors. Early on, during his reading of Clair's notebook, T.S. draws several stranded sea creatures to visualize a scene at Woods Hole harbor. Below the image, he comments, "Without knowing what I was doing, I found myself drawing a little illustration in the margin of her notebook. I know, I know—it was terrible. This was someone else's property. But I couldn't help myself" (149). The visual properties of the EOE notebook hereby become the first draft for the final layout of Larsen's book. A little while later, T.S. even finds a brief marginal note penned by his mother, stating, "T.S. will illustrate?" (152). This dialogue on the leaves of the notebook represents the most intimate conversation between mother and child in the entire book.

Readers can witness the repetition of Emma's spontaneous outburst "I should like to write ten volumes someday" almost 150 years later, as T.S. prepares himself for a reading session with the EOE notebook during his train ride: "I sat down at the little table and set up my workstation. As we traveled across Wyoming and then into Nebraska, I entered Emma's world and when I was moved to do so, I drew pictures next to my mother's text. Someday, we could make a book together" (181). Pivoting from this declaration of intent, we might speculate about the genesis of the final text. As T.S. repeatedly professes his aversion to literary prose and always prefers mapping to writing, it appears plausible to presume that his mother eventually becomes the ghostwriter who records T.S.'s oral account. Finally, Larsen's novel takes on its full artifactual meaning. Within an extended, medial diegesis, the presence of the book signifies the published embodiment of the curious relationship between mother and son, and between science and literature. Instead of passively representing it, *The Selected Works of T.S. Spivet* actively creates a fictional American life world.

In a way, Larsen's book is a small literary echo of the founding documents of the American nation. As Frank Kelleter points out, through the documents of the Declaration of Independence and the Constitution, the American nation is "*self-made*, not in the congratulatory sense of having freed itself from outside influences but in the sense of conjuring up its own presence" (106). The documents themselves figure strongly in this process, as they perform their intent already by their sheer existence; this discursive agency contributes to the quasi-sacred status the printed Declaration has in the American national consciousness. The Continental Congress had also been acutely aware of the material dimension of the Declaration that was supposed to create a nation out of nothing, commissioning a handcrafted manuscript version on parchment weeks after the broadsides had been printed. The same recursive performativity also figures throughout the history of American literature, which according to Kelleter "has always been concerned with the conditions of its own possibility: with the power of words and narratives to create what they describe" (101).

Admittedly, the comparison between Larsen's novel and Jefferson's text seems far-fetched. Yet, ever so subtly, the novel evokes this connection—not by telling it, but by showing it visually. The font of the EOE notebook is Caslon, a British Old Style typeface commonly used up to the mid-nineteenth century. Larsen and designer Ben Gibson modified the Caslon characters to emulate movable type printing (see fig. 8). The letters contain minuscule white specks that suggest the imperfections that may result from inferior lead types or flaws in the printing process. This typographic design subtly brings Clair's handwriting into chronological proximity to the story that commences with Emma Osterville's birth in 1845. It also references the Caslon typography of the famous Dunlap broadside of the Declaration of Independence. The Philadelphia printer John Dunlap had printed about 200 of these

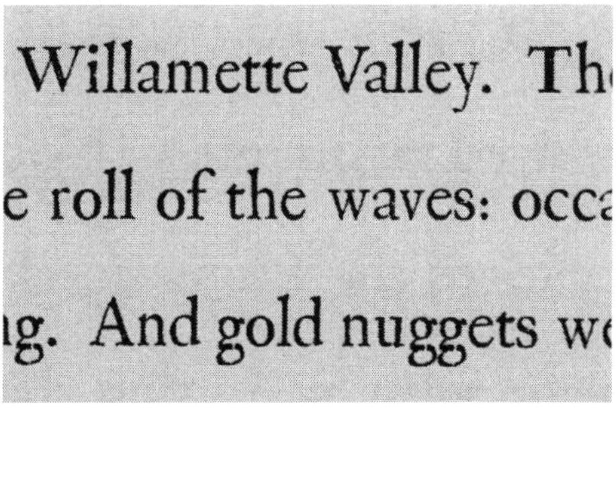

Fig. 8. Detail from Reif Larsen, *The Selected Works of T.S. Spivet* (New York: Penguin, 2009), p. 147. Courtesy of the Penguin Press, a division of Penguin Group (USA) LLC. Photograph by Alexander Starre.

broadsides on the night of July 4, 1776. The little imperfections that designer Ben Gibson added to the digital Caslon type correspond to those on Dunlap's broadside.[15] By extending the conjuring power of words to its material aura, Larsen's novel inscribes itself into the national imaginary of the United States. The mass-produced artifact of T.S. Spivet's *Selected Works* memorializes Layton's evanescent presence and the Spivets' tacit contribution to American cultural history. With its metamedial devices, the book finally includes the communicative tools for the reflexive description of this whole process.

## ¶ Bibliophiles 2.0

By framing Kidd, Plascencia, and Larsen as literary bibliographers, this chapter has concentrated on narrative, aesthetics, and literary style. But just as novels are hybrid forms—simultaneously works of art and commodities—so are authors bound to the logic and logistics of the marketplace. In the paper fetish endorsed in *The People of Paper* and the pedagogic impulse behind *The Cheese Monkeys*, book fictions depict more than ideas; they feed into ideologies. These novels update the reification of beauty and truth within the pages of a book that had informed earlier waves of bibliophilia. In the United States, a peculiar fashion of fine printing emerged in the interwar years of the 1920s, importing the production ideology of British Arts and Crafts, as exemplified in William Morris's Kelmscott Press. According to Megan L. Benton, however, the transatlantic passage of this ideology added an important factor to the equation: commercialism (*Beauty* 46). In the United States, fine printers did not see themselves as operating outside the market, but at its aesthetic helm, where they wanted to lead by example and inspire their colleagues to improve the quality of mass-market publishing. Springing from elitist gentlemen clubs and catering only to a small, but wealthy part of the reading public, American fine printing "revitalized a growing sense of hierarchy—of status and expense, as well as material quality and purpose—in the postwar world of books" (47). Within the creative networks of young writers I have described so far, metamedial writing carries similar ideological potential.

While merely implied in literary texts and graphic design, this ideology comes to the fore in the self-theorizations that writers circulate through public appearances, interviews, or on their own Web sites. In his *Nashville Review* interview Salvador Plascencia complained about the dominance of the "standard formatted book," which consists of "a single column of prose spread over 500 pages" (M. Baker). He observes that the publishing houses have pushed literary production ever further into this standardized format, promising frictionless delivery in various forms—hardback, paperback, e-book. "Somewhere along the evolutionary line of the novel," he contends, "we opted for faster flips of the page over a more varied typography. We opted for velocity." Like Plascencia, Reif Larsen sees hypertext and e-books as a threat to literary quality. He holds that the dilemma of screen-based hypertext lies in its structural opposition to authorial control. By granting the reader more control, hypertext fictions intentionally allow their precarious communicative mechanics to degenerate into chaos. In his work, Larsen argues, he aims for a balance between "volition and orchestration" ("Crying" 9). A literary text that achieves this balance invites the reader to become active while retaining a sense of willing subjugation under the storytelling architecture. Rejecting the mechanics of the mass market while profiting from its proceeds, both writers underline the inverse relationship between monetary and cultural capital in the literary field.

So, do contemporary writer-designers merely continue the conflicted heritage of cultural distinction exemplified by American fine printing? In one important sense they do, as they counter mass-production with a call for control. The outset of the fine printing craze of the 1920s occurred in a rapidly expanding book market, which sacrificed quality for quantity, resulting in the "blatantly commercial design" of mass-produced books (Benton, *Beauty* 27). Typographers and book designers such as William Addison Dwiggins, Bruce Rogers, and Daniel Berkeley Updike attempted to rein in these excesses and regain control over the look and feel of books.[16] Beyond its origin in a time of drastic technological change, however, contemporary metamedial literature has little in common with fine printing and traditional bibliophilia. For the early-twentieth-century bibliophiles, finely printed books quickly became a means to an end, a material embodiment of their own desired cultural distinction. As such, Benton argues, "fine books were produced and purchased primarily as complex (if sometimes clichéd or incoherent) material symbols of bookness; their textual function was secondary" (*Beauty* 241). The culture of fine printing is a culture of the edition; the most notable achievements in this arena are elaborate and pricey reeditions of the classics.[17] Such fine printings unabashedly fetishize the commodity, something we can still see in the output of the Folio Society or in the current classics lineup of Penguin. Here, the well-known (and affordable) "Penguin Classics" imprint has recently been complemented by such new (and expensive) formats as "Penguin Ink," "Penguin Threads," "Graphic Deluxe Editions," and "Penguin Drop Caps." The refined consumer can now pick and choose a Jane Austen novel in several of these formats.

In the novels of contemporary writer-designers, print culture evolves from crafted editions to multifaceted artworks. Within the emergent bibliophile ideology, a lingering book fetish has merged with a neo-modernist fixation on authenticity, albeit with a twist. Where modernist writing searched for a more immediate relationship between language and the experience of the individual subject, the metamedial impulse attempts to authenticate literary expression through its material form. Accordingly, Plascencia envisions a fusion of writing and design that would make paper "the site of the novel, not just some container" (M. Baker). This struggle for authenticity simultaneously figures as a struggle for authorization. Almost a century ago, the relationship between fine printers and literary authors was often antagonistic. If writers cared for the look of their books at all, they often found fault with it and quarreled with designers (Benton, *Beauty* 141). In the present, writers have started to either learn the tools of the trade themselves or to enlist professional designers as deputies. This is another indicator of the literary dialects of digitization: just as new tertiary media arise that promise unprecedented fidelity for recording and reproducing "real" experience, secondary media of inscription gain a distinctive cachet of authentic expression.

Perhaps graphic design may turn out to be the missing link between medium and content, a link that would prove the insufficiency of Jenkins's notion of fluid convergence between media systems. William Addison Dwiggins, influential designer and public spokesman at Knopf from the late 1920s, defined medial embodiment as a founding concern of all graphic design in his pioneering book *Layout in Advertising* (1928): "This difference of mental attitude—the difference between thinking about paper merely as a background upon which one draws or paints or prints, and thinking about it as an active element of design—is radical and important. It is a touchstone by which you can determine whether or not you are properly a printing designer" (5). From the inception of his publishing house, Alfred A. Knopf had a strong investment in book design, attempting to reconcile the electrified printing plant with the aesthetic tenets of fine printing. In their creative appropriations of dust jackets and typography, Knopf designers Barbara deWilde, Chip Kidd, and Peter Mendelsund have continued Dwiggins's ethos—with radically improved tools. Most of Dwiggins's writings have sunken into obscurity because they appeared in out-of-the way places like typophile journals or limited editions by small presses. The writer-designers of the present post paratextual essays, pictures, and videos to their personal Web sites or publisher's blogs, attempting to guide readers toward appreciating design, materiality, and mass-produced craft.

Even though the specific interpersonal dynamics among authors, designers, and editors at Knopf and other firms are well beyond the scope of this book, I would suggest that editorial policies may foster the work of medially sensitive authors. It is no coincidence, then, that Mark Z. Danielewski's works have been and continue to be published under the Pantheon imprint, whose list also carries graphic novels. While Danielewski's strong author persona disavows any external influence, his relationship to Pantheon critically informs the manufacture, design, and distribution of his work. The somewhat elusive but not less pronounced house style at Knopf performs important cultural work in its own right. Modern literature has always sprung from a complex media ecology, and it still does. Since its emergence a century ago, graphic design has taught us that visuality is only one segment of communication. Embodied literature enacts medial differentiation, not transmedia convergence.

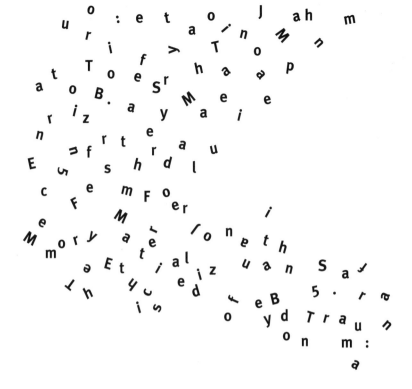

# 5. Beyond Trauma:
# The Ethics of Materialized Memory in Jonathan Safran Foer

WITH HIS BEST-SELLING DEBUT *Everything Is Illuminated* (2002) and his follow-up novel *Extremely Loud & Incredibly Close* (2005), Jonathan Safran Foer ranks as the most widely read author among the group of novelists discussed so far. Both of his novels have been adapted into successful films, further increasing the influence of his storytelling in American culture. Following his two best sellers, Foer published the experimental book *Tree of Codes* with the London-based publishing start-up Visual Editions in 2010. *Tree of Codes* takes the form of a bibliographic sculpture, consisting of roughly 130 die-cut sheets of paper. Foer used the text of *The Street of Crocodiles* (1934/1963), a collection of short stories by the Polish writer Bruno Schulz, to carve a new narrative out of its pages. The back cover of Foer's modified edition features an endorsement by the Danish artist Olafur Eliasson. In this brief snippet of text, Eliasson ponders the mediality of books and the embodied act of reading. In the end, he credits Foer for creating a timely aesthetic object: "In our world of screens, he welds narrative, materiality, and our reading experience into a book that remembers it actually has a body" (*Tree*, back cover).

As a radical experiment in bibliographic form, one might be tempted to perceive *Tree of Codes* as a significant departure from Foer's unconventional but accessible earlier novels. Conversely, I contend that this book sculpture merely foregrounds and intensifies a unifying theme underlying both his 9/11 novel and his fictionalized memoir of Holocaust remembrance. A literary author's cumulative oeuvre takes on new meanings with the publication of each subsequent text. This evolutionary process is never entirely prospective; new publications also do retrospective cultural work, as they build upon and renegotiate the impact of their predecessors. From such a retrospective angle, Jonathan Safran Foer appears to have followed a thematic thread that falls in line with the works discussed in the previous chapters. With profound attentiveness to his preferred artistic medium, Foer writes books that contain their own self-descriptions. Instead of being mere publishing accidentals, such entities as paper, inscription, and typography become cardinal points within his narratives.

As we have seen, the concept of metamedia helps to reframe recent developments in the American magazine scene, in experimental literature, and in the realist novel as systemic reactions to media change. This final chapter exemplifies how medial close reading helps us unearth a common denominator in the oeuvre of a best-selling novelist. Rather than pigeonholing Foer's novels into the respective genres of "Holocaust literature" and "9/11 literature," we may recognize his work as a series of meditations on bibliography, memory, and the world-creating function of literature. Such a reading is neither more accurate nor "better" than other interpretations that currently circulate. Reading Foer's three main fictional works as a series, I merely wish to shift perspectives. As discussed above, evolutionary communicative processes may be thought to occur as oscillations between variety and redundancy. Within their compositional and imaginative variety, Foer's works stage and restage a recurrent theme: the active role of books within the life-worlds of historically and geographically diverse people. For many postwar writers, the mass-manufactured final product of the book must have seemed like one of the most redundant aspects of their work. The new generation of tech-savvy American authors, however, has noticed the unlikely network of technological infrastructures and human activity that is necessary for book-based literature to emerge. As Foer tests out both the standard procedures of bookmaking and its innovative possibilities, the ethical import of his oeuvre lies not only in the content of his engaging narratives. Foer also tackles ethics at the level of material form, showing that to preserve memories always entails making media. "What remains of people," as Friedrich A. Kittler writes, "is what media can store and communicate" (*Gramophone* xl). Foer's books are books of the dead—but extremely lively ones.

## ¶ Tactile Typefaces

Before engaging with Foer's semiautobiographical debut novel, I wish to follow a minor intertextual path that diverges from this work. In *Everything Is Illuminated*, the author clones himself in the character Jonathan Safran Foer, a young writer searching the Ukrainian countryside for traces of his family history. His ancestral ties to the Jewish shtetl Trachimbrod inspire Jonathan to rewrite the town's history as a folkloric tale stretching back into the eighteenth century. Seven generations prior, Jonathan imagines, the roughly three hundred residents of the shtetl regularly convened in the street for heated debates on current events and other contentious matters. They argued about anything from "Polish identity" to the question of whether or not "to plug, finally, the bagel's hole" (12). Rounding up this hilarious portrayal of public disputes, Foer mentions one final issue that unsettled many Trachimbrodians: "[T]here had been the cruel and comic debate over the question of typesetting" (12). As compared to Polishness and the shape of a bagel, typesetting makes for a rather odd topic of town-wide deliberation. But in the fictional cosmos of Trachimbrod, forms of inscription stimulate disputes as reliably as anything else. The "question of typesetting" provides an intertextual link between *Everything Is Illuminated* and a piece of short fiction Foer published in the same year in the British newspaper *The Guardian*.

The story "About the Typefaces Not Used in This Edition" pretends to be an inverted "Note on the Type," as included by some publishers in the back matter of their books. Instead of explaining the aesthetic choice of a specific font, however, this extended notice describes eight typefaces that were not used in the final layout of a fictional book. Foer neither gives the title of this ominous publication, nor does he specify which font was used in the final layout. A few particulars can be grasped from the text, however. Presumably, the book that carries this typographic note contains a romantic novel, the love story of Henry and Sophy. Henry appears to die at the tragic end, right after a final conversation with his brother. Foer's typographic notice also lists the word count of the whole book, which at 237,983 words must be quite a tome. Aside from these scarce bits of information, readers learn nothing about the overall book. The story thus challenges the entrenched hierarchy of text and paratext; it is a paratext whose text has disappeared. Furthermore, "About the Typefaces" charts the contingent territory of possible choices that have been overturned in the design process of an artifact.

Foer imagines eight bizarre fonts, all of which approach the mediality of signification from a different angle. The fonts fall into three categories: bibliographic, screen-based, and corporeal. The two bibliographic typefaces provide peculiar aesthetic solutions for non-verbal communication. "Elena, 10 point" reifies language usage patterns and maps the frequency of word use: "The more a word is used, the more it crumbles and fades—the harder it becomes to see. By the end of this book, utilitarian words like *the*, *a* and *was* would have been lost on the white page" (42). Elena thus foregrounds little-used words at the expense of more common expressions. The phrase "this book" refers to the unnamed romance of Henry and Sophy; yet, the expression is double coded. Foer informs us that a typographer named Leopold Shunt created the typeface on the night his wife died. His font design links the ontological levels of the book's narrative with his real life. Letters formatted in his font slowly perish, just as his wife gradually fades away. Ultimately, the unnamed narrator fuses reader, book, and character by envisioning the physical form of the mise-en-abymic book. The peculiar typographic note is supposed to exist on the endpapers of a romantic novel. To touch this place in the book—or to imagine touching it—means to engage in a structural and tactile imitation of the typographer's gestures, who comforts his wife on her deathbed.

Second in line after the degenerating font Elena is "Tactil, Variable point," which does not represent semantic structures. Instead, the digital font Tactil reacts to the pressure applied to the keys on the keyboard when writing a text. As Foer informs us, the artist who invented this type—a Basque woman named Clara Sevillo—thought of the keyboard as a recording mechanism similar to the phonograph, registering what Kittler calls the "serial data flows" of real-life experience (*Gramophone* 10). The only difference lies in the type of data. While the phonograph records sound, the Tactil font is designed to transcribe the writer's emotions. However, it does not stop there. Tactil also notices the slightest movements of air that pass across the keys, even when no one is present. The narrator enchants the computer keyboard into an infinitely susceptible recording mechanism that can transcribe much of the complex data floating around in its environment. For the fictional book within Foer's story, the Tactil font still proved inadequate. The author of this book—another unnamed entity, possibly Foer's authorial persona—aimed for the same representational largesse that Reif Larsen's protagonist T.S. Spivet claims for his grand mapmaking project. If printed in Tactil, the fictional world would be represented by printed words on paper that correspond exactly to the size of their real world referents.

Foer's second group of fonts directly engages with the discourse of flexible digital information flows in and between devices and storage media. "Trans-1," "Trans-2," and "Trans-3" are screen-only fonts that rely on computation for their visual display. Each of these fonts refreshes constantly according to a preprogrammed algorithm. The first two versions attempt to "illuminate the richness of language" (42) by exchanging words for their synonyms (Trans-1) or their antonyms

(Trans-2). The narrator criticizes these two fonts because they do not reveal the connectedness of linguistic patterns, as their creator had hoped, but instead foreground only communicative disruptions and impasses. Even Trans-3, the ultimate attempt at a screen font, falls short of its goal. This font continually refreshes the same words without changing them. Ever-refreshing screen textuality, he implies, contains an inherent claim for newness. The dominant American discourse on new media usually presents screens as fast and books as slow. Trans-3 embraces this notion and tries to create the definitive form of flickering signifiers that can catch up with the present moment. The narrator skeptically remarks that the act of reading will always be situated in time and will therefore always immediately fall back into the past and that any given phrase "will never mean what it does, but what it did" (43).

The final set of fonts pushes the idea of typographic representations further into the corporeal realm. "Aviary, Variable Point" has to be tattooed on a flock of birds, following the hierarchy and the order of the flock in flight. The finished book will then reveal itself in the sky, but only in the ideal constellation of all birds. This outrageous scheme is reminiscent of Shelley Jackson's experimental tattoo project, Skin, as discussed in Chapter 2. With his last font, Foer collapses the ontological levels of his story completely. The narrator claims that the evolution of pictorial representation—from symbols, to sketches, to photographs, to sculpture—will ultimately bring forth the representation of a story in the font "Real Time, Real World, To Scale." Yet, the publishers of Henry and Sophy's romance felt that the aesthetic experience would suffer, as readers would certainly confuse fiction and reality.

In the end, "About the Typefaces" deploys yet another self-referential complication: we are told that the fictional romance novel starts with the word "Elena" and ends with "free." Foer's short story itself in fact begins and ends with just these words. The reversed typographic note at first pretends to explain elements of a text that do not turn up in its final edition. Ultimately, however, the typographic note is the only thing that actually exists. While this last twist delivers the final blow to the precarious narrative construction, "About the Typefaces" figures as much more than a creative exercise in recursive metafiction. Foer here presents a humorous, yet ultimately sincere, poetological essay on the representational craft of writing. In the process, he upsets the hierarchies of text and paratext, and of bibliographical substantives and accidentals. From this angle, choosing the typographic format and the medial carrier for a literary work of art is never a neutral act.

## ¶ The Illuminated Typescript

Reading "About the Typefaces" as a companion piece to the novel *Everything Is Illuminated* also provides us with a specific interpretive perspective for the latter text. In her perceptive analysis, Mita Banerjee has recently examined the novel's precarious balancing of the virtual and the real with regard to sites of memory. However, the crucial communicative function of Foer's book at the time of its publication is only partially connected with its representation of geographic and architectural sites of memory and heritage, as Banerjee holds (161). In the autopoiesis of American literature, the novel's function lies less in depicting sites of cultural memory than in presenting the book medium itself as a site of just such memory. From an anthropocentric view, one can summarize the plot of the book as Banerjee does: "Jonathan, an American Jew, goes on a 'heritage tour' to the Ukrainian [sic] to find Augustine, the woman who saved his grandfather from the Nazis. He is accompanied by Alex, a young Ukrainian, and his grandfather, also named Alex" (149–50). Once we add the agency of objects into this ensemble of subjects, the summary will read differently. Here, *Everything Is Illuminated* becomes a reflexive personal account of recording past events in written form. The narrative tracks the intergenerational history of collective documents such as *The Book of Antecedents* and *The Book of Recurrent Dreams*. These artifacts uphold communicative networks both of communal and individual memories that sustain the small trans-generational community of the Jewish shtetl Trachimbrod from 1791 to 1941. Faced with the impossibility of representing the real-life atrocities of the Holocaust, Jonathan Safran Foer relates the extinction of his supposed ancestral home via the desecration and destruction of primary documents.

"It was March 18, 1791, when Trachim B's double-axle wagon either did or did not pin him against the bottom of the Brod River" (8). Thus begins the draft of the novel written by the character Jonathan. With this ambiguous beginning—"did or did not"—Jonathan erects a shaky foundation for his fictionalized account of Trachimbrod. Deeply steeped in myth, folklore, and the genre of magical realism, the novel relegates authenticity and historical accuracy to the backseat from the very beginning. From the waters of the Brod River, the author's ancestor Brod B emerges as an immaculate baby. This miracle becomes the creation myth for the whole town, a legend soon celebrated in an annual festival, the Trachimday. The inexplicable origin of the baby nevertheless poses a problem for the town's written history. The "Well-Regarded Rabbi" decides against submitting an "official interpretation of her origins" for inclusion in The Book of Antecedents (16). As we can infer, the ongoing usage and production guidelines for this specific town record are well in place on the date chosen as the start of Jonathan's story.

The town's history, therefore, extends much farther back than the dates indicate. As readers later learn, a predecessor of the "Well-Regarded Rabbi"—the "Venerable Rabbi"—had written the ur-text roughly two centuries before. Jonathan explains the book's tangled history at some length: "The Book of Antecedents began as a record of major events: battles and treaties, famines, seismic occurrences, the beginnings and ends of political regimes" (196). Soon after its inception, however, the archive of Trachimbrod takes on a hybrid form. Initially dedicated to essential public information, the inhabitants appropriate the foundational book for their own purposes. In subsequent editions, they start to include "family records, portraits, important documents and personal journals," eventually recording even the most tedious details of town life (196). On the ensuing fifteen pages, Jonathan transcribes entries from the book that collectively make up a chaotic assortment of brief anecdotes and definitions.

A particularly telling cluster of entries concerns the town's relationship to art. The headword "Art" provides a curious definition: "Art is that thing having to do only with itself—the product of a successful attempt to make a work of art" (202). This constructivist explanation of art closely resembles Luhmann's functional definition.[1] The Book of Antecedents immediately points to the aporia resulting from this recursive formula. Given that all cultural creations inevitably have external purposes such as money, fame, or education, the authors claim that "there are no examples of art, nor good reasons to think that it will ever exist" (202). Nevertheless, the impossibility of total autonomy does not seem to worry artists much: "And yet we continue to write, paint, sculpt, and compose. Is this foolish of us?" (202). In and through The Book of Antecedents, the Jewish shtetl Trachimbrod evolves as a tightly knit, literate community—a book culture in microform. Even though art itself appears to be beyond the reach of citizens, artistic creation still takes place as a self-referential set of practices carried out between authors and their medium. If art has to do "only with itself," Foer seems to imply, literature should constantly stay aware of what "itself" is. In Trachimbrod's idealized book culture, the value of literature fuses with its bibliographic form. It is a small wonder, then, that the debate on typesetting—possibly connected to a new edition of The Book of Antecedents—becomes a matter of supreme importance. The citizens' convoluted records constitute a site of memory in the ever-expanding book; altering the typographic form of this site would always also alter the memories themselves.

In several places, Jonathan emphasizes how the all-embracing book culture at Trachimbrod resembles a veritable cult. A section on pages 212–13 is a fitting emblem for this; it merely contains the phrase "We are writing . . ." reprinted dozens of times. Books demand to be written and books demand to be read. The citizens of Trachimbrod cannot help but obey these demands. Ever since the beginning of The Book of Antecedents, the Jewish town had been split into two sections, the Slouchers and the Uprighters. The rift between these groups also originated with a liturgical practice, during which half of the ancestors dropped their prayer book and the other half held on to it (17–18). The Slouchers, more secular and relaxed in their rites, left the synagogue to convene at varying locations from that point onward. As their liturgical book, the Slouchers later adopt *The Book of Antecedents*, which preserves the sermons and the ritual practices of preceding generations.

One weekly meeting acutely renders the full extent to which books figure as Latourian mediators in the community of Trachimbrod. The Sloucher service consists exclusively of sections devoted to either the reading or the writing of books (36–37). Their members have started a companion volume to *The Book of Antecedents* in which they record common dreams that occur in their congregation.[2] Alongside the history of empirical events, *The Book of Recurrent Dreams* endeavors to protect the imagined histories of Trachimbrod from oblivion. Through the authoritative format of the "heavy leather-bound book" (37), the members can fetishize the object, which also feeds into Trachimbrod's secular cult of the book. Even for Jonathan's grandfather Safran, books were more than delivery vehicles for texts. To him, they imply a reassuring sense of order. Accordingly, his ordering methodology for his little home library does not follow the subject matter of the book, the publication year, or the name of the author. Instead, he sorts his books by color. The external order radiates tranquility back into his mind and body: "His books were properly stacked, according to color. (He pulled one off the shelf, to have something to hold)" (236). As T.S. Spivet remarks in Larsen's novel, the ordering of books in one's private space is "an intimate thing" (*Selected* 153). In the routinized, sometimes ritualized, interaction with books, individual agency is dispersed across human subjects and carrier media—books write the residents of Trachimbrod, just as much as the residents write books.

For Jonathan's protagonist Brod, writing and reading are even more existential matters. With Brod, Foer anticipates Salvador Plascencia's characters Merced de Papel and Baby Nostradamus. For one, his text surrounds this woman with symbolic instances of reading and writing, suggesting that she is like a book herself. Also, Brod uses her imagination to penetrate book pages and arrive at prophetic visions of the future. Soon after she has mysteriously risen from the waters of the Brod River, the old man Yankel D adopts her. Lacking furniture, he improvises a cradle with a baking pan that he stuffs with newspaper. The newsprint leaves its marks on the baby's white skin, so that Yankel D can read her: "If it wasn't written on her, it wasn't important to him" (44). Yankel educates the little girl in literature, science, and mathematics, buying up all the books that he can get his hands on and spending excessive amounts of money on them. Brod is left to sort out the finances, which she achieves by returning many of the books and by founding a circulating library for the town—the Yankel and Brod Library—whose fees put bread on the odd pair's table. From the day of her birth, Brod weaves herself into the collective history of the town. She provides a mythic creation story, acts as namesake, and finally also lends her body as a receptacle for daily news of the town. Like Merced de Papel, she is a woman made of paper.

Jonathan's mythical story of Trachimbrod ends with the Nazi firebombing of the village on March 18, 1942. Tragically, this is also the town's annual "Trachimday," celebrating Brod's legendary rise from the waters of the river. In the midst of the festivities, Nazi planes unload their bombs onto the village. Most of the residents either die directly from the explosions or drown in the river, where hundreds of villagers seek shelter from the heat. For this passage, Jonathan makes use of the description of the events that an old woman named Lista related to him and his guide Alex during his trip to the Ukraine (184–86).[3] However, Jonathan also alters her narrative and invents new details. The most consequential change concerns the book of the Sloucher congregation. Jonathan writes that after locking all of the Jews into the synagogue and setting the building on fire, the Nazis threw random objects into the flames, including all volumes of *The Book of Recurrent Dreams*. During the haste of the raid, one of the pages falls out and comes to rest "like a veil on a child's burnt face" (272). Jonathan's narrative ends by reprinting the contents of this page in the typical column format used throughout for articles from *The Book of Recurrent Dreams*. The speaker of this entry turns out to be the superhuman presence of Brod, who describes in visceral detail how masses of villagers drown "in that river with my name" (272). In the waters, Jonathan's grandfather Safran loses his wife, Zosha, and their unborn baby. In Brod's dream, the death of

Zosha's baby completes the historical cycle that had begun with her own birth in 1791. Already under water, Zosha gives birth to the child, but the umbilical cord drags the little baby downward with her mother. Trachimbrod, Jonathan seems to suggest, will not see a second mythical creation after the Holocaust.

For all the human cruelty and the sacrilege the Nazis commit by having the surviving Jews spit at the Torah, the final image of the story is one of endurance and survival. A shred of the primary document survives long enough to be transcribed by the authorial persona, thus bearing archival testimony to the history of Trachimbrod. Other documents appear to persist as well. During one of her prophetic visions, Brod travels 140 years into the future to witness a domestic scene in which a young boy reads to a girl. This particular passage is set in 1943, after the mysterious picture was taken that shows Jonathan's grandfather with Augustine, the woman who supposedly saved his life. Through several indicators, we can assume that the boy in the scene is Jonathan's grandfather and the girl is Augustine. Like Plascencia's Baby Nostradamus, Brod can penetrate walls with her all-seeing gaze and watches Safran and Augustine reading: "And even from such a distance she can see that it is a copy of The Book of Antecedents from which he is reading to her" (89). An edition of this definitive record of Trachimbrod appears to have survived the 1942 Nazi raid.

Similarly, the book turns up in Alex's chronicle of the events that occurred during their search for Augustine in the Ukraine. Having shown her visitors several historical keepsakes from Trachimbrod, Lista gives Jonathan a storage box as a present. When Jonathan opens it, he finds an old book. Alex describes the wondrous object: "I moved the dust off of the cover. I had never previous witnessed a book similar to it. The writing was on both covers, and when I unclosed it, I saw that the writing was also on the insides of both covers, and, of course, on every page. It was as if there was not sufficient room in the book for the book" (224). The book also bears a title that Alex translates as The Book of Past Occurrences. He starts to translate a section from the Ukrainian, and readers will immediately notice that it is a slightly altered excerpt from the longer selection of *The Book of Antecedents* reprinted in an earlier chapter. While Foer's narrative immediately questions the accuracy of Alex's description, the overall effect remains: as long as the book survives, the town of Trachimbrod still exists as a collective memory.

Returning once more to Brod's vision of the boy reading to the girl, we now begin to understand the cryptic monologue of Jonathan's superhuman ancestral mother figure:

> His mouth, her ears. His eyes, his mouth, her ears. The hand of the scribe, the boy's eyes, his mouth, the girl's ears. She traces the causal string back, to the face of the scribe's inspiration, and the lips of the lover and palms of the parents of the scribe's inspiration, and their lovers' lips and parents' palms and neighbors' knees and enemies, and the lovers of their lovers, parents of their parents, neighbors of their neighbors, enemies of their enemies, until she convinces herself that it is not only the boy who is reading to the girl in that attic, but everyone reading to her, everyone who ever lived. (89)

Brod's imagination brings forth the specters of Trachimbrod's past to speak through the medium of the book and through the medium of Safran, Jonathan's grandfather. In Friedrich A. Kittler's media historiography, the advent of electric recording changes the storage function of printed documents so that "the realm of the dead has withdrawn from the books in which it resided for so long" (*Gramophone* 10). Brod and Foer rebel against the idea that the material book as a connective tissue between the living and the dead belongs to a historical paradise lost that can never be regained. From their perspective, embodiment is the key link between humans and their books. Through the asyndetic collocation of body organs ("His eyes, his mouth, her ears."), Foer foregrounds the immediate cohesion of bodily activity that unifies the writing and reading processes. These embodied actions provide a link between readers and (dead) authors, even after new recording apparatuses have been introduced.

This link is of course strongest when there are real traces of a unique inscription process. In Brod's imagination, scribes produced *The Book of*

*Antecedents*, not professional typesetters. The epiphanic reading scene, however, shows the constructivist component of embodied reading. The copy of the book in Safran's hands might well be a printed one and not a manuscript; after all, there had been a town debate on type-setting. Nevertheless, the aesthetic experience of the book nurtures Brod's vision of embodiment, as it protrudes from a medial replica of the original writing scene. In essence, Foer's book attempts to do the same: in its bibliographic shape, it provides the content and the form for active historicization during every individual reading experience. The blend of bibliographic and semiotic codes in *Everything Is Illuminated* forms the path to understand and to remember the lost book culture of Trachimbrod.

The illumination topos, finally, provides Foer's book with a guiding metaphor that resonates with the metamedial reading experience. Collado-Rodriguez argues that Foer uses the idea of illumination in a "poststructuralist sense," which subjects it to "the Derridean non-referential play of signifiers" (55). Therefore, the term "illumination" supposedly becomes a multipurpose signifier with "different meanings in line with diverse contexts in which it appears" (55). This interpre-tation seems hardly adequate, as even Collado-Rodriguez's own close readings of the text show. He aptly outlines how the term fluctuates be-tween the practical notion of lighting something or making something glow and the figurative sense of understanding or clarifying something. This simple double meaning of the term hardly qualifies it as an emblem of the post-structuralist agenda. In light of the book's overall aesthetic perspective, deconstructive terminology drastically misrepresents the function of illumination as Foer's guiding trope.

This suggestive trope only realizes its full creative potential when we add to it a third dimension. Foer consciously uses the term in its book-historical significance as referring to medieval manuscripts and other bibliographic artifacts that have been hand decorated with colors or gold. As a contemporary author, he also hints at the possibility of transporting aspects of illumination into the standardized manufac-turing process of mass-market books. Foer is not a nostalgic adherent to a lost art. Rather, he belongs to a small lineage of innovators who attempted to reconcile typesetting with illumination practices. The leading figure in this arena is once more William Morris, who employed professional artists as illuminators of his printed books (Ovenden 810). To reconcile pictorial illumination with the novelistic form, however, Foer rejects the notion of pure ornamentation. Instead, his manipulations of typography and page design contribute an essential level of signification to the fictional world.

As embellishment, illumination functions both in a figurative and in a concrete sense. Aside from referencing the visual decorations of a printed artifact, the term figuratively applies to the discursive embellishments of storytelling. While the historical practice of illumination foregrounds the mediality of texts, narrative embellishment forces readers to confront the inevitable effects of mediation. What does it mean, then, to claim, "everything is illuminated"? For one, Foer reformulates Hayden White's seminal thesis on the formative role of narrative structures in historiography. As White explains, any historical account written in prose will "emplot" a given set of events so as to render a causal chain in an intelligible form (7–11). Even scholarly historiographies therefore present a mediated version of the facts that is, in a way, embellished through its narrative form. On the textual level, the unreliable narrators Jonathan and Alex openly emplot their historical sources and further enhance the narrative by inventing new ones. Similarly, the ancestral citizens of Trachimbrod alter their personal histories into "thinly veiled memoirs" (Foer, Everything 201)—a direct allusion to Foer's own decision to fictionalize his journey to the Ukraine. None of this, however, calls into question the historical magnitude of the Holocaust. While the unceasing activity of writing and remembering will never fully explain the Shoa, it may still help present generations in continually confronting its incommensurability. For individual identity construction and sensemaking, the authenticity of memories sometimes matters less than the sheer act of remembering itself.

Beyond this, the claim that everything is illuminated also refers to the concrete practices of bookmaking in the present. Just as verbal representations of history are always already emplotted, material, textual artifacts are always already illuminated. They can never contain pure language, as writing down and setting in type inevitably transfer language into a different medial form. So, finally, there is no such thing as an unembellished book—every page is an iconic page.[4] Usually conceived of as either present or absent, bibliographic illumination thus becomes a matter of degree. With its anecdotes of manic chroniclers and illustrated diaries, *Everything Is Illuminated* contains promises of visual experimentation that the book itself never actually fulfills. The novel depicts the colorful life of Trachimbrod through the bottleneck of black-and-white typography. These aesthetic seeds of the illumination topos would however soon sprout in Foer's second novel.

## ¶ Ethics of the Page

*Extremely Loud & Incredibly Close* tells, yet again, the story of a book. The nine-year-old Oskar Schell records his life in a long-running scrapbook project after the traumatic loss of his father in the 9/11 attacks. Instead of the manic bibliophiles of Trachimbrod, Foer now ventriloquizes a young digital native who has a functional attitude to the medium of the paperbound diary. After finding a mysterious key in his father's closet, Oskar goes on a treasure hunt through New York City. In the scrapbook that he calls *Stuff That Happened to Me*, he collects "maps and drawings, pictures from magazines and newspapers and the Internet," all of which chronicle his pursuit of traces that his father left before he died (42).[5] In his ferocious determination to map his day-to-day experience and to understand his environment, the precocious boy resembles Larsen's T.S. Spivet.

An informational omnivore, Oskar casually uses Web interfaces and mobile technologies during his quest. Toward the end of the novel, he has become skeptical of paper-based storage media, as they purportedly fueled the collapse of the twin towers:

> I felt in the space between the bed and the wall, and found *Stuff That Happened to Me*. It was completely full. I was going to have to start a new volume soon. I read that it was the paper that kept the

towers burning. All of those notepads, and Xeroxes, and printed e-mails, and photographs of kids, and books, and dollar bills in wallets, and documents in files . . . all of them were fuel. Maybe if we lived in a paperless society, which lots of scientists say we'll probably live in one day soon, Dad would still be alive. Maybe I shouldn't start a new volume. (325)

While Oskar spends little thought on the material value of his personal diary, the position of the implied author at this late point in the book differs considerably. Jonathan Safran Foer deliberately frames his first novels as literary metamedia. Both books enforce second-order observation on the medial processes of writing and reading. *Everything Is Illuminated* and *Extremely Loud & Incredibly Close* are foremost documents that incorporate other documents. This transposition onto a higher plane of observation crucially figures in the novel's aesthetic impact.

Foer's 9/11 novel has sparked an extensive array of scholarly essays and book chapters. The majority of these readings tap into a distinctive branch of research that fuses psychological and medical theories of trauma with literary narratives of 9/11. In one of these essays, Sien Uytterschout makes a seemingly obvious statement on Foer's book, which recurs in similar form in several other studies: "With his latest novel, *Extremely Loud & Incredibly Close*, Jonathan Safran Foer has ventured to represent the traumatic events of September 11" (61). Similarly, Ilka Saal asks whether or not Foer's "trauma narrative" fosters "narrative access to one's own trauma" (463, 455). Philippe Codde sets out to tackle "the question of the accuracy and suitability of Foer's novels as traumatic histories" (241). Codde appears to enlist the actual 9/11 victims as the ultimate reference point for Foer's text: *Extremely Loud & Incredibly Close* can only succeed as a literary work, he implies, if it presents an accurate and suitable rendition of the survivors' real-life experience. Saal likewise predicates her evaluation of Foer's novel on its ability to initiate "empathetic understanding" (455) for actual 9/11 trauma victims in the reader.

Seen as a metamedium, however, the novel refuses to be pinned to mimetic renderings of traumatization. I concur with S. Todd Atchison, who approaches Oskar Schell's story as an ensemble of metatexts that fosters "a self-conscious awareness of constructed realities" (67). Foer's second novel, much as his first one, correlates the conflicted bonds of a family with a complex network of primary documents. The stability and resistance of inscription media eventually overcomes the traumatic ruptures and representational impasses within the genealogy of the Schell family. Starting with a primal scene at the home of Oskar's great-grandfather, Foer constructs a continuous personal narrative—a literal paper trail—that eventually provides the traumatized boy with a renewed sense of identity.

Extremely Loud & Incredibly Close lacks a central narrative voice; instead, it tells the interweaving stories of Oskar and his grandparents in the first person. Whereas both grandparents relate their autobiographical anecdotes in epistolary form, Oskar appears to record the events directly in his scrapbook. The plot converges on the second anniversary of the 9/11 attacks in 2003, when several consequential things happen. For one, Oskar's grandfather, Thomas Schell Sr., composes a letter that is intended more or less directly for his grandson (262–86). As a young man, Thomas Sr. had survived the firebombing of Dresden, but lost his fiancée Anna, who was pregnant with their child. Years later in New York, Thomas Sr. encountered Anna's sister, Oskar's grandmother, and they subsequently married. After confronting the fact that he only married her as a substitute for Anna, Thomas Sr. ran away from his new life just as Oskar's grandmother was about to give birth to their son. Foer underscores the status of the grandmother as the stand-in for her dead sister by strictly excluding her proper name from the narrative. Anna's name, on the other hand, recurs frequently throughout Thomas Sr.'s letters. The grandfather resettled in Dresden and started writing letters to his son, all bearing the title "Why I'm not where you are." Eventually, he would write one every day from May 31, 1963 to the day of his son's death on September 11, 2001; almost all of them remain unsent. On the second 9/11 anniversary, however, Thomas Sr. sits down once more and composes a final letter, which takes a unique form, as discussed below. That same night, he and Oskar dig up Thomas Jr.'s grave, which contains nothing but an empty coffin. In a highly symbolic ceremony that Oskar does not fully comprehend at that moment, Thomas Sr. fills the empty coffin with his unsent letters.

Afterward, Thomas Sr. briefly revisits the grandmother's apartment before embarking to the airport. Once there, he cannot decide whether to depart or to stay. Oskar's grandmother quickly follows him. As she relates, she only takes "a suitcase with the typewriter and as much paper as would fit" (309). At the airport, she locates Thomas Sr. at the international terminal. They find a comfortable table, and since neither of them is able to decide what to do, the grandmother suggests that they stay at the airport. After all, she argues, they have everything they need at their disposal: "I told him, There are pay phones, so I could call Oskar and let him know I'm OK. And there are paper stores where you could buy daybooks and pens. There are places to eat. And money machines. And bathrooms. Even televisions" (312). This final scene at the end of the book links up with the grandmother's initial chapter. There, she begins writing to Oskar in the form of a letter. She dates the paper "12 September 2003" and starts as follows: "Dear Oskar, I am writing this to you from the airport. I have so much to say to you. I want to begin at the beginning, because that is what you deserve" (75). Only at the very end, however, will readers learn why she is at the airport.

The first letter the grandfather writes to his unborn son relates the story of how the traumatic experience of the Dresden firebombing took away his ability to speak. As substitute for speech, he uses "YES" and "NO" tattoos in the palms of his hands in combination with a notebook into which he scribbles what he wants to say: "I started carrying blank books like this one around, which I would fill with all the things I couldn't say . . . at the end of each day I would take the book to bed with me and read through the pages of my life" (17–18). For both the grandfather and the grandmother, writing proves to be an existential, but ultimately frustrating exercise. Thomas Sr. fills daybook after daybook with his manic inscriptions, without ever achieving a sense of completion. To the grandfather, these books are more than mere diaries. They are also his medium of interpersonal communication into which he

scribbles what he would ordinarily tell people with his voice. Throughout the book, the layout metamedially imitates this usage by rendering
little snippets of transcribed speech on otherwise empty pages.

The biggest shortcoming of writing for Thomas is the ever-encroach-
ing lack of space, be it in his daybooks or in the New York apartment
where he covers walls, floor, and ceilings with words and sentences.
His final letter renders this motif to astonishing effect (262–84). In
the beginning, the grandfather makes lavish use of the pages, yet as
his writing progresses toward the end of his daybook, he has to cram
more and more words onto every page. Panicked, Thomas Sr. constantly
interrupts the flow of his writing: "There won't be enough pages in this
book for me to tell you what I need to tell you, I could write smaller, I
could slice the pages down their edges to make two pages, I could write
over my own writing, but then what?" (276). Shortly before his tiny
letters become illegible, he cries out, "I want an infinitely blank book
and the rest of time" (281). The book's typography mimics the spatial
arrangement of his handwriting. Pages 282–84 appear as if various
layers of text have been printed on the surface of the book. In the end,
the grandfather's agitated writing erases itself in an incomprehensible
landscape of blackness (284).

Oskar's grandmother struggles with the writing of her own history
and ends up producing the mirror image of the grandfather's unfathom-
able blackness. At one point during the brief period they spend together
in New York in the late 1950s and early 60s, Thomas Sr. sets her up with
his old typewriter and encourages her to write in order to "relieve the
burden" (119) of her past. Hesitant at first, she quickly embraces the
new writing machine and soon spends most of her free time typing
away in her private room. Years later, she presents her husband with two
enormous stacks of typing paper. The grandfather is stunned to see the
mass of almost a thousand sheets. But his wife's "crummy" eyes (119)
have seemingly kept her from perceiving a crucial detail—the paper is
blank: "I picked up the pages and wandered through them, trying to
find the one on which she was born, her first love, when she last saw
her parents, and I was looking for Anna, too, I searched and searched,

I got a paper cut on my forefinger and bled a little flower onto the page on which I should have seen her kissing somebody, but this was all I saw" (120). This statement ends with a colon, after which readers are confronted with two-and-a-half empty pages. As the impact of these empty pages hits the grandfather, he can barely speak.

He recognizes that his own past actions, with which he intended to punish himself after Anna's death, have also deprived his wife of the means to express her own life. After his fiancée's death, he had pulled the ribbon out of the machine in an "act of revenge against the typewriter and against myself" (124). Thomas Sr. decides not to tell his wife that her writing has left no marks on the pages. He will stick to this tragic memory of failed communication for decades, yet readers of the novel soon learn another side to the story. Typing out long letters to Oskar at the airport, the grandmother finally confesses that her eyes had been good enough to notice the missing typewriter ribbon. She intentionally produced blank pages, pretending to write while only hitting the space bar "again and again and again" (176).

Both grandmother and grandfather attempt to hurt and manipulate each other by producing documents that stress absence and emptiness. For almost forty years, Thomas Sr. dispatches empty envelopes to his wife, envelopes that were supposed to carry letters for his son. At one point, Oskar accidentally discovers hundreds of these symbolic envelopes in his grandmother's closet: "They were tied together in bundles. I opened the next drawer down, and it was also filled with envelopes. So was the drawer underneath it. All of them were" (235). Oskar sees that they were all postmarked and mailed from Dresden, but to his disappointment, they are empty. Anna's death haunts both her sister's and her lover's life as a recurring absence. Anna had given the typewriter to Thomas Sr. shortly before her death in the firestorm. Consequently, the writing machine appears to solely produce stalled communications and noise. After the death of Oskar's father, however, the machine evolves from a Kittlerian "discursive machine gun" (*Gramophone* 191) that determines the actions of its operator into a flexible tool dependent on human agency. At the airport, the grandmother uses the typewriter to round out her letter to Oskar with a simple affirmation of her love for the little boy.

In the chronology of the plot, the scene of writing at the airport ends the book. The last chapter, however, belongs to Oskar, who relates the ceremony at the graveyard and finishes his story during the early morning hours of September 12, 2003. Lying in bed, he has the ingenious idea—discussed at length in almost all reviews and critical essays—to rearrange a series of photographs depicting one of the famous World Trade Center "falling men." In the rearranged order of a flip-book, which forms the last sixteen-page spread of the novel, the anonymous man appears to be soaring upward, suggesting "a retrieval of a lost pre-9/11 innocence" (Saal 472). As Saal points out, many reviews have castigated Foer for ending the novel with such a presumably melodramatic finale. Visions of undoing horrible tragedies do not automatically signal simplistic closure, as Billy Pilgrim's hallucinations of reversing the Dresden firebombing in Kurt Vonnegut's *Slaughterhouse-Five* show. Rachel Greenwald Smith calls the reversal of the falling man "disturbingly regressive" and charges Foer with ignoring the "larger geopolitical frame" of 9/11 in favor of "U.S.-centric values and experience" (157). Smith ignores that *Extremely Loud & Incredibly Close* features a historical plot that is much less concerned with the geopolitical context of the present than with the historical evolution of communication and memory. Her reading overlooks the entire backstory surrounding the letters written by Oskar's grandparents, most likely because these transcend the narrow genre boundaries of 9/11 literature.

In any case, the final flip-book pages are not the end of the diegesis. Saal too closely follows the classical conception of the book, which holds that the end of the story is contained within the covers and excludes the paratext. She holds, "It is Oskar's narrative, and his alone, that concludes the novel and, in this manner, also provides the overall narrative frame for Foer's exploration of trauma" (Saal 471). The grandmother's plan to call Oskar from the airport strongly suggests that she will either send him her long, typewritten letter or give it to him personally. This would trigger a cascade of follow-up events, pointing to an extratextual resolution. The finalized, material form of the 2005 Houghton Mifflin edition itself guarantees narrative closure. Readers are asked to assume that Oskar's grandmother, after finishing her letter, calls Oskar at his home. In all likelihood, Oskar and his mother will pick up grandmother and grandfather from their exile at the airport. Afterward, the nine-year-old will have the chance to read through his grandmother's writing, which would then lead him back to his father's grave once more. At long last, Oskar should then possess the full archive of his family's tragic history, so that he can collate the whole ensemble into the book *Extremely Loud & Incredibly Close*. Foer thus carefully inserts the resolution at the level of the medial diegesis. As a fully formed codex book, Oskar Schell's text at last closes the lid on a half-century of failed communication through manuscripts.

Foer's book also fills a symbolic hole within the diegesis and completes the narrative cycle by returning to a suggestive episode of bibliophile creation. Thomas Sr. frequently reminisces about the place where he and Anna made love for the first time, behind the shed of her father, who was a collector of books and a sophisticated art aficionado. With compassionate humor, the grandfather remembers his father-in-law, who killed himself shortly after the war: "literature was the only religion her father practiced, when a book fell on the floor he kissed it, when he was done with a book he tried to give it away to someone who would love it, and if he couldn't find a worthy recipient, he buried it" (114). Anna and her father clearly evoke Lista, the Holocaust survivor in *Everything Is Illuminated*, whose father would also have his children kiss every book that fell to the floor (185).

In *Extremely Loud & Incredibly Close*, the bibliophile ancestor spends his leisure hours reading in a miniature library housed in his shed. The walls of this shelter, however, finally succumb to the weight of the bookshelves and fall down. Anna's father takes the opportunity to improve the place with new shelves full of books that replace the outer walls. The paper walls shield the inside from the weather, with the books freezing during the winter and thawing in the spring. Thomas Sr. remembers: "He made a little salon of the space, carpets, two small couches, he loved to go out there in the evenings with a glass of whiskey and a pipe, and take down books and look through the wall at the center of the city. (126) Shortly before the young couple has sex, Thomas Sr. meets Simon Goldberg, a Jewish intellectual who will soon seek refuge from the Nazis in the shed. This scene encapsulates the idea of procreation—both in the bodily and the mental sense. As Oskar's paternal great-grandfather and Simon Goldberg conjure up possible futures inside, Anna and Thomas Sr. beget a child outside of the wall. World War II and the Holocaust will halt these creations on either side of the Cartesian divide between mind and body, eradicating both Goldberg's lofty predictions and Anna's embryo.

For Thomas Sr., Anna's father takes on superhuman proportions. With the grandfather's fledgling interest in sculpture and writing, the old bibliophile comes to epitomize everything he wants to be. Tragically, he soon has to witness how the deportation of Simon Goldberg to Westerbork transit camp breaks the old man. Thomas Sr. finds him "with his face in his hands" (209), indicating the onset of anguish that later drives him to suicide. The whole scene, however, possesses a unique bibliographic framing, as he has to peer through a hole in the paper wall:

> When I think back on that moment, I never see him with his face in his hands, I won't let myself see him that way, I see the book in my hands, it was an illustrated edition of Ovid's Metamorphosis [sic]. I used to look for the edition in the States, as if by finding it I could slide it back in the shed's wall, block the image of my hero's face in his hands, stop my life and history at that moment. (209–10)

As a concrete symbol for the trauma that imprisons both grandmother and grandfather, Foer employs the empty space a missing book leaves on a shelf. Essentially an exteriorized representation of the intellectual identity of Anna's family, the bookshed thus signifies stability, learning, and—as Simon Goldberg's sanctuary—interethnic tolerance. The void in the wall, left by the missing Ovid volume, foreshadows its collapse.

Returning to post-war Dresden after leaving Oskar's grandmother, Thomas Sr. revisits the symbolic site. While there, he pens a letter to his son, in which he relates—aside from the scene involving the Ovid book—the horrors and atrocities of the bombings that destroyed Dresden. This letter will turn out to be the only he ever actually sends to his son. The site has been transformed, much to the grandfather's delight: "I'm writing this from where your mother's father's shed used to stand, the shed is no longer here, no carpets cover no floors, no windows in no walls, everything has been replaced. This is a library now, that would have made your grandfather happy, as if all of his buried books were seeds, from each book came one hundred" (208). Unlike the lost Yankel and Brod Library at Trachimbrod, the rickety shed at Dresden was merely an overture to the erection of a much larger literary institution.

Sometime after 9/11, Thomas Sr. appears to run into Simon Goldberg again. Their chance meeting takes place in a bookstore on the Upper West Side, possibly while the grandfather is looking for the illustrated Ovid edition. Still unable to fill the void in the bookshelf, he receives some solace from the fact that Goldberg has survived the Nazi camps. Some of the most crucial scenes in *Extremely Loud & Incredibly Close* are therefore set in the typical localities of book culture: private collections, book stores, public libraries. Even its guiding motif—the communicative void—morphs into the tangible symbol of a missing codex. For Philippe Codde, this void remains empty: "Foer suggests, then, that the aporia at the heart of the traumatic experience can, indeed, only be filled with words to ease the pain (think of his own literary attempt to fill the void of Trachimbrod), but the words can never really capture or represent the traumatic past" (245–46). Neither Foer nor his novel will provide an adequate answer as to whether or not words can heal traumatic disorder. Instead, the text shows an acute awareness of its status as fiction. *Extremely Loud & Incredibly Close* is not the testimony of a 9/11 victim or a World War II survivor. Instead of proposing therapeutic solutions or ethical guidelines, it explores the role of communication and its media in the face of trauma.

Codde somewhat hastily assumes that Thomas Sr.'s struggle to replace the void on the bookshelf remains unsuccessful (248). During the pivotal scene, the grandfather remembers how he held on to the illustrated edition of Ovid. While reading the final Houghton Mifflin edition, the reader can deduce that Thomas Sr. does manage after all to recover, or rather replace, the missing volume that will fill the void in the bookshelf of his mind. In a recursive metamedial loop, this missing piece turns out to be the very artifact the reader is holding. The American Houghton Mifflin hardcover edition and subsequent Mariner paperback editions feature an iconic cover design by the British artist Jon Gray depicting two hands on the front and back. Each hand is inscribed in handwritten lettering with the book's title, the author's name, and other snippets of text. Uytterschout holds that these hands are radically different from Thomas Sr.'s hands as photographed in the book (68). Däwes also explicitly comments on the cover, arguing that it "introduces the novel's central topic: the fragile conjunction of communication and agency" (529). While Däwes reproduces the front cover within her essay, she analyzes it as a dislocated image. Yet, as I hope to have shown in the course of these chapters, medial close readings should pay attention to the placement of pictorial or verbal matter on the finite artifact. The hand on the front is only half of the complete design of the dust jacket.

As opposed to Uytterschout, I would argue that the jacket design does depict Thomas Sr.'s hands. His "yes" and "no" tattoos are not visible because the jacket shows the backsides, not the palms, of his hands, as they would look were he to hold the book (see fig. 9). Textual evidence also connects the cover to Thomas Sr., as he confirms in one of his letters that he frequently writes on his body during his manic states: "my arms are books, too" (132). Thus, the two iconic hands—only one of which turns up as a single image in clippings and reproductions on the Web—have a specific function on the cover of Foer's work. The designer Jon Gray has created the covers for all of Foer's major books; the sustained collaboration of the two underscores the deep integration of narrative and graphic design in the author's oeuvre. The narrative function of Gray's design dwindles when the image becomes divorced from its original placement. *Extremely Loud & Incredibly Close* ultimately fills the void it tears open. The illuminated book of Thomas Sr.'s life comes to replace the illustrated edition of the ancient Roman *Metamorphoses*. All instances of thwarted communication coalesce into a final

Fig. 9. Dust jacket of Jonathan Safran Foer, *Extremely Loud & Incredibly Close*
(Boston: Houghton Mifflin, 2005). Cover design by Jon Gray / Gray318.
Courtesy of the artist. Photograph by Harald Wenzel.

moment at which the central characters and the reader may declare in
unison, "I see the book in my hands."

With and through his first two novels, Jonathan Safran Foer sheds
light on the medial basis underlying networks of memory that stretch
across personal and national histories. He portrays written artifacts as
highly personal, but omnipresent entities that can spark communication, connect individuals across time and space, and store threads of
meaning. The systemic interrelation between operative closure and
communicative openness, as theorized by Niklas Luhmann, underlies
Foer's contribution to the uneasy literary heritage of modernism and
postmodernism. Material borders and limitations, formerly the antag-

onists of postmodernist writers and post-structuralist critics, become the creative catalyst of his metamedial novels. Foer's ethics of communication and memory embraces closure and material resistance; it is a second-order ethics that does not lay claim to the truth about trauma, politics, and history. All the more, these novels encourage the reader to perceive cultural memory as an embodied process that needs active engagement with texts and things to endure. Published in the early twenty-first century, the novels also aim to make visible a medium that has become an invisible object throughout mainstream American culture. To repeat Latour's dictum, "To be accounted for, objects have to enter into accounts" (79). Foer has produced two literary accounts that imbue intratextual books with agency to a degree where they stand at eye-level with the traditional anthropomorphic literary agents, the characters. Neither novel, however, announces this idea with great fanfare, and reviews were split evenly on the value of typographic "gimmicks" and pictorial flourishes.

## ¶ Vanishing Materiality

With *Tree of Codes*, published in 2010, Foer has given his media theory of the book a definitive shape that radiates backward across his entire oeuvre. In many ways, *Tree of Codes* is a prestige project corresponding to the trajectory of Foer's career. The book represents the philosophy of the McSweeney's publishing manifesto discussed in Chapter 2. The London-based publisher Visual Editions gave Foer full control over the project and utilized digital design tools, dispersed manufacturing, and online marketing, while aiming for only a small profit. In its experimental form, Foer's book sculpture fits well with the other early publications of Visual Editions. The publisher debuted in 2010 with a redesigned edition of the metamedial ur-text *The Life and Opinions of Tristram Shandy, Gentleman*. Enlisting the services of the visual design studio APFEL, the publisher's founders Anna Gerber and Britt Iversen reissued Laurence Sterne's text in a thoroughly polished form. The guiding color in the two-tone book is a glaringly neon orange that visually sets off the novel's nine volumes, its footnotes, and Sterne's excessive use of em-dashes.

The designers freely improvised on the famous design elements of the book—the marbled page, Yorick's black page, the inserted "Slawkenbergius's Tale"—while adding a number of unique features such as a page-spread that appears wet with tears. After *Tree of Codes*, Visual Editions published another redesigned version of an experimental classic, Marc Saporta's *Composition No. 1*. The loose-leaf collection of this text comes in a sturdy yellow box. The designers of this artifact have used flexible design algorithms to adorn the backside of each page with a unique cloud pattern derived from thousands of small letters.

The publisher's Web site, in sleek Web 2.0 format, outlines an aesthetic framework for what Gerber and Iversen call "visual writing." They define it as "writing that uses visual elements as an integral part of the writing itself. Visual elements can come in all shapes and guises: they could be crossed out words, or photographs, or die-cuts, or blank pages, or better yet something we haven't seen" ("Visual Writing"). In an accompanying photo gallery, the editors provide samples of this kind of writing, incorporating books by Mark Z. Danielewski, Dave Eggers, Jonathan Safran Foer, and B.S. Johnson. The publisher has not yet issued any original fiction, but it can still be said to form a British counterpart of McSweeney's. Gerber and Iversen actually surpass Eggers's self-conscious interest in book production, as the special Web sites for each of their books contain elaborate descriptions of the design and manufacturing process. Employing slide shows and YouTube videos, the digital presentation for *Tree of Codes* chronicles the collaboration with the Belgian printer Die Keure ("VE2"). One such video features commentary by the author and close-up shots of the die-cut pages. Beyond this, readers can find a full "Making Of," a three-and-a-half minute clip that depicts meticulous workers and imposing machinery in the Die Keure print shop. As Visual Editions depends on direct marketing through their Web site, such paratexts are closely interwoven with the primary artifact. Just as the playful pleasure of early *McSweeney's* issues rested in part with the production in Iceland, so the aura of Foer's book sculpture benefits from this filmed presentation of hypermodern bookmaking craft.

Where Foer's prior novels celebrated illumination and ornament, *Tree of Codes* is an exercise in reduction. The novelist uses die-cutting radically, excising about half of the surface of each page (see fig. 10). Picking up the book, readers will be surprised by its unexpected lightness. The outward design mimics a regular paperback book and thus subverts the standardized usage parameters that would lead the average reader to expect greater weight. Applying some pressure to the center of the book, one can indent the cover easily; the book feels hollow. The overall

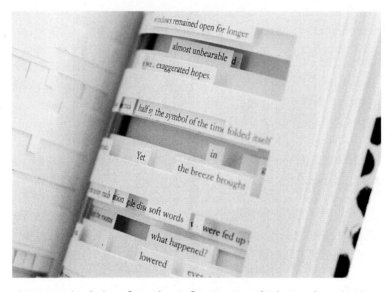

Fig. 10. Interior design of Jonathan Safran Foer, *Tree of Codes* (London: Visual Editions, 2010). Copyright © by Visual Editions. Cover design by Jon Gray, book design by Sara de Bondt Studio. Courtesy of Visual Editions.

reading experience reinforces this sensation of lightness and fragility. Each page feels simultaneously delicate and unwieldy, budging at the slightest touch, yet impeding fluent reading. To navigate through the text, the reader needs a piece of white paper as a tool to shield the few snippets of text from those on the ensuing pages, which peer through the large die-cut holes.

From the business angle, a die-cut in a book significantly drives up the cost per copy. Modifying individual pages with anything else but standard printing slows the production process as it disrupts the streamlined operations of high-volume printing, cutting, and binding machinery. As detailed above, Salvador Plascencia used a small number of die-cuts in The People of Paper, all of which functioned mimetically to represent the erasures performed by the author persona in the text. In an interview, Plascencia explains how this device figured within the editing process at McSweeney's: "The diecut seemed like the most reasonable solution. As far as the wider publishing culture goes, no, the majors won't invest the four cents it costs to punch a hole into a page" (M. Baker). As mentioned earlier, the follow-up paperback editions of The People of Paper graphically document how the economics of publishing figure into the look and feel of the novel, as die-cuts were replaced with ink splashes. In an anecdotal aside, Plascencia divulges a significant detail about Jonathan Safran Foer: "I know Safran Foer wanted diecuts in Extremely Loud & Incredibly Close and Houghton Mifflin wouldn't do it" (M. Baker). Again, we can see that Foer approaches the book not merely as a flat surface for visual material to be printed on. He is also deeply invested in the physical properties of pages and the tools of shaping and transforming them.

Oskar Schell's narrative does in fact contain an episode that could have been reinforced using die-cuts. As the result of his fascination with the physics of bombs and explosions, Oskar at one point gives a class presentation on the nuclear bombing of Hiroshima. Aside from using recorded first-hand testimony by a Japanese survivor, Oskar also relates several scientific oddities. He explains that the fierce light of the Hiroshima explosion burned dark materials more forcefully than light ones. During his research, he found out about pieces of paper strewn on the ground in Hiroshima, on which the black letters were "neatly burned out" (190) while the white paper remained intact. As an illustration for the class, he attempts to recreate such an artifact: "I became extremely curious about what that would look like, so I first tried to cut letters on my own, but my hands weren't good enough to do it, so I did some research, and I found a printer on Spring Street who specializes in die-cutting, and he said he could do it for two hundred fifty dollars" (190). The opposing recto page features an image of a falling cat against a black background. Instead of illustrating the class presentation, this image only refers to one of Oskar's tangential thoughts. In all likelihood, this is the place in which Foer would have inserted a die-cut representation of the perforated page. Ironically, Oskar himself describes the difficulties in finding a printing specialist for this type of job and paying the enormous price for it—something Houghton Mifflin obviously declined to do.

In *Tree of Codes*, die-cuts transcend the idea of a narrative device or an illustrative component. Here Foer reinterprets the work of someone else, thus acting less as a writer than a manipulator. In the domain of artists' books, this strategy has well-known precedents. One of the most widely known artist's books, Tom Phillips's A Humument (1980), represents a similar interest in the erasure and recompilation of a complete textual artifact.[6] Phillips used a little-known Victorian novel called A Human Document and painted over each page, leaving only a few words or lines of texts intact. Foer directly emulated Phillips's creation of the book's title, erasing letters from "The Street of Crocodiles" to form the words "Tree of Codes." In creating a unique painting of each page, Phillips unearths a wholly different plot from the base material of the original novel. Simultaneously, he illuminates each page with pictorial matter that resonates with the text. His technique works exceptionally well as the novel itself already contains the device of a fictional editor who merely collated journal entries and letters into a scrapbook (Hayles, *Writing* 78). Johanna Drucker usefully groups A Humument and several similar works under the rubric "transformed books" that reduce, restructure, or fragment "the presence of the original" (*Century* 109). Compared to A Humument, Foer's *Tree of Codes* stresses this "presence of the original" to a much higher degree, while revealing the work of the intervening artist only *ex negativo*. Aside from the excessive amount of die-cuts, the book's external form resembles a standard paperback volume. Where artist's books commonly attempt to surpass the raw material of the book via disruptive drawings, intricate folding techniques, or handcrafted customization, *Tree of Codes* submits itself entirely to the external format of a mass-produced book.

*Tree of Codes* does not exercise the mechanics of die-cutting on random material. Foer is an ardent admirer of Bruno Schulz, the provincial avant-garde writer and painter, whose entire literary oeuvre fits into a small volume. Foer in fact supplied the preface for the Penguin reedition of Schulz's fiction in 2008. In 1942, during the Nazi occupation of his hometown, a Gestapo officer shot Schulz in the street; the writer was 50 years old on the day of his death. Schulz's writings are steeped deeply in myth and symbolism. They transform his native town of Drohobycz into a place of cosmological fantasies in which the borders between the living and the dead or humans and nonhumans exist only to be transgressed from either side. In Schulz's symbolic repertoire, the trope of the book occupies a central position. As David A. Goldfarb explains, his frequent recourse to the semantic field of bibliography rotates around the central idea of the book, an idealized, sacred text that lends meaning to life. Goldfarb holds, "The image of The Booke in Schulz's mythic world is like a book of the Talmud—a large folio volume, worn from age and use, where a central text appears in large type at the center surrounded by layers upon layers of commentary and debate among great rabbis and their disciples over centuries, and a wide margin" (xix). This mythic quality can then assume an infinitely wide range of physical forms in everyday life, as Schulz's story "The Book" shows (Schulz 115–28). Here, the narrator searches for a book he saw during his childhood—not unlike Thomas Sr. in his quest for the illustrated Ovid. In the end, it turns out that the hallowed book is merely a full-color magazine that the family tore apart to wrap lunches.

The stories in *The Street of Crocodiles* all loosely cohere. The narrator, an unnamed little boy, relates family scenes sketched out against the background of the changing seasons. In the small spaces of the family home, the narrator's father engages in strange metamorphoses and psychic rituals while slowly descending into madness. Beyond the tightly knit group of protagonists—son, mother, father, and the maid

Adela—several brothers, uncles, store hands, and town characters drift in and out. Schulz depicts a central conflict between the father's entropic antics and Adela's attempts at sustaining order in the house. In its mythological enchantment with the book, The Street of Crocodiles is already a thoroughly metamedial source text. In one chapter, Schulz portrays the eponymous street as a modern shopping district appended to the otherwise sleepy, archaic village. To render this quarter of the town, Schulz constructs an allegory of papery illusion. Visitors to this area feel like they are merely "turning the pages of a prospectus" (Schulz 64); the windows resemble "the pages of a ledger" (64); the faces of the saleswomen appear as "gray parchment" (65); passersby are a "row of pale cutout paper figures" (69). In short, the modern commercialism of the Street of Crocodiles is just a "montage of illustrations cut out from last year's moldering newspapers" (72). In other episodes, Schulz freely extends this allegory, writing of "the enormous book of holidays" (3) and of tiresome days that resemble "an apocrypha, put secretly between the chapters of the great book of the year" (83). The Polish modernist exposes the precarious, medium-bound emergence of fictive worlds and mental constructs which may collapse at any given point. Showing himself as a true constructivist, Schulz questions the value of "reality" as a descriptive category that humans will never be able to penetrate as their minds can only observe this reality and not participate in it. In the mytho-poetic landscape of Drohobycz, stories thus merge with truth, and living organisms with dead matter. "Reality," Schulz's narrator concludes, "is as thin as paper and betrays with all its cracks its imitative character" (67).

The heavy symbolism and the vast metaphorical reservoir of The Street of Crocodiles allow Foer to use the die-cutting technique like a semiotic mechanism capable of variable paradigmatic selection. Throughout the book, he physically unhinges the respective donor and target in dozens of metaphors and recombines them. Words that seemed far apart in the narrative stream suddenly huddle close together. To give just one example: In the section "Tailor's Dummies," the narrator remembers the approach of a gray winter that slows down everything within his

house. In the original, the boy depicts the beds, which remained un-
made and disordered, assuming the look of "deep boats waiting to sail
into the dank and confusing labyrinths of some dark starless Venice"
(Schulz 26). Foer condenses parts of this sentence with fragments from
the entire paragraph into the following, "like boats waiting to sail into
the starless dawn, we were full of aimless endless darkness" (Tree 43).
Elsewhere, the same strategy of transferring the image from inanimate objects or animals onto the main characters turns the narrator's
father, a tailor, into "an enormous featherless dignity" (38). Explicitly
correlating the physical elimination of material from the book with the
deletion of narrative components, Foer exhumes a thoroughly altered,
truncated plot from The Street of Crocodiles. Here, the young narrator exclusively chronicles the strange relationship between his parents—all
other characters have been erased. The father's madness, which has
multiple, obscure causes in Schulz's version, now solely stems from
his unhealthy infatuation with his wife: "he would spend whole days
in bed, surrounded by Mother. he became almost insane with mother.
he was absorbed, lost, in an enormous shadow" (24–26). Throughout,
the narrator's voice wavers with the moods and longings of his parents.

Even though Tree of Codes succeeds mostly at the level of individual,
poetic phrases, a vague leitmotif pervades the text. On the whole, Foer
has cut references to tangible objects and to concrete phenomena from
the stories. The fragmented book thereby represents three characters
desperately trying to cope with the fleeting, transitory process of living.
In Schulz's version of the chapter "Tailors' Dummies," the father developed the heretic doctrine of a second creation, at the helm of which
he saw himself and his seamstresses. Manically raving about the "Second Demiurgy," during which biblical creation will reoccur in a more
materialist fashion, he distances himself from the original creator god:
"Demiurge, that great master and artist, made matter invisible, made it
disappear under the surface of life. We, on the contrary, love its creaking,
its resistance, its clumsiness" (Schulz 33). He also professes to love
discarded materials and trash and celebrates "the cheapness, shabbi-
ness, and inferiority of material" (33). In this whole section, the father

denounces metaphysics and proposes a thoroughly materialistic cosmogony. Foer, on the other hand, reduces the father's speech to a brief celebration of transience. In the beginning, he cuts part of a sentence out of its context to set the tone. "[W]hat relief it would be," the father exclaims, "for the world to lose some of its contents" (Tree 48). In this altered version, the material experience of the word matters little. The father celebrates the fleeting sense of the present as the essence of life and admits that "our creations will be temporary" (51). Accompanying the disappearance of materiality in the hollowed-out codex, the story mutates into a suitable parable on evanescence. Instead of fantasizing about "ectoplasm," "rarefied tissue," and "multifarious matter" (Schulz 39), the father chases the fleeting ideas of words, gestures, and instances.

As we have seen, metamedial forms of expression stress the material nature of writing and the heft of the physical volume that ground the abstract idea of the literary work in the empirical world. In the delicate form of Tree of Codes, however, metamediality ultimately shows that it can also function in the reverse. By accentuating the holes and absences that physically mark the book, Foer's book sculpture expresses itself both through linguistic codes and through the absence of specific bibliographic codes. The effect of this fleeting emptiness fluctuates throughout the brief story. First intimidated by his father's embrace of emptiness, the narrator later appears to accept and embrace evanescence: "The feeling of no permanence in life transformed into an attempt to express wonder" (67). Perhaps, we can assume that the poetics of both Schulz and Foer merge in this autoreferential statement. Simultaneously speaking for his own writing and for American fiction at large at the end of the 2000s, Foer's "attempt to express wonder" effectively encapsulates both the futility and the enduring creativity of this thing we call literature.

## Conclusion: Print Culture and the Dialectic of Digitization

"EVERYTHING DEPENDS UPON THE WAY in which material is used when it operates as medium," John Dewey declared in his major study on aesthetic theory, *Art as Experience* (66). In keeping with the sentiment of Dewey's assertion, I have argued throughout this book that the mediality of the book matters in artistic communication. Yet it does not matter in and of itself. As multifaceted and chronically instable cultural artifacts, books continue to function as mediators within an extensive field of interactions. If we approach books in their relationship to literature, we should distinguish this perspective through what it does not address. For one, it does not provide an outlook on the role of printed communication outside the social context of art. There are plenty of issues surrounding the evolution of printed and digital texts in spheres such as politics, economics, or science: Are there forms of participatory democracy that work better in online communities than in exchanges of printed newsletters or party programs? What does it mean for copyright and author compensation when revenue shifts from the exchange of things to the licensing of content? How do electronic forms of publishing affect and possibly redirect established academic practices surrounding the evaluation of research? All of these fields, and many others, have been affected by recent transformations in communications technologies. Each of these spheres, however, has begun to adapt differently, on a different scale and with recourse to different discourses. In the realm of literature, the advent of the e-book in 1998 registered deeply not because it entailed financial or technological changes, but because it constituted an aesthetic challenge.

The stakes of my overall argument necessarily traverse the territories of aesthetics, literary history, hermeneutic methodology, and even pedagogy. At its best, the idea of metamedia disrupts neat categorizations. The individual artifacts covered throughout this book belong to widely dispersed traditions and genres. *McSweeney's Quarterly Concern* continues the history of the little magazine in the U.S., *House of Leaves* forms an addition to the canon of experimental novels, and *The Cheese Monkeys* is a run-of-the-mill bildungsroman. As metamedia, however, these book fictions form an important cluster within contemporary American literature. To closely engage with such works should not remain a purely academic exercise. In the digital age, metamedial works also matter as learning devices. The increasing technologization of humanities education at the university level—fuelled most recently by the exponential growth of the digital humanities—has led to a tacit consensus that media literacy equals *new* media literacy. Curricular reforms that attempt to bring media into the literature classroom mostly concentrate on digital devices and software that are meant to enhance "traditional" forms of reading. As Andrew Piper reminds us, however, the media ecology of the presence has all but obliterated the notion that reading is a simple, mundane activity (ix–xi). Metamedia expose the full complexity of this cultural technique and demand us to stay close, to focus, and to be patient in decoding them. To understand and value them—whether in private or in the classroom—we have to do more than read in books. We have to relearn how to read books.

So how can we make sense of the confluence between a socio-historical domain called "print culture" and the aesthetic system of literature? Based on the theoretical considerations and the readings that form the core of this book, I believe that a productive strategy to build bridges between these domains has two very general characteristics: it moves from the bottom up and from the inside out. As print culture ceases to be equivalent to such formations as "Western Culture" or "Modernity," it transforms into a subculture in which only specific forms of discourse occur on paper. Elizabeth L. Eisenstein's *The Printing Press as an Agent of Change* gave shape to print culture studies, yet it also contained a consequential media-historical axiom.[1] According to Eisenstein, print culture figures on the uppermost level of historical developments and its effects trickle down into specific contexts (Renaissance aesthetics, the Reformation, emerging discourses of science). Modeled in this fashion, such attributes as widespread dissemination, standardization, and extended preservation hover above the individual arenas of social exchange. The lessons of media change in contemporary literature, however, point to the waning applicability of top-down models of book history. This limitation has to do with the unresolvable specificity of art discourse: the practices of book production and consumption figure in different ways once we enter the literary. To return to Luhmann once more: "The social autonomy of the art system rests on its ability to define and use resources in ways that differ from those of society at large" (Art 80). Print culture in the present, then, is a much more complex and fine-grained phenomenon than the aggregate constellations of print and scribal culture that Eisenstein traces through centuries. In light of differentiated societies and multimedia platforms, it makes little sense anymore to speak of print culture in the singular, but a lot of sense to inquire into formally and geographically diverse print cultures. Since book history is not a unified domain occurring as the context of literature, we may work from the inside outwards to uncover a specific strand of print culture *through* literature.

There is an argument to be made that the experience of printing, instead of falling away from our social horizon, has penetrated deeper into contemporary life than ever before. Whereas printed matter—term papers, forms, certificates, invitations—used to be manufactured elsewhere and brought into the home, the private inkjet or laser printer has democratized the printing profession. Barbara A. Brannon has recently considered the immense scope of this technological shift. While Brannon emphasizes the digital malleability of laser printing technology—words and images blend seamlessly in the form of tiny dots—I would highlight the ubiquitous presence of printing processes and materials it entails both at home or in the office. Formerly relevant only to professionals in publishing and advertising, design protocols such as fonts, line spacing, or page borders now belong to the toolbox of common cultural techniques, way beyond the social confines of professional-managerial classes. In similar form, the raw materials of printing such as toner cartridges and standardized paper stock have taken their place among mundane commodities. If we look to artifacts and not merely to production technologies, we perceive an extended culture of print that is deeply tied to digitization, instead of being its antagonist.

In the Introduction, I called this convoluted relationship between the computer and the printed page the literary dialectic of digitization. This dialectic shows itself in several forms. While consumers increasingly access media content through screens, they also have the tools on hand to become lay publishers at home. In academia, the digital humanities currently develop methods of algorithmic analysis that parse literary texts in the form of large digital corpora. At the same time, the archival branch of digital humanities has exploded the range of scanned historical material available in library repositories or online, thereby accentuating the materiality and the visual design of manuscripts, incunabula, and early modern print books. In the literary variant of this dialectic, authors and designers employ state-of-the-art digital tools to produce some of the most elaborately crafted and narratively complex book fictions in American literary history. Thanks to InDesign, Pantone matching, and extensive digital font libraries, Mark Z. Danielewski can now submit finished print files with detailed instructions on how to manufacture the book to his publisher. Even Dave Eggers, whose recent novel *The Circle* (2013) leans toward blunt expressions of technophobia, relies heavily on the new media ecology of digitized printing and e-commerce to create, advertise, and sell his own books and those put out by his publishing house.

In the aesthetic practices of today's print culture, the dialectical trajectory of digitization has opened up a window far into the past of bookmaking, graphic design, and publishing. With recourse to Harold Innis's famous distinction between "time-binding" and "space-binding" media, Striphas argues that the electronic transmission of texts relegates the printed book into the realm of time-binding media (xiii). Andrew Piper has likewise differentiated between digital files and printed texts, asserting that books via their materiality "bear time within themselves" whereas digital code overwrites temporality (107). Literary texts supplement this binding function with aesthetic adaptations of time, as digital modes of book design and printing activate and extend historical webs of significance. Throughout this book, I have located several features of contemporary literature as extensions of modernism, for example in the institution of the little journal or the avant-garde experiments with graphic design. As we have seen, the metamedial mode in narrative texts reaches at least as far back as *Tristram Shandy* or *Clarissa*. Janine Barchas contends that these early-eighteenth-century explorations of the printed book owed to the status of the novel as an emerging, not-yet-conventionalized genre, whose readers "still needed to be lured over the threshold" of fictionality: "It was then that novelists used the developing novel's graphic presentation as printed book to entice readers and guide their interpretation" (Barchas 18). In this period, however, it took a master printer like Samuel Richardson to stage creative interventions on the printed page. Compared to the ever-strenuous métier of creative writing, bookmaking has become refreshingly simple, as Dave Eggers pointed out in the first hardcover issue of *McSweeney's Quarterly*: "We are fascinated by how easy it all is" (*McSweeney's* 5, 12).

Echoing the attitudes of American pioneers of graphic design and typography such as Frederic W. Goudy and William Addison Dwiggins, the writer-designers of the present see printing tools and machinery as means to an end. In a form of print pragmatism still common to graphic designers, Goudy refuted bibliophile technophobes in his seminal compendium, *Typologia* (1940):

> Too often they confuse the thing itself and the method of its production. The machine has not killed good craftsmanship; the machine in the hand of the craftsman is merely a more intricate tool than any that was available to the earlier worker, and enables him to carry out his own creative idea more exactly than can be done when the work is passed into the hands of artisans employed to perform the various processes singly . . . I hold that if the final printed result is satisfactory to the creator of it, and to the viewer of it as well, the method of its production is in a sense immaterial. (2–3)

Reading such self-descriptions, we may be tempted to critique and deconstruct the aesthetic practices of bookmaking as determined by economics, false ideologies, or technology. Inspired by Bruno Latour's sociology of associations and Rita Felski's recent reflections on the uses of literature, however, I hesitate to simply dismiss or debunk the investment of both writers and readers in the pleasure of making and experiencing well-designed book objects.[2] Very often, technology-centered perspectives introduce a teleological drift into literary history—and historiography—which can turn any literary text produced in the so-called digital age into an emblem of digitization.

In the metamedial experiments of recent American novels, however, literature attempts to construct a new semantics for coping with media change. Publishing institutions such as Alfred A. Knopf, McSweeney's, or Visual Editions disseminate multiple minority reports about the role of printed communication in the digitized present, providing alternative ways to speak about book literature. Social semantics, Luhmann holds, can either "anticipate or even initiate potentials for development in society," but "they can also conserve obsolete traditions" (*Theory* 172).

Times of rapid technological shifts often include an intermediate stage, in which old usage protocols inform strategies to make sense of the new. In a way, the act of naming a digital file an "electronic book" recalls the early phase of the automobile, in which motorcars were labeled "horseless carriages." To think of electronic texts in terms of an e-book means to direct an entire discourse toward emulation: the e-book is best if it can replicate and thus eventually replace the printed book. Johanna Drucker cogently criticizes the imitative design philosophy arising from this premise: "There has been too much emphasis on formal replication of layout, graphic, and physical features and too little analysis of how those features affect the book's function. Rather than thinking about simulating the way a book *looks*, then, designers might do well to consider extending the ways a book *works*" (*SpecLab* 166). Drucker points out that emulation may lead to an impasse in innovation as the fundamental medial difference between "the malleable electronic display of data" and "material object familiar to us as the codex book" cannot be overcome (166). Aside from the flexible, medium-independent design underlying effective Web sites—coded in mark-up languages that separate between content and form—medium-specific design pursues the difference between page and screen. In their practices of medium-specific design, the most bibliophile of contemporary authors are simultaneously innovators in digital literature, as the independent mechanics of e-texts by Mark Z. Danielewski and Reif Larsen show.

This book engaged with American literature in its cultural and discursive specificity without aiming to make global claims concerning media change. On these final pages, I nevertheless wish to point to several metamedial artifacts that have emerged outside the American literary scene. In 2011, Scottish novelist A.L. Kennedy published *The Blue Book*, an intricately designed book fiction rivaling the work of Danielewski and Foer in its complex medial diegesis. In *The Blue Book*, the two former lovers Elizabeth and Arthur reunite on a cruise ship after a long separation. In the past, both pretended to be spiritual mediums and performed petty magic tricks on unsuspecting customers. The book itself poses as a magical compendium; it is completely covered in blue ink, including its outer edges. As the memorable opening lines show, the narrative voice focalizes on the physical artifact: "But here this is, the book you're reading. Obviously. Your book—it's started now, it's touched and opened, held . . . And, quite naturally, you face it" (Kennedy 1). In the end, the book turns out to be compiled by Elizabeth herself, who uses it to write down an extended confessional that she never dared to relate to Arthur. Chief among Elizabeth's confessions is the fact that she gave birth to a child after their separation—a boy who died in an accident in his infancy.

The stirrings of metamedial aesthetics have also appeared on the German literary scene. Directly influenced by McSweeney's, the literary magazine Bella Triste published its thirtieth issue in 2011 as a box full of print objects.[3] Showing the material diversity of contemporary print culture, Bella Triste 30 contains, among other things, a questionnaire, a doorknob hanger, a satchel with playing cards and a piece of bark, along with numerous short fiction and nonfiction pieces printed on large posters, overhead transparencies, and postcards. The contributors to the issue were mostly born in the 1970s and 80s and thus fall into the same generation of digital natives as the writers discussed earlier. Among them is Judith Schalansky, a successful novelist and designer, whose career resembles that of recent American writer-designers. For the special Bella Triste issue, Schalansky supplied a small pamphlet that contains a mini-manifesto akin to the programmatic inserts and paratexts written by Dave Eggers for McSweeney's Quarterly Concern. In the essay "Wie ich Bücher mache" ("How I Make Books"), Schalansky compares herself to an auteur filmmaker who controls all aspects of film production. The essay describes the ultimate ambition of her craft as "a book, in which all parts are fused so that they cannot be separated from each other, and in which the result is more than the sum of its parts" (my translation).

Schalansky has published two novels with the prestigious German press Suhrkamp. Her more recent work Der Hals der Giraffe (2011; The Giraffe's Neck) was one of the first volumes put out by Suhrkamp that bore a stamped hardcover design instead of a dust jacket. Another one of Schalansky's experimental book projects is the *Atlas of Remote Islands* (2010), which reinvents the geographic atlas as a literary form, bearing cartographic renditions of fifty small islands, each accompanied by a fictional vignette imagined to have taken place on this island. The *Atlas* shows how the literary system uses the resource of the material book to different ends than other communicational contexts. With the scientific usage of maps migrating into the digital realm, the printed map becomes available for aesthetic appropriation. The same holds for *Naturkunden*, a bibliophile monograph series of natural history books Schalansky curates and designs for the Berlin publishing house Matthes & Seitz.

Schalansky's metamedial aesthetics have found their most accomplished form to date in her collaboration with Austrian author Clemens J. Setz. For Setz's novel *Indigo* (2012), Schalansky developed a design scheme that reinforces the book's detective story about a rare gene defect in children. The story's protagonist, an autobiographical version of Setz himself, amasses evidence concerning the secret internment of such children, resulting in a wealth of documents that rivals Johnny Truant's collection in *House of Leaves*. Through typography, illustrations, and photorealistic renditions of fictional documents, Schalansky intensifies the reading experience of the book by manipulating the very stuff it is made off. The book's hardcover wrapping consists of exactly the same gray marbled paper used in standard-issue ring binders in Germany. While formally there seems to be a transnational continuum in literary expression, the cultural discourses surrounding evolving media ecologies are decidedly more local, as embodied in this marbled paper. As part of everyday material culture, its semiotic significance would largely be lost on the average American reader. The designers of the English-language edition that appeared in 2014 accordingly chose a more conventional, pictorial cover design. For the release of *Indigo*, Suhrkamp hosted a special blog on their Web site that featured interviews, photo galleries, and videos analogous to the ones produced for Foer's *Tree of Codes*. Readers could here follow the entire manufacturing process of the novel from offset printing to binding and wrapping. Schalansky stages her designer's craft, with several photos showing her bent over drafts and fine-tuning the printed artifact. Such paratextual glances into the workshops of contemporary print culture attest both to the convergence of writing and design and to the divergence of secondary and tertiary media.

As all these cases from the U.S. and elsewhere show, digitization allows authors unprecedented control over the design and manufacture of printed texts. The reverse is true in the current publishing ecosystem for e-books. Apple, Amazon, and Google each offer closed, proprietary systems for electronic dissemination. These delivery systems work so well because they offer relatively seamless user experiences. Yet, as novelist Nicholson Baker complains, the prime reason for the success of their reading devices is their rigorous enforcement of software standards. Referring to licensing agreements, Baker holds that buying a Kindle book translates to acquiring "the right to display a grouping of words in front of your eyes for your private use with the aid of an electronic display device approved by Amazon" ("A New Page"). To enter fenced-in Web marketplaces, authors have to relegate parts of their textual performance to machines and IT-engineers. While writers like Eggers and Kidd openly attest to their expertise with digital design tools, no literary author can credibly claim to have a decisive say in the development of devices like the Kindle or the iPad. Innovation in digital technologies passes over the heads of novelists. Unless this process changes radically in the future—as it well might—literary authors cannot fully exploit the potentials of their tertiary, digital display media.

According to Jerome McGann, a similar situation unfolds in the realm of humanities scholarship, where pioneering digital projects such as Project Muse and JSTOR were designed without consulting scholars from the field: "Indeed, to this day our scholarly community continues largely to hang back, reacting to the rapidly changing scene rather than working to shape policy and exert control over events" ("On Creating" 183–84). One of the key goals in the evolving field of digital humanities, McGann argues, should be to correct this imbalance. Aside from direct activism in this arena, literary and cultural critics have a decisive stake in this ongoing conversation, because they produce accounts of the aesthetic operations of art production and reception. The power of criticism, therefore, is also the power of redescribing and recreating. I put forward the descriptive tool of "metamedia" to be used for representations that in some way bind themselves to a specific storage and display medium. Metamedial forms of presentation are in the first sense neutral: they do not presuppose a specific historical relationship between "old" and "new" forms of expression. Neither do they highlight a specific technology of production or reception, or a peculiar practice of writing. My account of American literary print culture since the late 1990s should therefore not be understood as a direct intervention in the debate on the relative use value, functionality, or beauty of books as compared to screens. Instead, I hope to have provided a fuller portrait of the human and nonhuman actors, sites, and institutions that have fueled a recent renaissance of book culture.

Against the overwhelming discourse surrounding the agon between books and screens, *Metamedia* has attempted to shift the focus to their mutual influence, and thus to move from a rhetoric of competition to one of coevolution. To invoke media change as an overarching historical determinant means to disregard the feedback loops between discourse and technologies. Who knows whether the engineers at Apple and Amazon were not struck by the idea of the "electronic book" before even drawing the first blueprints of paper-thin devices and writing the first lines of code for their emulative visual interfaces? So perhaps, the idea of a robust and innovative post-digital print culture may seep into the workshops and laboratories where the next steps in the production of paper, ink, layout software, and printing equipment are imagined. The question of the future of the book promises to remain a question—albeit a productive one. The e-book has turned printed paper from a medium of necessity into a medium of choice. As the veneer of neutrality falls away from the media of literature, writers and readers will need to constantly renegotiate the nature and the boundaries of these very media. Competing answers to this question are formulated daily in the minds of those who write and those who read. Yet, they also occur in publishing houses, software corporations, printing shops, bookstores, classrooms, and libraries. Metamedial literature extends into all of these arenas as it emerges to become an aesthetic mode of reflection on the materiality, the borders, the limitations, and the possibilities of this ancient contraption of paper and ink, which has never appeared more modern than now.

# Notes

### Introduction: From Text to Book

1. All italics in quotations are those of the original.

2. The English translation of "*il n'y a pas de hors-texte*" as "there is nothing outside of the text" effectively eradicates the ambiguity of the French phrase "*hors-texte*," which is also a printer's term for pages carrying illustrative plates without printing on their verso side.

3. On the media ecology concept and its various theoretical origins, see Punday, esp. 11–19.

4. For a succinct discussion of what the notion of autopoiesis in social communication is—and what it is not—see Luhmann, *Theory* 32–35 and "Autopoiesis." See also Chapter 1.

5. See Sussman (esp. 138–45, 163–93) for an extended discussion of *Glas* and Derrida's investment in the book form.

6. I understand artifact here as an "object made or modified by human workmanship" ("Artifact" def. A.1.a).

7. One standard textbook, *New Media: A Critical Introduction*, does not address the screen itself as an influential display medium—even as it constantly refers to all kinds of screens (Lister et al.). The authors appear to be interested in a more wholesale description of media as cultural products, as ideologies, and as aggregations of various technological processes.

8. Appropriated by software engineers for various electronic contexts, the notion of digital content has cycled back into everyday language. Yet, to employ "con-

tent" to describe works of art, Lev Manovich notes, suggests that the essence of an artwork exists outside its medium: "Situated in some idealized medium-free realm, content is assumed to exist before its material expression" (66). This definition falters, Manovich writes, as soon as the artwork activates the medial dimension within its aesthetic totality. He further differentiates between new media "art" and new media "design," depending on whether or not the artifact creates a localized, materialized aesthetic experience: "In contrast to design, in art the connection between content and form (or, in the case of new media, content and interface) is motivated; that is, the choice of a particular interface is motivated by a work's content to such degree that it can no longer be thought of as a separate level" (67).

9. Umberto Eco's concept of the *opera aperta*, the open work, best articulates this idea. See Eco, *Open*.

10. Robert Darnton, whose contributions to the field of book history I briefly discuss in Chapter 1, is another important public figure in the American debate on the book in the digital age. In the course of the 2000s, Darnton authored numerous essays and opinion pieces for the *New York Review of Books*, which were later collected in revised form in *The Case for Books: Past, Present, and Future* (2009). Since 2007, Darnton has served as director of the Harvard University Library, where he was entangled from the start in the intricate legal struggles over Google Books. Also relevant are Jason Epstein's writings in the *New York Review of Books*, in which he outlines a future print-on-demand system. See, for example, his "Publishing: The Revolutionary Future" (2010).

11. As if to prove his own argument, Anthony Grafton published an extended version of his essay as *Codex in Crisis* with the New York–based fine-printing publisher The Crumpled Press. Each copy of the small print run is, as Janneke Adema reports, numbered and handbound. The copyright page contains a detailed description of the paper stock: "Cover paper Neenah Classic Laid in Peppered Bronze; Text paper Mohawk Superfine in Bright White; Flyleaf paper Frazier Pegasus in Black" (qtd. in Adema). While this publication clearly caters to a small audience of bibliophiles, I perceive it less as an essay than as an embodied message. In his *New Yorker* article, Grafton presents the New York Public Library as the prototype of future libraries—a place where digital information converges with rare book rooms. And sure enough, copy no. 213 of *Codex in Crisis* now sits on the shelves of the NYPL Rare Book Collection, as the library's online catalogue shows.

12. In the following, the shorthand *McSweeney's* refers to the literary journal. The non-italicized version McSweeney's indicates the San Francisco–based publishing house.

266

## 1. Reading Metamedia

1. For Luhmann, the notion of "semantics" denotes a "supply of themes" (*Social* 163) that enables easy integration into communicative processes. Social semantics constantly adapt to the changes in the environment of a system. Luhmann posits a direct connection between the development of new media and the ensuing volatility in social semantics (*Theory* 187–89).

2. The term "metamedium," to note this in passing, has recently received some attention in new media studies. In *Software Takes Command*, Lev Manovich discusses the influential work of computer scientists Alan Kay and Adele Goldberg from the 1970s. Kay and Goldberg described the computer as a metamedium, meaning that it gathers in one location previously separate expressive modalities (such as writing, images, sound). With recourse to this formulation, Manovich uses the prefix "meta" merely in a descriptive sense to indicate various levels of media content. Against this immaterial, data-centered formulation, I aim to align metamedia with the analytical and reflexive tradition of metafiction research. This well-established field of literary studies hearkens back to the seminal volumes *Narcissistic Narrative* (1980) by Linda Hutcheon and *Metafiction* (1984) by Patricia Waugh. For a more formalist approach to metafiction and a summary of recent work on this topic, see Wolf.

3. My perspective on Scarry is indebted to Leah Price's *How to Do Things with Books in Victorian Britain* (32–33).

4. On improbability as a foundational premise for systems theory see Luhmann's essay "The Improbability of Communication."

5. Luhmann's first complete outline of his theory is *Social Systems*. For literary studies, *Art as a Social System* and the essay collection *Essays on Self-Reference* are valuable resources. Moeller provides an excellent, concise introduction to Luhmann's thought. See also Wellbery, "Systems" for a short discussion of the uses of systems theory for the study of media in the humanities.

6. The term "autopoiesis" derives from the Greek *autos* ("self") and *poiein* ("create"). Where former sociological theories have called similar, but less fundamental operations "self-organization," Luhmann through this term stresses the creationary nature of self-reference. The idea of "autopoiesis" was originally developed within a theory of living systems by the Chilean neurobiologists Humberto R. Maturana and Francisco J. Varela. Hayles explains, "While an observer may posit causal links between events in the environment and an animal's behavior, autopoietic theory argues that within the living system as such, everything takes place in terms of the system's own organization, which always operates so as continually to produce and reproduce itself" ("Cybernetics" 147).

7. Luhmann comments at length on the notion of "dynamic stability" within

the chapter "Evolution" in *Art as a Social System* (211–43). For more on this debate, see Schweighauser 14–15.

8. Also see Henry Sussman's *Around the Book*, which suggestively pairs theoretical vocabularies from a wide array of systems philosophers and theorists with bibliographic analyses of works by Benjamin, Kafka, and Derrida.

9. On the systemic position of literature and of the genre of the novel see Luhmann, *Reality* 56–57.

10. Luhmann speaks of "*Anschlusskommunikation*," a term that is, like large parts of his terminological toolbox, hard to translate. "Connecting communication" as used in the standard translation of *Social Systems* (143) adequately conveys the sense of linkage inferred in the German original. Yet, the aspect of sequentiality would come across better if one thought of "follow-up communication."

11. Notably, the German word *Buchdruck* references both the technology (*Druck*) and the medium (*Buch*). In English translations, succumbing to the scarcity of compound nouns, the word "book" is mostly dropped so that it appears as if Luhmann was solely interested in the technology. His insistence on "book printing," however, indicates that he is also keenly aware of how material formats add dimensions to printed communication that cannot solely be explained by the technological apparatus needed to produce the medium.

12. The effects of digitization remain a footnote in Luhmann's oeuvre. Written two decades ago, *Theory of Society* contains an explicit consideration of the role of the computer in media evolution, but it could not yet describe the vast communications grid of the Internet. While Luhmann's specific speculations about the computer are less helpful in this context, his aerial view of twentieth-century media evolution is much more germane. He holds that new dissemination media have considerably heightened the potential for communication. These media have drastically increased the discrepancy between communication that could take place and communication that actually occurs (*Theory* 184–87). Thus, contemporary social systems have to face hyper-complex environments by becoming hyper-selective. This holds for every individual who has to maneuver the information overload, as well as for systems as a whole, which have only a finite capacity to render environmental aspects in system-internal operations.

13. All page numbers refer to the University of Toronto Press edition from 2002, though a new edition was released by the same press in 2011.

14. In her media-based close reading of *The Gutenberg Galaxy*, Jessica Pressman likewise holds that the text "is not only about media but also about depicting and embodying its own printed materiality" (*Digital* 45).

15. McLuhan's most widely read book *Understanding Media*, in contrast, has been published in various editions by several presses over the years. A recent

Routledge edition is typeset in Eric Gill's modernist fonts Joanna (regular text) and Gill Sans (headlines and long quotations), thus imbuing the volume with a clean, unobtrusive look that blends well with the graphic design tenets of the present. Gill's typefaces are even farther away from the pictorial flourishes of Gothic script that McLuhan seemed to favor. In fact, the availability of the essayistic, utopian *Understanding Media* in print forms that please the eyes of contemporary readers may help to sustain the high standing accorded to McLuhan in new media circles.

16. See Eisenstein's remarks on "typographical fixity" (113–26). She holds that the permanence of printed records "helps to explain much else that seems to distinguish the history of the past five centuries from that of all prior eras" (113).

17. This integrative potential is on display in the recent collection *Comparative Textual Media*, edited by Hayles and Pressman. The research agenda presented here aims to establish comparative media studies as an interdisciplinary approach for mostly text-based fields of the humanities.

18. The significance of the book's title as well as Kittler's contribution to post-hermeneutic criticism are cogently explained in David Wellbery's foreword to *Discourse Networks 1800/1900* (vii–xvi).

19. See McCaffery and Gregory.

20. On the interrelation between media-specific analysis and close reading in the realm of electronic literature see also Pressman's *Digital Modernism* (28–55).

21. See Adams and Barker, whose main grievance is Darnton's exclusive focus on the anthropological level of the communications circuit. They propose re-thinking Darnton's scheme and locating the book as artifact at its center, with the individuals and the influx of matter and energy around the perimeter. Accordingly, they rephrase Darnton's anthropocentric terminology as four "separate zones" (53) or procedural stages: publishing, manufacturing, distribution, and reception. While my perspective owes more to Adams and Barker's work, I believe that their model merely specifies a number of details that Darnton's well-structured framework already implies.

22. Even though "bibliographic" and "bibliographical" may be used inter-changeably, I will limit the term "bibliographical" to those instances where it applies to scholarly conventions and practices of bibliography. "Bibliographic" then refers to the wider arena of issues relating to the design, structure, and pro-duction of books, especially in the case of the deliberate artistic use of the book medium. McGann himself occasionally uses the phrase "bibliographic codes" (*Radiant* 258).

23. Scholarship on the post-postmodern in American literature includes Hol-land, esp. 11–17, as well as Timmer.

24. There has been a distinct uptick in interest surrounding modernist mag-

azine culture. See Scholes and Wulfman, who reiterate the importance of Ezra Pound, calling him the founder of periodical studies. George Bornstein's *Material Modernism* also locates modernist networks of small presses and little magazines within material texts.

25. See Lothar Müller's *Weiße Magie*, which attempts to resituate the Gutenberg era within the larger context of an "epoch of paper." Müller criticizes the contemporary division between the eras of print and of the Internet. This standard pairing impedes, he argues, a larger historical view on paper-based "cultural techniques," which extend beyond the effects of printing technologies (14–15).

26. I have taken the oft-cited explication of metafiction by Patricia Waugh as my inspiration for the first part of this definition: "*Metafiction* is a term given to fictional writing which self-consciously and systematically draws attention to its status as an artefact in order to pose questions about the relationship between fiction and reality" (2).

27. As Joseph North argues, however, there is a lineage of New Critical aesthetic theory that does not conceptualize the experience of literary texts as taking place in an immaterial, purely idealist frame. In his pioneering writings from the 1920s, the British literary critic I.A. Richards developed what North calls "an incipiently materialist practice of close reading," stressing the continuity of embodied experience between art and everyday life (142). Only in later work from John Crowe Ransom onward did close reading morph into the radically decontextualized and dematerialized method that first became the gold standard and later the whipping post of literary studies. To practice close reading on material texts would thus constitute a return to the most fundamental concerns that originally sparked the New Criticism.

## 2. A Bookish Institution: The McSweeney's Universe

1. Along these lines, Brouillette wonders: "Is it a business, a general cultural network, a literary clique, or a movement?" (fn. 1). In a course on McSweeney's at the University of Göttingen taught by Frank Kelleter in 2008, in which I served as teaching assistant, the group agreed at some point to the phrase "McSweeney's Universe." I adopt this phrasing, since the term "universe" transports a sense of the expansiveness without presuming a specific aesthetic or political project.

2. While there is a growing number of essays and book chapters on Eggers's novels, scholarly interest in the quarterly and the publishing house has been sparse so far. Aside from Hamilton's account, Brouillette and Hungerford provide the most helpful perspectives on the early years of McSweeney's.

3. Four out of five authors covered in the following chapters have in some way appeared in one or more McSweeney's publications. The jacket designer and

novelist Chip Kidd has contributed to *McSweeney's* 13 and 33. Salvador Plascencia's novel *The People of Paper* was published by McSweeney's and his work has also appeared in *McSweeney's* 12 and 22. Reif Larsen wrote an essay about books for the *Believer*, which I discuss in Chapter 4. Jonathan Safran Foer contributed to two collections published by McSweeney's.

4. See Pearson (147–49) for a historical discussion of this shift in bookbinding practice.

5. While I reproduce italics as in the original, I do not replicate the extensive use of all-caps, as frequently performed on *McSweeney's* title pages.

6. Many items in *McSweeney's* issues, specifically in the paratexts, are not attributed to individual authors or editors. Since it is hard to confirm that Dave Eggers wrote all of these, I will cite such passages simply by providing the number of the issue and the page.

7. In passing, we need to note the inaccurate identification of Garamond 3 with Claude Garamond. As print historical research has shown, the designs of another sixteenth-century type designer, Jean Jannon, were misidentified as the work of Garamond in the nineteenth century, leading to an entire strain of revivals that falsely call themselves Garamond. This includes the work of Benton and Cleland (Bringhurst 235).

8. It is therefore misleading to accord this book supreme innovative significance as Bran Nicol does when he claims, "the metafictional *McSweeney's* 'house style' was first adopted in *A Heartbreaking Work of Staggering Genius*" (102).

9. Tête-bêche refers to a form of binding in which one part of the book is rotated by 180 degrees so that the ends of both texts meet somewhere in the middle of the book. Eggers later employed a similar binding for *McSweeney's* 24. This hardcover, clothbound issue features a cardboard division in the middle in order to create the effect of a book with two spines. The issue can be folded outward to reveal continuous illustrations on both sides of the three cardboard covers. The two sections of text, bound on opposite sides of the book, contain a regular short-story issue and a thematic section on Donald Barthelme.

10. Hansen's *Embodying Technesis* confronts the common philosophical and theoretical process during which material technologies become only a metaphor for the impact of objects on human thought. Hansen calls this process "technesis" or "the putting-into-discourse of technology" (4).

11. My reading is based on the extended Vintage paperback, for both quantitative and qualitative reasons. The Vintage edition that includes *Mistakes* is the longest of all three editions, encompassing significant additions and design enhancements. As to qualitative improvements, Eggers announces that he corrected a number of errata and factual mistakes for the paperback edition.

12. On the life-giving book as a trope in Western literary history, see Assmann (171–205).

13. On the issue of irony and the interrelation between *A Heartbreaking Work* and David Foster Wallace's essay "E Unibus Pluram: Television and U.S. Fiction" (1993), see Nicol 103–05 and Timmer 222–24.

14. For the concept of "material metaphors," see Hayles, *Writing* 22–23.

15. The verso page of the front endpaper carries the page number 2. Thus, I count the front cover as page 1. In common bookmaking practice, the numbered pages start after the endpapers. Traditionally, endpapers do not fall into the domain of the book's printer, since they are decorative elements added during the binding process.

16. On hyper attention as a behavioral pattern resulting from the evolution of screen media, see Hayles, *Electronic* 117–18. Hayles further develops the notion of hyper attention, as opposed to deep attention in *How We Think*. Here, she explicitly points to a generational divide that separates children and young adults who encountered screen media at a formative age from older age groups who did not (96–103).

17. The description above is based on images of this rare first edition available at the personal book collector's Web site, *this book is collectible* ("Sacrament").

18. To complicate things further, the Vintage paperback edition of 2003 reprints Hand's "Interruption" only in parts of its print run. In this Vintage edition, the title again reverts to *You Shall Know Our Velocity*, though added to the end of the title is an exclamation point that was not part of the original title. Only the minuscule print on the copyright page references it as having been "Previously retitled as *Sacrament*." Depending on whether readers buy the text online or in a store, receiving an edition that reprints *Sacrament* is entirely up to chance. Obtaining such a copy through online retailers has proven to be a hit-and-miss operation. I was able to locate a copy containing the additional sections only on the third attempt. The following readings are based on the PDF file of *Sacrament*, which I checked against the Vintage paperback edition. Both texts have the same pagination and layout. In the color-printed McSweeney's hardcover, Hand's section bears a red outer frame.

19. For Assmann, storage spaces figure strongly among the cultural metaphors of memory. In her broad historical survey, the "fusion of memory and architecture" is best exemplified in "temples of fame, memorial theaters, and libraries" (147). The cultural practice of putting something in storage, is—at least in the U.S.—an everyday form of space management, during which individualized decisions of mnemonic importance are made. Assmann's notion of inhabited and uninhabited memory (123) corresponds neatly to the division between the inhabited home, which has the more valuable artifacts in it, and the uninhabited storage unit that

retains an intermediate class of possessions: too precious to discard, too distant from daily life to be kept close at hand.

20. As with many other terms, Niklas Luhmann took pains to distinguish the systems-theoretical meaning of "self-description" from the term's everyday usage. He presents self-descriptions as a driving force of a system's autopoiesis but simultaneously as a paradoxical operation because these descriptions are "contingent upon themselves" (Moeller 47). See Luhmann, *Theory of Society*, chapter 5.

21. See Starre, "American Comics Anthologies" and "Teaching the Comics Anthology."

22. *McSweeney's* 12 (2003) contains a section of "twenty-minute stories," including pieces by Jonathan Lethem, Jennifer Egan, and Douglas Coupland, all purportedly composed in a few minutes. *McSweeney's* 28 (2008) features fables, all written with the requirement to be very short and have a clear moral. These strict guidelines on the form of writing are reminiscent of Oulipo writers like Georges Perec, who used quasi-scientific constraints to compose their texts. For *McSweeney's* 22 (2006), guest editor Michelle Orange sent the contributors brief conceptual ideas for short stories culled from the notebooks of F. Scott Fitzgerald—such as "Fairy who fell for a wax dummy"—and had writers flesh these out. In *McSweeney's* 32 (2009), the task was to write from different geographical locations and envision those places in the year 2024. The overall idea that creativity often results from constraints echoes Luhmann's openness-from-closure principle. Once clear frames are established, one might argue, the creative process works better. The playful potential of serial publishing is evident in the competitive mechanics of the writing contest, a pastime that even the supposedly elitist modernist magazines did not shy away from. Margaret Anderson's *Little Review*, for example, conducted a vers-libre contest in 1917, with the winning submissions printed in the April issue of that year.

23. I adopt the suggestive term "testing ground" from Jenkins (87), who introduces it casually in a wholly different context. Nevertheless, the term perfectly encapsulates the cultural function of a small literary journal.

24. The recent reedition of *Composition No. 1* by the British publisher Visual Editions follows this book-like format and omits Saporta's introduction. I briefly address this reedition in Chapter 5.

25. While praise may flatter the editors, the overall autopoiesis of the larger communication system also feeds from disapproval and reproach. In 2004, the 32-year-old author Benjamin Kunkel and a number of his friends founded the journal n+1, a direct competitor less to the *Quarterly Concern* than to the McSweeney's journal *The Believer*. To distinguish themselves from McSweeney's, the editors at n+1 published a fierce polemic against the "Eggersards" in their first issue ("Re-

gressive"). Despite internal competition, the success of *McSweeney's* and *n+1* along with other new independent little magazines like *A Public Space* or *The Point* speaks for the continued attraction of print culture in the United States.

26. See for example Wutz and Punday.

27. Rubrics used here include "multimodal novels" or novels that bear the "mark of the digital." For the multimodal perspective, see Gibbons. The latter phrase stems from Hayles, *Electronic* 159–86.

### 3. Mark Z. Danielewski's Complex Codices

1. See Pressman, who uses the images of the "node" and the "network" as central concepts in her reading of Danielewski's novel and its place in a group of related works, such as the accompanying text *The Whalestoe Letters* and the record *Haunted* by Danielewski's sister Poe ("House").

2. Hayles's extensive body of work on Danielewski includes "Saving the Subject," *Writing Machines*, *Electronic Literature*, and *How We Think*. To a certain extent, I would argue, many of Hayles's insightful literary-theoretical conceptualizations have their point of origin in Danielewski's work. *House of Leaves* has sparked a large body of critical essays, virtually all of which closely engage with Hayles's readings. For a good selection of essays and references to further sources, see the collection *Mark Z. Danielewski*, edited by Bray and Gibbons.

3. Hayles writes about the "four different editions" (*My Mother* 105), while Little only doubts the authenticity of the "Incomplete" edition (195).

4. The "Black & White" version, however, was published with Doubleday Books in Britain and Ireland. On the U.S. market, readers could only purchase the Pantheon "2-Color" edition, which featured blue printing in the mass-market paperback and red printing in the limited hardcover release.

5. See the thread "Comprehensive guide to printings/editions/ISBN's etc." on www.houseofleaves.com. Within this thread, some fans of the book also chronicle their attempts to collect all existing editions. A user named "heartbreak" wrote in 2007: "Finally! I've got it! A book shelf containing all published editions of *House of Leaves*! Well . . . until it gets translated again that is" (post #319). Below these lines, the fan posted an image that depicts his home bookshelf, carrying more than ten editions of the book in several languages.

6. For the interplay of constrictions and improvisations in the field of American popular culture, Kelleter and Jahn-Sudmann propose the concept of "play-enhancing constraints" (206). They argue that the remarkable productivity of popular genres such as television series relies equally on the standardizing frameworks inherent in each serial narrative and on the creative play with these strictures.

Notably, the same nexus of complexity reduction and increasingly complex effects characterizes the work of Oulipo writers.

7. My use of the term "forensic fandom" is indebted to Jason Mittell, who employs it in conjunction with the hyper-attentive viewing and reviewing activities common to fans of the TV show *Lost*. See Mittell, "*Lost*" 130.

8. The novel did have a significant prerelease circulation. On a personal Web site, now defunct, Danielewski posted excerpts in PDF format for easy download by friends, family, and anyone who found the site by accident (Brookman). After securing the publication deal with Pantheon, Danielewski agreed with the Barnes and Noble–owned online publisher iUniverse to publish the novel in serial form as a promotional event. The press announcement by the company reads: "This serialization enables Pantheon and iUniverse.com to reinvent the historic, Dickensian publishing formula—serialization of an entire work prior to publication—using a new technology" ("iUniverse.com"). From the e-publisher's Web site, readers were directly rerouted to the forums hosted on Danielewski's Web site, which explains the immediate outpouring of fan commentary on the site.

9. In British and American Studies, influential volumes are Gutjahr and Benton; Moylan and Stiles; Drucker, *Visible*. In German Studies, the pioneering monograph is Wehde, which combines a thorough account of the aesthetic basics of typography with more detailed explorations of crucial stylistic schools and debates within German literature.

10. The German Italian typographer Giovanni Mardersteig originally designed this Renaissance-revival typeface in 1954. For Alexander S. Lawson, this "book type" is "eminently suited both to the antique finish of most book papers and to the dull-coated stocks, used for illustrations" (108).

11. It fits the picture that the only instance in which the text proper uses the color purple addresses the topic of memory. At the very end of his autobiographical footnotes, Johnny strikes out a brief phrase before relating a final anecdote. The struck-out words rendered in purple ink read: "what I'm remembering now" (518). This passage indicates that his memories will no longer rest in the gray matter of his head, but in the pages of the novel. As such, it would be inadequate to claim possession of these memories, which is why Johnny decides to strike this line out.

12. In *How We Think*, Hayles argues that *Only Revolutions* experiments with the spatialized display of data on the surface of pages. In her most Kittlerian analysis to date, she claims that the "writing-down system" (223) is of utmost importance for this novel even though the narrative systematically excludes technology. Hansen focuses similarly on the technological realm, as he engages with the chronological function of books as artistic media. He holds that *Only Revolutions* is a prototypical

example of a print book that allows its readers "an opportunity to engage with the collective, digital archive of history" ("Print" 197). Both essays rely extensively on authorial comments about the production process of the book. To wit, Danielewski fuels such commentary through his rare, but extensive interviews. In the case of *Only Revolutions*, his extended conversation with the literature scholar Kiki Benzon published on the Web site *Electronic Book Review* provides ample material that Hayles and Hansen use to corroborate their readings. McHale ("Only Revolutions") opts for a less author-centered perspective as he analyzes the form of the poem with recourse to Roman Jakobson's theory of the poetic function of language.

13. Incidentally, Apple Inc. chose Myriad Pro as their corporate font around 2002, thus influencing the typographic look of its most commercially successful products such as the iPod, the iPhone, and the iPad.

14. Founded by Donald Barthelme, the magazine *Gulf Coast* is run by students at the University of Houston. The publication of Danielewski's drafts in this journal continues the author's habit of dispersing parts of his work across a broad array of nonmainstream publishers. Aside from the "Spoiler" poster that appeared only in France, this practice also occurred with *The Fifty Year Sword* (2005), which was printed in two limited editions of 1,000 copies with the Dutch publisher De Bezige Bij. The book is very tall and narrow and contains a fractured ghost story told through the voices of five individual narrators. In 2012, Pantheon produced an American edition of *The Fifty Year Sword* for the general market, which returns to the metamedial style of *House of Leaves*. The short story surrounding the seamstress Chintana plays out on the surface the book, where photographs of specially crafted embroideries adorn the recto pages. *The Fifty Year Sword* also foregrounds the fact that book binding entails sewing, using thick red thread plainly visible at the midpoint of each signature.

15. Immediately preceding *House of Leaves*, the metamedial pursuits of William H. Gass's *The Tunnel* (1995) and Lee Siegel's *Love in a Dead Language* (1999) stand out.

## 4. Convergences of a Different Order: Immersive Book Fictions and Literary Bibliographers

1. "The writing of books" is an obsolete meaning of the word bibliography in the English language. It is derived from the Greek βιβλιογραφία, which also signified "book-writing" ("Bibliography" def. 1).

2. The willingness to supplement immersion with formal attentiveness may be a general characteristic of contemporary audiences. Thinking beyond the immersion/defamiliarization binary, the television scholar Jason Mittell proposes to think of this receptive posture in terms of an "operational aesthetic"—a term he borrows from Neil Harris. With regard to increasingly complex forms of tele-

vision narrative, Mittell holds: "We watch these shows not just to get swept away in a realistic narrative world (although that certainly can happen) but also to watch the gears at work, marveling at the craft required to pull off such narrative pyrotechnics" ("Narrative" 35).

3. Tanselle presents an extensive overview of the scarce scholarly work done specifically on book jackets ("Dust-Jackets"). He attests to the importance of Chip Kidd, both as designer and as public advocate of book jacket art (49–50), while slyly noting that professional bibliographers have until recently deemed the idea to study dust jackets "a trifle frivolous" (46).

4. Aside from the large illustrations, the external design of the book also contains several small, playful experiments. For one, Kidd credits a number of his friends and associates in a ribbon of white text that runs along the outer edges of the hardcover. Central aphorisms and one-liners are excerpted from the narrative and reprinted on the top and bottom edges of the spine ("Whatever you do, don't think of elephants!") and on the spine itself ("Good Is Dead"). The mock-Nietzschean "Good Is Dead" embellishes the fore-edge of the book, along with the question "Do You See?" One has to twist the whole block of pages in opposite directions to reveal either of these slogans. Hayles's *Writing Machines* uses a similar design, as discussed in Chapter 1.

5. Happy's admiration for Sorbeck has a distinctly erotic component from the very beginning. Still somewhat insecure in his sexual orientation, Happy comes closer to accepting his homosexual leanings during his collegiate career.

6. See, for example, the following pages in the *The Learners*: 29, 43, 57, 61, 105, 141, 251.

7. This is yet another area in which the field of book history provides productive impulses. Many studies in the field accord the publisher the central position en route to explicating cultural networks of information exchange. Recent work in this area includes Gregory Barnhisel's account of Ezra Pound's relationship with New Directions Press as well as Amy Root Clements's book on Alfred A. Knopf, Inc.

8. By way of anecdote: Bill Bell, professor of book history at Cardiff University, showed me a copy he obtained of Frank Harris's infamous autobiography *My Life and Loves* (4 vols., 1922–1927). The one-time owner of the book had left marks on the text that chronicle his sexual fixation on the artifact. For one, he had underlined and earmarked the raunchiest passages, so that he could return to the explicit descriptions of intercourse with relative ease. Finally, the title page of the book had a large stain, likely bearing permanent witness to masturbation that took place decades ago.

9. This planetary metaphor reverberates throughout the novel. The citizens of

the book associate the hovering presence of the authorial creator with the ringed planet of Saturn and closely observe the sky for signs of him. At one point, the novel features a visual illustration of Saturn and its characteristic rings (218). Since the middle ages, the planet Saturn has also been associated with melancholia, a fitting allusion in the case of Plascencia's fictional alter ego.

10. The claim for authorship on behalf of a fictional character at times confuses librarians and bibliographers. The largest German interlibrary catalogue GVK lists T.S. Spivet as coauthor of Larsen's novel, just as it features Johnny Truant as a real person who contributed to *House of Leaves*. In the digital databases of modern libraries, the characters of immersive book fictions come alive and share the ontological status of their creators. I wish to thank Stephen Burn for alerting me to the double-coded meaning of "T.S."

11. See Hallet and Fjellestad, neither of whom comments on the interpolated story.

12. Nicholas Carr usefully explains the coevolution of neural structures and representational tools with the scientific concept of neuroplasticity. Studies of neuroplasticity reveal, he holds, "that the tools man has used to support or extend his nervous system . . . have shaped the physical structure and workings of the human mind" (48). Resonating deeply with Larsen's novel, Carr uses the example of mapmaking as an "intellectual technology" that virtually all children practice via scribbles and drawings. Notably, a map always positions the observer: "The map is a medium that not only stores and transmits information but also embodies a particular mode of seeing and thinking" (41). The personal nature of maps is furthermore evident in T.S.'s habit to include his brother's name in each map he produced since Layton's accidental suicide.

13. While the excerpt shown here is Larsen's invention, the famous photographer Jackson did indeed join the expedition led by Ferdinand Vandeveer Hayden.

14. See especially the discussion in Adams and Barker, 62.

15. For an insightful account of the competing fonts Caslon and Baskerville used during the American revolutionary period, see Martin McClellan's essay published on *McSweeney's Internet Tendency* in 2009. With regard to the imperfect look of many American documents of the time, McClellan comments: "If you can imagine a piece of printing from revolutionary America (with the funny-to-our-eyes use of an f in the place of an s), you're most likely looking at Caslon. If, in your mind's eye, the letters appear rough around the edges, some say that's because the sea air eroded the type somewhat on its trip from England." See also Lawson, who holds that the omnipresence of this typeface in the print culture of the early republic initiated a "tradition of enthusiasm for Caslon on the part of American printers" (176).

16. As Benton points out in her essay "Typography and Gender," the proponents of fine printing at this time also frequently resorted to gendered rhetoric, distinguishing carefully handcrafted, "masculine" printing from mass-marketed, machine-made, "feminine" productions.

17. Specifically during the modernist period, however, limited first editions of new poetry or prose were an important aesthetic and economic tool for authors and publishers. See Rainey for a discussion of James Joyce's and T.S. Eliot's relationship to fine printing.

## 5. Beyond Trauma:
### The Ethics of Materialized Memory in Jonathan Safran Foer

1. See for example the circular definition in Luhmann's essay "Work of Art": "We could therefore suppose: art consists of works of art and what a work of art is is determined by art" (193).

2. Haselstein calls The Book of Recurrent Dreams a record of the collective unconscious, in which acts of writing, dreaming, remembering, and repeating merge (202–03). Repetition is a central structural feature of the book as individual lives parallel each other across generations. Haselstein argues that this also undermines the presentation of the Holocaust as a singular event; instead, it is a recurrent nightmare of the townspeople, the likes of which may happen again (203). The dust jacket of the first edition hardcover takes up this cyclical conception of history. It features white-on-black lettering that imitates the irregular brush of handwriting on the front. On the back, it presents a rotated, inverted black-on-white version of the same design, so that one cannot at first determine which side of the book is the proper front. The design references forms of tête-bêche binding, as used in the Vintage edition of Dave Eggers's A Heartbreaking Work. In Everything Is Illuminated, the inverted back cover resonates with the novel's insistence on repetition, suggesting that readers can start the book anew once they have finished it.

3. Jonathan bases his search on a photograph, probably owned by his grandfather, who had written on the back: "This is me with Augustine, February 21, 1943" (60). The old woman they end up finding, though, knows about the history of Trachimbrod and seems to have been an eyewitness to the massacre. Her name, Lista, aligns her with a character from Jonathan's fictionalized history. Jonathan imagines a woman named Lista as one of his grandfather's several lovers before the destruction of Trachimbrod. Ostensibly, Jonathan bases this storyline on old Lista's description of Safran's brief visit to her after the war. During the trip to the Ukraine, both Alex and Jonathan repeatedly confess that they desperately want her to be Augustine. Alex even carries this name throughout his narrative, speaking of her as "the woman we continued to think of as Augustine, even though we

knew that she was not Augustine" (181). Ironically, Alex succeeds in concealing the name Lista so well that even contemporary critics keep referring to the woman as Augustine.

4. See the essays in Bornstein and Tinkle on the notion of the "iconic page" in illuminated manuscripts and printed artifacts.

5. Foer follows the formatting conventions for a finite volume of text when he italicizes the title of Oskar's scrapbook throughout the novel. He thus enlists the cultural protocol that will have reader's decode "italic text" as "book title." *Stuff That Happened to Me* is not the only personal book Oskar uses. He also owns a "feelings book," in which he records and updates his current emotional state. During a conversation with his mom, for example, he first writes "mediocre" onto the current page, then strikes out the word and writes "optimistic, but realistic," before ending up "extremely depressed" (170–71). In the struck passages, his feelings book thus serves as a permanent record of his past moods.

6. On Phillips's work, see Hayles, *Writing* 78–99, and Drucker, *Century* 109–16.

## Conclusion: Print Culture and the Dialectic of Digitization

1. Within the field, Eisenstein's work is of course far from undisputed, as seen for example in the work of Adrian Johns. In *The Nature of the Book*, Johns dismisses the broad concept of print culture as an inadequate construct, specifically with regard to Eisenstein's emphasis on fixity and stability.

2. Felski's manifesto, *Uses of Literature*, contains a stimulating discussion of literary immersion. Felski criticizes the common assumption that immersion always entails forgetting the mediated nature of reading. She holds: "What such an argument overlooks is the possibility of an emotional, even erotic cathexis onto the sounds and surfaces of words. Here language is not a hurdle to be vaulted over in the pursuit of pleasure, but the essential means to achieve it" (63). If we accept this enchantment by the surface of words as a prime use of literature, we should pay more attention to the emotional responses triggered by the surface of books as well.

3. Victor Kümel, one of the editors, explains the impulse behind this design in an interview: "We didn't want to force any formal gimmicks onto the texts, we wanted the text itself to seek out its genuine form, for its physical appearance to be an integral part of what it's trying to express. A running joke we used to motivate ourselves during the long work on the issue—especially in the difficult phases: We're going to make Dave Eggers cry with this issue" (De Marco).

# Bibliography

Aarseth, Espen J. *Cybertext: Perspectives on Ergodic Literature.* Baltimore: Johns Hopkins UP, 1997.

"About the Series." *Mediawork Pamphlet Series.* MIT Press, 2005. Web. 2 Apr. 2012.

Adams, Thomas R., and Nicolas Barker. "A New Model for the Study of the Book." 1993. Finkelstein and McCleery, *Book* 47–65.

Adema, Janneke. "Ancient Texts in New Worlds." *Open Reflections.* 6 Feb. 2009. Web. 10 Sep. 2014.

Anderson, Margaret C., ed. "The Vers Libre Contest." *The Little Review* 3.10 (1917): 11–23. *The Modernist Journals Project.* Web. 10 Sep. 2014.

"Artifact." *Oxford English Dictionary Online.* Oxford UP, 2011. Web. 10 Sep. 2014.

Assmann, Aleida. *Cultural Memory and Western Civilization: Functions, Media, Archives.* New York: Cambridge UP, 2011.

Atchison, S. Todd. "'Why I Am Writing from Where You Are Not': Absence and Presence in Jonathan Safran Foer's *Extremely Loud & Incredibly Close.*" *Journal of Postcolonial Writing* 46 (2010): 359–68.

Baker, Matthew. "An Interview with Salvador Plascencia." *Nashville Review* (Spring 2010): n. pag. Web. 10 Sep. 2014.

Baker, Nicholson. "Can a Paper Mill Save a Forest?" *The San Francisco Panorama* [*McSweeney's 33*] (2009): Opinion, 1–2.

———. *Double Fold: Libraries and the Assault on Paper.* 2001. London: Vintage, 2002.

———. "A New Page: Can the Kindle Really Improve on the Book?" *The New Yorker* 27 July 2009: n. pag. Web. 10 Sep. 2012.

Banerjee, Mita. "Roots Trips and Virtual Ethnicity: Jonathan Safran Foer's *Everything Is Illuminated.*" *Transnational American Memories.* Ed. Udo J. Hebel. Berlin: de Gruyter, 2009. 145–69.

Barchas, Janine. *Graphic Design, Print Culture, and the Eighteenth-Century Novel.* Cambridge: Cambridge UP, 2003.

Barnhisel, Greg. *James Laughlin, New Directions, and the Remaking of Ezra Pound.* Amherst: U of Massachusetts P, 2005.

Barthes, Roland. *The Pleasure of the Text.* 1973. New York: Farrar, 1989.

Baym, Nina. "Melodramas of Beset Manhood: How Theories of American Fiction Exclude Women Authors." *American Quarterly* 33.2 (1981): 123–39.

Benjamin, Walter. "The Work of Art in the Age of Its Technological Reproducibility." *The Work of Art in the Age of Its Technological Reproducibility, and Other Writings on Media.* Cambridge, MA: Belknap-Harvard UP, 2008. 19–55.

Benton, Megan L. *Beauty and the Book: Fine Editions and Cultural Distinction in America.* New Haven, CT: Yale UP, 2000.

———. "Typography and Gender: Remasculating the Modern Book." Gutjahr and Benton 71–93.

Benzon, Kiki. "Revolution 2: An Interview with Mark Z. Danielewski." *Electronic Book Review.* 20 Mar. 2007. Web. 10 Sep. 2014.

"Bibliography." *Oxford English Dictionary Online.* Oxford UP, 2011. Web. 10 Sep. 2014.

Bolter, Jay David. *Writing Space: Computers, Hypertext, and the Remediation of Print.* 2nd ed. Mahwah, NJ: Erlbaum, 2001.

Bolter, Jay David, and Richard Grusin. *Remediation: Understanding New Media.* Cambridge, MA: MIT, 1999.

Borges, Jorge Luis. "On Exactitude in Science." 1960. *Collected Fictions.* New York: Viking, 1998. 325.

Bornstein, George. *Material Modernism: The Politics of the Page.* Cambridge: Cambridge UP, 2001.

Bornstein, George, and Theresa Tinkle, eds. *The Iconic Page in Manuscript, Print, and Digital Culture.* Ann Arbor: U of Michigan P, 1998.

Brannon, Barbara A. "The Laser Printer as an Agent of Change: Fixity and Fluxion in the Digital Age." *Agent of Change: Print Culture Studies after Elizabeth L. Eisenstein.* Eds. Sabrina A. Baron, Eric N. Lindquist, and Eleanor F. Shevlin. Amherst: U of Massachusetts P, 2007. 353–64.

Bray, Joe, and Alison Gibbons, eds. *Mark Z. Danielewski.* Manchester: Manchester UP, 2011.

Brick, Martin. "Blueprint(s): Rubric for a Deconstructed Age in *House of Leaves.*" *Philament* 2 (2004): n. pag. Web. 10 Sep. 2014.

Bringhurst, Robert. *The Elements of Typographic Style.* 4th ed. Vancouver: Hartley & Marks, 2012.

Brookman, Rob. "E-Publishing Is Here: Now, What About E-Reading?" *Book Magazine* 11 (2000): n. pag. Web. https://web.archive.org/web/20040201000000*/ http://www.bookmagazine.com/issue11/eread.shtml. 10 Sep. 2014.

Brouillette, Sarah. "Paratextuality and Economic Disavowal in Dave Eggers' *You Shall Know Our Velocity.*" *Reconstruction: Studies in Contemporary Culture* 3.2 (2003): n. pag. Web. 10 Sep. 2014.

Brown, Bill. "Introduction: Textual Materialism." *PMLA* 125.1 (2010): 24–29.

———. "Thing Theory." *Critical Inquiry* 28.1 (2001): 1–22.

Burn, Gordon. "The Believers." *The Guardian.* Guardian News and Media Ltd., 27 Mar. 2004. Web. 10 Sep. 2014.

Carr, Nicholas. *The Shallows: What the Internet Is Doing to Our Brains.* New York: Norton, 2010.

Chabon, Michael, ed. "The Editor's Notebook: A Confidential Chat with the Editor." Chabon, *McSweeney's* 10, 5–8.

———. *McSweeney's 10: McSweeney's Mammoth Treasury of Thrilling Tales.* London: Penguin, 2004.

Chanen, Brian W. "Surfing the Text: The Digital Environment in Mark Z. Danielewski's *House of Leaves.*" *European Journal of English Studies* 11.2 (2007): 163–76.

Chartier, Roger. "Laborers and Voyagers: From the Text to the Reader." 1992. Finkelstein and McCleery, *Book* 87–98.

———. "Languages, Books, and Reading from the Printed Word to the Digital Text." *Critical Inquiry* 31.1 (2004): 133–52.

Chielens, Edward E., ed. *American Literary Magazines.* Westport, CT: Greenwood, 1992.

Clarke, Bruce, and Mark B.N. Hansen, eds. *Emergence and Embodiment: New Essays on Second-Order Systems Theory.* Durham: Duke UP, 2009.

———. "Introduction: Neocybernetic Emergence." Clarke and Hansen, *Emergence* 1–25.

Clements, Amy Root. *The Art of Prestige: The Formative Years at Knopf, 1915–1929.* Amherst: U of Massachusetts P, 2014.

Codde, Philippe. "Philomela Revisited: Traumatic Iconicity in Jonathan Safran Foer's *Extremely Loud & Incredibly Close.*" *Studies in American Fiction* 35 (2007): 241–54.

Collado-Rodriguez, Francisco. "Ethics in the Second Degree: Trauma and Dual Narratives in Jonathan Safran Foer's *Everything Is Illuminated.*" *Journal of Modern Literature* 32.1 (2008): 54–68.

"Comprehensive Guide to Printings/Editions/ISBN's etc." *House of Leaves Online Forum.* Mark Z. Danielewski, 2005. Web. 10 Sep. 2014.

Coover, Robert. "Heart Suit." *McSweeney's Quarterly Concern* 16 (2005): n. pag. [deck of cards].

Coupland, Douglas. "Survivor." *McSweeney's Quarterly Concern* 31 (2009): 43–59.

Cuddon, J.A. "Ekphrasis/Ecphrasis." *The Penguin Dictionary of Literary Terms and Literary Theory*. 4th ed. London: Penguin, 1999. 252.

Danielewski, Mark Z. *The Fifty Year Sword*. New York: Pantheon, 2012.

———. *House of Leaves*. New York: Pantheon, 2000.

———. *House of Leaves: The Remastered Full-Color Edition*. New York: Pantheon, 2006.

———. "Only Evolutions." *Gulf Coast* 19.2 (2007): 176–84.

———. *Only Revolutions*. New York: Pantheon, 2006.

———. "A Spoiler: Route & Legend & Other Unfinished Manners of Direction & Boundary." *inculte* 14 (2007): poster.

———. *The Whalestoe Letters*. New York: Pantheon, 2000.

Darnton, Robert. *The Case for Books: Past, Present, and Future*. New York: Public, 2009.

———. "What Is the History of Books?" 1990. Finkelstein and McCleery, *Book* 9–26.

Däwes, Birgit. "On Contested Ground (Zero): Literature and the Transnational Challenge of Remembering 9/11." *Amerikastudien/American Studies* 52.4 (2007): 517–43.

De Marco, Amanda. "Inspired by McSweeney's, German Lit Mag Wins Big." *Publishing Perspectives* 3 Jan. 2012. Web. 10 Sep. 2014.

Derrida, Jacques. "The Book to Come." Derrida, *Paper* 4–18.

———. *Of Grammatology*. 1967. Baltimore: Johns Hopkins UP, 1998.

———. *Paper Machine*. Stanford: Stanford UP, 2005.

———. "Paper or Me, You Know . . . (New Speculations on the Luxury of the Poor)." Derrida, *Paper* 41–65.

———. "The Word Processor." Derrida, *Paper* 19–32.

Dewey, John. *Art as Experience*. 1934. New York: Perigree, 2005.

"Directions for Use." *McSweeney's Quarterly Concern* 6 (2001): 5.

Dixler, Elsa. "Paperback Row." *New York Times Sunday Book Review* 16 Mar. 2008: n. pag. Web. 10 Sep. 2014.

Drucker, Johanna. *The Century of Artists' Books*. New York: Granary, 1995.

———. *SpecLab: Digital Aesthetics and Projects in Speculative Computing*. Chicago: U of Chicago P, 2009.

———. *The Visible Word: Experimental Typography and Modern Art, 1909–1923*. Chicago: U of Chicago P, 1994.

Dwiggins, William Addison. *Layout in Advertising*. New York: Harper, 1928.

Earle, David M. *Re-Covering Modernism: Pulps, Paperbacks, and the Prejudice of Form*. Farnham, UK: Ashgate, 2009.

Eco, Umberto. "Interpreting Serials." *The Limits of Interpretation*. Bloomington: Indiana UP, 1994. 83–100.

———. *The Open Work*. Cambridge: Harvard UP, 1989.

The Editors of McSweeney's. *Art of McSweeney's*. San Francisco: Chronicle, 2010.

Eggers, Dave. *The Circle*. San Francisco: McSweeney's, 2013.

———. *A Heartbreaking Work of Staggering Genius*. New York: Simon and Schuster, 2000.

———. *A Heartbreaking Work of Staggering Genius*. New York: Vintage, 2001.

———. *How We Are Hungry: Stories*. San Francisco: McSweeney's, 2005.

———. "Introduction." *The Best of McSweeney's*. London: Hamish, 2004. vii–xiii.

———. *Mistakes We Knew We Were Making*. New York: Vintage, 2001.

———. "Notes and Background." *McSweeney's Quarterly Concern* 4 (2000): i–xii.

———. *Sacrament*. San Francisco: McSweeney's, 2003.

———. *What Is the What: The Autobiography of Valentino Achak Deng, A Novel*. San Francisco: McSweeney's, 2006.

———. *You Shall Know Our Velocity*. San Francisco: McSweeney's, 2002.

———. *You Shall Know Our Velocity!* New York: Vintage, 2003.

———. *Zeitoun*. San Francisco: McSweeney's, 2009.

Eisenstein, Elizabeth L. *The Printing Press as an Agent of Change: Communications and Cultural Transformations in Early-Modern Europe*. Cambridge: Cambridge UP, 1980.

Epstein, Jason. "Publishing: The Revolutionary Future." *The New York Review of Books* 57.4 (2010): 4–6.

Felski, Rita. *Uses of Literature*. Malden, MA: Blackwell, 2008.

Finkelstein, David, and Alistair McCleery, eds. *The Book History Reader*. 2nd ed. London: Routledge, 2006.

———. *An Introduction to Book History*. 2nd ed. New York: Routledge, 2012.

———. "Introduction." Finkelstein and McCleery, *Book* 1–6.

Fitzpatrick, Kathleen. *The Anxiety of Obsolescence: The American Novel in the Age of Television*. Nashville, TN: Vanderbilt UP, 2006.

Fjellestad, Danuta. "Resisting Extinction: The Pictorial in Contemporary American Literature." Rapatzikou and Redding 11–24.

Foer, Jonathan Safran. "About the Typefaces Not Used in This Edition." *The Guardian* Guardian News and Media Ltd., 7 Dec. 2002. Web. 10 Sep. 2014.

———. *Everything Is Illuminated*. Boston: Houghton Mifflin, 2002.

———. *Extremely Loud & Incredibly Close*. Boston: Houghton Mifflin, 2005.

———. Foreword. Schulz vii–x.

———. *Tree of Codes*. London: Visual Editions, 2010.

Foucault, Michel. *The Archaeology of Knowledge*. 1969. London: Routledge, 2002.

———. "What Is an Author?" 1969. Finkelstein and McCleery, *Book* 281–91.

Gass, William H. *Fiction and the Figures of Life*. 1970. 2nd ed. Boston: Nonpareil, 1980.

Genette, Gérard. *Narrative Discourse: An Essay in Method.* Ithaca, NY: Cornell UP, 1980.

———. *Paratexts: Thresholds of Interpretation.* 1987. Cambridge: Cambridge UP, 1997.

Gibbons, Alison. *Multimodality, Cognition, and Experimental Literature.* New York: Routledge, 2012.

Gitelman, Lisa. *Always Already New: Media, History, and the Data of Culture.* Cambridge, MA: MIT, 2006.

Goldfarb, David A. Introduction. Schulz xi–xxv.

Goudy, Frederic W. *Typologia: Studies in Type Design & Type Making, with Comments on the Invention of Typography, the First Types, Legibility, and Fine Printing.* 1940. Berkeley: U of California P, 1977.

Grafton, Anthony. *Codex in Crisis.* New York: Crumpled, 2008.

———. "Future Reading: Digitization and Its Discontents." *The New Yorker* 5 Nov. 2007: n. pag. Web. 10 Sep. 2014.

Greenberg, Clement. "Towards a Newer Laocoon." 1940. *Perceptions and Judgments: 1939–1944.* Ed. John O'Brian. Chicago: U of Chicago P, 2008. 23–38.

Gumbrecht, Hans Ulrich. "A Farewell to Interpretation." 1988. Gumbrecht and Pfeiffer 389–402.

———. *Production of Presence: What Meaning Cannot Convey.* Stanford: Stanford UP, 2004.

Gumbrecht, Hans Ulrich, and Karl Ludwig Pfeiffer, eds. *Materialities of Communication.* 1988. Stanford, CA: Stanford UP, 1994.

Gutjahr, Paul C., and Megan L. Benton, eds. *Illuminating Letters: Typography and Literary Interpretation.* Amherst: U of Massachusetts P, 2001.

Hallet, Wolfgang. "Visual Images of Space, Movement and Mobility in the Multimodal Novel." *Moving Images, Mobile Viewers: 20th Century Visuality.* Ed. Renate Brosch. Berlin: Lit, 2011. 227–48.

Hamilton, Caroline D. *One Man Zeitgeist: Dave Eggers, Publishing and Publicity.* New York: Continuum, 2010.

Hansen, Mark B.N. "The Digital Topography of Mark Z. Danielewski's *House of Leaves.*" *Contemporary Literature* 45.4 (2004): 597–636.

———. *Embodying Technesis: Technology Beyond Writing.* Ann Arbor: U of Michigan P, 2000.

———. "Print Interface to Time: *Only Revolutions* at the Crossroads of Narrative and History." Bray and Gibbons 178–99.

Haselstein, Ulla. "Rücksicht auf Darstellbarkeit: Jonathan Safran Foers Holocaust-Roman *Everything Is Illuminated.*" *Literatur als Philosophie, Philosophie als Literatur.* Eds. Eva Horn, Bettine Menke, and Christoph Menke. München: Wilhelm Fink, 2006. 193–210.

Hayles, N. Katherine. "Cybernetics." Mitchell and Hansen, *Critical* 145–56.

————. *Electronic Literature: New Horizons for the Literary.* Notre Dame, IN: U of Notre Dame P, 2008.

————. *How We Became Posthuman: Virtual Bodies in Cybernetics, Literature, and Informatics.* Chicago: U of Chicago P, 1999.

————. *How We Think: Digital Media and Contemporary Technogenesis.* Chicago: U of Chicago P, 2012.

————. *My Mother Was a Computer: Digital Subjects and Literary Texts.* Chicago: U of Chicago P, 2005.

————. "Saving the Subject: Remediation in *House of Leaves.*" *American Literature* 74.4 (2002): 779–806.

————. *Writing Machines.* Cambridge, MA: MIT, 2002.

Hayles, N. Katherine, and Jessica Pressman, eds. *Comparative Textual Media: Transforming the Humanities in the Postprint Era.* Minneapolis: U of Minnesota P, 2013.

Holland, Mary K. *Succeeding Postmodernism: Language and Humanism in Contemporary American Literature.* New York: Bloomsbury, 2013.

Hungerford, Amy. "McSweeney's and the School of Life." *Contemporary Literature* 53.4 (2012): 646–80.

Hutcheon, Linda. *Narcissistic Narrative: The Metafictional Paradox.* 1980. New York: Methuen, 1984.

————. *A Poetics of Postmodernism: History, Theory, Fiction.* 1988. New York: Routledge, 2000.

"Information Pamphlet." *The San Francisco Panorama* [*McSweeney's* 33] (2009): n. pag.

"iUniverse.com and Pantheon Present *House of Leaves*, by Mark Z. Danielewski." iUniverse.com. iUniverse.com, 15 Feb. 1999. Web. 2 Apr. 2012. http://markzdanielewski.info/hol/content1482.html.

Jackson, Shelley. "Consuetudinary of the Word Church, or The Church of the Dead Letter." *McSweeney's Quarterly Concern* 31 (2009): 131–50.

————. *Patchwork Girl.* Watertown, MA: Eastgate Systems, 1995. CD-ROM.

————. "Stitch Bitch: The Patchwork Girl." Thorburn and Jenkins 239–52.

————. "Who Is Is." *Shelley Jackson's Ineradicable Stain*, n. d. Web. 10 Sep. 2014.

Jakobson, Roman. "Closing Statement: Linguistics and Poetics." *Style and Language.* Ed. Thomas A. Sebeok. Cambridge: Technology Press, 1960. 350–77.

Jenkins, Henry. *Convergence Culture: Where Old and New Media Collide.* New York: New York UP, 2006.

Johns, Adrian. *The Nature of the Book.* Chicago: U of Chicago P, 1998.

Junod, Karen. "Artist's Book." Suarez and Woudhuysen 484–85.

Kelleter, Frank. "Early American Literature." *English and American Studies: Theory and Practice.* Ed. Martin Middeke et al. Stuttgart: Metzler, 101–10.

Kelleter, Frank, and Andreas Jahn-Sudmann. "Die Dynamik serieller Überbietung:

Zeitgenössische amerikanische Fernsehserien und das Konzept des Quality TV." *Populäre Serialität: Narration-Evolution-Distinktion.* Ed. Frank Kelleter. Bielefeld: transcript, 2012. 205–24.

Kelly, Kevin. "Scan This Book!" *New York Times* 14 Mar. 2006: n. pag. Web. 10 Sep. 2014.

Kennedy, A.L. *The Blue Book.* London: Cape, 2011.

Kidd, Chip. *Book One: Work, 1986–2006.* New York: Rizzoli, 2006.

———. *The Cheese Monkeys: A Novel in Two Semesters.* New York: Scribner, 2001.

———. *The Learners.* New York: Scribner, 2008.

Kilgour, Frederick G. *The Evolution of the Book.* New York: Oxford UP, 1998.

Kittler, Friedrich A. *Discourse Networks 1800/1900.* Stanford: Stanford UP, 1990.

———. *Gramophone, Film, Typewriter.* Stanford: Stanford UP, 1999.

Klepper, Martin. "The Emergence of Literature as Art and the Refinement of Literary Perspective." *Addressing Modernity: Social Systems Theory and U.S. Cultures.* Eds. Hannes Bergthaller and Carsten Schinko. Amsterdam: Rodopi, 2011. 38–62.

Kun, Josh. "The Full El Monte." *Los Angeles Magazine* 9 (2005): 78–84.

Landow, George P. *Hypertext 3.0: Critical Theory and New Media in an Era of Globalization.* Baltimore: Johns Hopkins UP, 2006.

Lanier, Jaron. *You Are Not a Gadget: A Manifesto.* New York: Knopf, 2010.

Larsen, Reif. "The Crying of Page 45: How Will a Page without Limits Change the Way We Tell Stories?" *The Believer* 77 (2011): 3–9.

———. *The Selected Works of T.S. Spivet.* New York: Penguin, 2009.

Latour, Bruno. *Reassembling the Social: An Introduction to Actor-Network-Theory.* Oxford: Oxford UP, 2005.

Lawson, Alexander S. *Anatomy of a Typeface.* Boston: Godine, 1990.

LeClair, Tom. *In the Loop: Don DeLillo and the Systems Novel.* Urbana: U of Illinois P, 1987.

Lerer, Seth. "Epilogue: Falling Asleep over the History of the Book." *PMLA* 121.1 (2006): 229–34.

Lister, Martin, et al. *New Media: A Critical Introduction.* London: Routledge, 2006.

Little, William G. "Nothing to Write Home About: Impossible Reception in Mark Z. Danielewski's *House of Leaves.*" *The Mourning After: Attending the Wake of Postmodernism.* Eds. Neil Brooks and Josh Toth. Amsterdam: Rodopi, 2007. 169–99.

Luhmann, Niklas. *Art as a Social System.* Stanford, CA: Stanford UP, 2000.

———. "The Autopoiesis of Social Systems." Luhmann, *Essays on Self-Reference* 1–20.

———. *Essays on Self-Reference.* New York: Columbia UP, 1990.

———. "The Improbability of Communication." Luhmann, *Essays on Self-Reference* 86–98.

———. "Modes of Communication and Society." Luhmann, *Essays on Self-Reference* 99–106.

———. *The Reality of the Mass Media*. Cambridge: Polity, 2000.

———. *Social Systems*. Stanford, CA: Stanford UP, 2005.

———. *Theory of Society*. 2 vols. Stanford: Stanford UP, 2012–2013.

———. "The Work of Art and the Self-Reproduction of Art." Luhmann, *Essays on Self-Reference* 191–214.

Maliszewski, Paul. "Paperback Nabokov." *McSweeney's Quarterly Concern* 4 (2000).

Manovich, Lev. *The Language of New Media*. Cambridge, MA: MIT, 2001.

———. *Software Takes Command*. New York: Bloomsbury, 2013.

Marchessault, Janine. *Marshall McLuhan: Cosmic Media*. London: Sage, 2005.

Maturana, Humberto R., and Francisco J. Varela. *Autopoiesis and Cognition: The Realization of the Living*. Dordrecht: Reidel, 1980.

McCaffery, Larry, and Sinda Gregory. "Haunted House: An Interview with Mark Z. Danielewski." *Critique: Studies in Contemporary Fiction* 44.2 (2003): 99–135.

McClellan, Martin. "Caslon, Baskerville, and Franklin: Revolutionary Types." *Timothy McSweeney's Internet Tendency*. McSweeney's, 30 Oct. 2009. Web. 10 Sep. 2014.

McGann, Jerome. *Black Riders: The Visible Language of Modernism*. Princeton: Princeton UP, 1993.

———. "On Creating a Usable Future." *Profession* (2011): 182–95.

———. *Radiant Textuality: Literature after the World Wide Web*. New York: Palgrave, 2001.

———. *The Textual Condition*. Princeton: Princeton UP, 1991.

McGrath, Charles. "Not Funnies." *New York Times* 11 Jul. 2004: n. pag. Web. 10 Sep. 2014.

McGurl, Mark. *The Program Era: Postwar Fiction and the Rise of Creative Writing*. Cambridge: Harvard UP, 2011.

McHale, Brian. "Only Revolutions, or, The Most Typical Poem in World Literature." Bray and Gibbons 141–58.

———. *Postmodernist Fiction*. London: Methuen, 1987.

McKenzie, Donald F. "Typography and Meaning: The Case of William Congreve." 1981. *Making Meaning: "Printers of the mind" and Other Essays*. Eds. Peter D. McDonald and Michael F. Suarez. Amherst: U of Massachusetts P, 2002. 198–236.

McLuhan, Marshall. *The Gutenberg Galaxy: The Making of Typographic Man*. 1962. Toronto: U of Toronto P, 2002.

———. *Understanding Media: The Extensions of Man*. 1964. London: Routledge, 2008.

McLuhan, Marshall, and Quentin Fiore. *The Medium Is the Massage*. 1967. London: Penguin, 2008.

"Medium." *Oxford English Dictionary Online*. Oxford UP, 2011. Web. 10 Sep. 2014.

Menand, Louis. *The Metaphysical Club*. New York: Farrar, 2002.

Mitchell, W.J.T, and Mark B.N. Hansen, eds. *Critical Terms for Media Studies*. Chicago: U of Chicago P, 2010.

———. "Introduction." Mitchell and Hansen, *Critical* vii–xxii.

Mittell, Jason. "Lost in a Great Story: Evaluation in Narrative Television (and Television Studies)." *Reading Lost: Perspectives on a Hit Television Show*. Ed. Roberta E. Pearson. London: Tauris, 2009. 119–38.

———. "Narrative Complexity in Contemporary American Television." *The Velvet Light Trap* 58 (2006): 29–40.

Moeller, Hans-Georg. *The Radical Luhmann*. New York: Columbia UP, 2012.

Morris, William. *The Ideal Book: Essays and Lectures on the Arts of the Book*. Ed. William S. Peterson. Berkeley: U of California P, 1982.

———. "The Ideal Book." 1893. Morris, *Ideal* 67–74.

———. "Printing." 1893. Morris, *Ideal* 59–66.

Mosley, James. "The Technologies of Printing." Suarez and Woudhuysen 89–104.

Moylan, Michele, and Lane Stiles. Introduction. Moylan and Stiles, *Reading* 1–15.

———, eds. *Reading Books: Essays on the Material Text and Literature in America*. Amherst: U of Massachusetts P, 1996.

Müller, Lothar. *Weiße Magie: Die Epoche des Papiers*. München: Hanser, 2012.

Murphy, Priscilla Coit. "Books Are Dead, Long Live Books." Thorburn and Jenkins 81–93.

Nicol, Bran. "Dave Eggers and the Memoir as Self-Destruction." *Modern Confessional Writing: New Critical Essays*. Ed. Jo Gill. London: Routledge, 2006. 100–14.

"A Note about the Type." *McSweeney's Quarterly Concern* 3 (1999): 205–208, 288.

North, Joseph. "What's 'New Critical' about 'Close Reading'?: I.A. Richards and His New Critical Reception." *New Literary History* 44.1 (2013): 141–57.

Ovenden, Richard. "Illuminated Book." Suarez and Woudhuysen 810.

Paulson, William R. *The Noise of Culture: Literary Texts in a World of Information*. Ithaca: Cornell UP, 1988.

Pearson, David. "Bookbinding." Suarez and Woudhuysen 147–55.

Peirce, Charles Sanders. "What Is a Sign?" 1894. *The Essential Peirce: Selected Philosophical Writings*. Ed. Nathan Houser. Bloomington, IN: Indiana UP, 1998. 4–10.

"Pelafina Is the Author of *House of Leaves*!!!" *House of Leaves* Online Forum. Mark Z. Danielewski, 2008. Web. 12 Sep. 2014.

Peters, John Durham. *Speaking into the Air: A History of the Idea of Communication*. Chicago: U of Chicago P, 1999.

Peterson, William S. "Introduction." Morris, *Ideal* xi–xxxv.

Phillips, Tom. *A Humument: A Treated Victorian Novel*. London: Thames, 1980.

Piper, Andrew. *Book Was There: Reading in Electronic Times*. Chicago: U of Chicago P, 2013.

Plascencia, Salvador. *The People of Paper*. San Francisco: McSweeney's, 2005.

———. *The People of Paper*. Orlando: Harcourt, 2006.

"A Pocket Guide to the Middle East." *McSweeney's Quarterly Concern* 19 (2006).

Poulet, George. "Phenomenology of Reading." *New Literary History* 1.1 (1969): 53–68.

Powers, Richard. *Galatea 2.2*. New York: Farrar, 1995.

Pressman, Jessica. *Digital Modernism: Making It New in New Media*. New York: Oxford UP, 2014.

———. "*House of Leaves*: Reading the Networked Novel." *Studies in American Fiction* 34.1 (2006): 107–22.

Price, Leah. *How to Do Things with Books in Victorian Britain*. Princeton, NJ: Princeton UP, 2012.

Price, Steven R. "The Autograph Manuscript in Print: Samuel Richardson's Type Font Manipulation in *Clarissa*." Gutjahr and Benton 117–35.

Pross, Harry. *Medienforschung: Film, Funk, Presse, Fernsehen*. Darmstadt: Habel, 1972.

Pruzan, Todd. "Hooper's Bathhouse: An Adventure Story Shaped by the Reader's Own Design." *McSweeney's Quarterly Concern* 2 (1999): 25–26, 41, 70, 104, 136, 142, 148, 152, 158, 164, 187.

Punday, Daniel. *Writing at the Limit: The Novel in the New Media Ecology*. Lincoln: U of Nebraska P, 2012.

Rabinowitz, Tova. *Exploring Typography*. Clifton Park, NY: Thomson-Delmar, 2006.

Rainey, Lawrence S. *Institutions of Modernism: Literary Elites and Public Culture*. New Haven: Yale UP, 1998.

Rapatzikou, Tatiani, and Arthur Redding, eds. *Representational and Literary Futures: American Writing in the New Millenium*. Spec. issue of *Writing Technologies* 3 (2010). Web. 10 Sep. 2014.

"A Regressive Avant-Garde: *McSweeney's/Believer*." *n+1* 1 (2004): n. pag. eBook.

Ryan, Marie-Laure. "Metaleptic Machines." *Semiotica* 150 (2004): 439–69.

Saal, Ilka. "Regarding the Pain of Self and Other: Trauma Transfer and Narrative Framing in Jonathan Safran Foer's *Extremely Loud & Incredibly Close*." *Modern Fiction Studies* 57 (2011): 451–76.

"Sacrament." *this book is collectible*. 3 May 2010. Web. 10 Sep. 2014. http://jamespreynolds.com/sacrament.

Saldívar, Ramón. "Historical Fantasy, Speculative Realism, and Postrace Aesthetics in Contemporary American Fiction." *American Literary History* 23.3 (2011): 574–99.

Saporta, Marc. *Composition No. 1*. 1962. London: Visual Editions, 2011.

Scarry, Elaine. *Dreaming by the Book*. Princeton: Princeton UP, 2001.

Schalansky, Judith. *Atlas of Remote Islands: Fifty Islands I Have Never Set Foot On and Never Will*. New York: Penguin, 2010.

———. *Der Hals der Giraffe: Bildungsroman*. Berlin: Suhrkamp, 2011.

———. "Wie ich Bücher mache." *Bella Triste* 30 (2011).

Scholes, Robert, and Clifford Wulfman. *Modernism in the Magazines: An Introduction*. New Haven: Yale UP, 2010.

Schulz, Bruno. *The Street of Crocodiles and Other Stories*. 1934. New York: Penguin, 2008.

Schwanitz, Dietrich. "Systems Theory According to Niklas Luhmann: Its Environment and Conceptual Strategies." *Cultural Critique* 30.1 (1995): 137–70.

Schweighauser, Philipp. *The Noises of American Literature, 1890–1985: Toward a History of Literary Acoustics*. Gainesville: UP of Florida, 2006.

Setz, Clemens J. *Indigo*. Berlin: Suhrkamp, 2012.

Silverman, Willa Z. *The New Bibliopolis: French Book Collectors and the Culture of Print, 1880–1914*. Toronto: U of Toronto P, 2008.

Smith, Dinitia. "Is This the End of the Story for Books?" *New York Times* 20 Nov. 1999: n. pag. Web. 10 Sep. 2014.

Smith, Rachel Greenwald. "Organic Shrapnel: Affect and Aesthetics in September 11 Fiction." *American Literature* 89.1 (2011): 153–74.

Starre, Alexander. "American Comics Anthologies: Mediality–Canonization–Transnationalism." *Transnational American Studies*. Ed. Udo J. Hebel. Heidelberg: Winter, 2012. 541–60.

———. "Teaching the Comics Anthology: The Readers, Authors, and Media of *McSweeney's 13*." *Teaching Comics and Graphic Narratives: Essays on Theory, Strategy and Practice*. Ed. Lan Dong. Jefferson, NC: McFarland, 2012. 40–52.

Sterne, Laurence. *The Life and Opinions of Tristram Shandy, Gentleman*. 1759. London: Visual Editions, 2010.

Stiegler, Bernard. "Memory." Mitchell and Hansen, *Critical* 66–87.

Striphas, Ted. *The Late Age of Print: Everyday Book Culture from Consumerism to Control*. New York: Columbia UP, 2009.

Suarez, Michael F., and H.R. Woudhuysen, eds. *The Oxford Companion to the Book*. 2 vols. Oxford: Oxford UP, 2010.

Sussman, Henry. *Around the Book: Systems and Literacy*. New York: Fordham UP, 2011.

Tabbi, Joseph. *Cognitive Fictions*. Minneapolis: U of Minnesota P, 2002.

Tanselle, G. Thomas. "Dust-Jackets, Dealers, and Documentation." *Studies in Bibliography* 56 (2003–2004): 45–140.

———. "Textual Criticism and Deconstruction." 1990. *Literature and Artifacts*. Charlottesville, VA: Bibliographical Society, 1998. 203–35.

They Might Be Giants. *They Might Be Giants vs. McSweeney's* [*McSweeney's Quarterly Concern* 6]. McSweeney's, 2001. CD.

Thorburn, David, and Henry Jenkins, eds. *Rethinking Media Change: The Aesthetics of Transition.* Cambridge, MA: MIT, 2003.

Timmer, Nicoline. *Do You Feel It Too? The Post-Postmodern Syndrome in American Fiction at the Turn of the Millennium.* Amsterdam: Rodopi, 2010.

Updike, John. "The End of Authorship." *New York Times Sunday Book Review* 25 Jun. 2006: n. pag. Web. 10 Sep. 2014.

Uytterschout, Sien. "Visualised Incomprehensibility of Trauma in Jonathan Safran Foer." *Zeitschrift für Anglistik und Amerikanistik* 56.1 (2008): 61–75.

"VE2 Tree of Codes." *Visual Editions* 2010. Visual Editions, 2010. Web. 10 Sep. 2014.

Vienne, Véronique. *Chip Kidd.* New Haven, CT: Yale UP, 2003.

"Visual Writing." *Visual Editions.* Visual Editions, 2010. Web. 10 Sep. 2014.

Wallace, David Foster. "Another Example of the Porousness of Various Borders (VI): Projected but Not Improbable Transcript of Author's Parents' Marriage's End, 1971." *McSweeney's Quarterly Concern* 3 (1998): spine.

Warde, Beatrice. "Printing Should Be Invisible." *Books and Printing: A Treasury for Typophiles.* Ed. Paul A. Bennett. Cleveland, OH: World Publishing, 1963. 109–14.

Warner, John. "The Circus Elephants Look Sad Because They Are." *McSweeney's Quarterly Concern* 3 (1999): 31–35.

Waugh, Patricia. *Metafiction: The Theory and Practice of Self-Conscious Fiction.* London: Methuen, 1984.

Wehde, Susanne. *Typographische Kultur.* Tübingen: Niemeyer, 2000.

Wellbery, David. "Foreword." Kittler, *Discourse* vii–xxxiii.

———. "Systems." Mitchell and Hansen, *Critical* 297–309.

White, Glyn. *Reading the Graphic Surface: The Presence of the Book in Prose Fiction.* Manchester: Manchester UP, 2005.

White, Hayden. *Metahistory: The Historical Imagination in Nineteenth-Century Europe.* 5th ed. Baltimore: Johns Hopkins UP, 1985.

Wimsatt, William K., and Monroe C. Beardsley. "The Intentional Fallacy." 1946. *The Norton Anthology of Theory and Criticism.* Ed. Vincent Leitch. New York: Norton, 2001. 1374–87.

Wolf, Werner. "Metareference across Media: The Concept, Its Transmedial Potentionals and Problems, Main Forms and Functions." *Metareference across Media: Theory and Case Studies.* Ed. Werner Wolf. Amsterdam: Rodopi, 2009. 1–85.

Wolfe, Cary. "Meaning as Event Machine, or Systems Theory and 'The Reconstruction of Deconstruction': Derrida and Luhmann." Clarke and Hansen 220–45.

Wutz, Michael. *Enduring Words: Literary Narrative in a Changing Media Ecology.* Tuscaloosa: U of Alabama P, 2009.

# Index

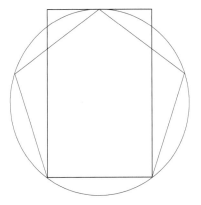

## Colophon

*Metamedia* was typeset in Quadraat and Meta fonts using Adobe InDesign page layout software. Quadraat, designed by Fred Smeijers, is a late twentieth-century digital font, yet many of its qualities are rooted in the letterforms printed from metal type in the sixteenth century. Meta, used in this book as the display type, is a humanist sans-serif designed by Erik Spiekermann. The rectangular dimensions of this book are derived from a regular pentagon (see above); the text block area is based on the the golden ratio. The paper scanned for the cover was handmade from cotton fiber at the University of Iowa Center for the Book. First digital printing at BookMobile in Minneapolis, Minnesota, on 60# Flambeau River text paper using a Océ VarioPrint 6320 press.